Colour Matters? by Anuranjita Kum for ages, skin colour has defined wh people are, and has invariably led to perceptions that may need to be challenged. This book puts the spotlight on how one's character is not defined by the colour of one's skin but by one's values and abilities. It captures extraordinary efforts of individuals as well as the stories of people who have battled to break out of these perceptions. A definitive read for individuals at all levels and an eye-opener to raise oneself from these shackles and see people for who they are. Humanity is about understanding and connecting with each other with compassion to defy such biases.

—**Johnny C Taylor, Jr**, *President and CEO,*
Society for Human Resource Management (SHRM)

Colour Matters? is a good read for every individual looking for growth in a global organisation and is working with a diverse set of teams. The book focuses on cross-cultural dynamic and presents possibilities to navigate through it. It enhances one's sensitivity and brings our unconscious beliefs to a conscious level, enabling us to deal with them.

—**Leena Nair**, *Chief HR Officer, Unilever*

Colour Matters? explores stories of resilience and optimism. It invites us to explore our own paradigm of thinking on how we engage with different people. Read the book with an open mind as it traverses across experiences to bring you some personal stories that touch a cord.

—**Shirish Apte**, *former Chairman*
(Asia Pacific region), Citibank

Colour Matters? encourages us to be open-minded to the diversity of people around us. It helps us explore how our local roots and inclusion can be a strong glue for human interactions, thereby making our collective experience richer and more meaningful. As the world is shrinking, a shared sense of belonging makes us stronger to face the challenges of life. Stories in this book are inspiring and will get you thinking!

—**Stefan Barot**, *Senior Business Director,*
Total Corbion PLA

COLOUR MATTERS?

C O L O U R
M A T T E R S?

The truth that no one wants to see

Reflections, thoughts and experiences of
working in a multi-ethnic environment

ANURANJITA KUMAR

Best Wishes

Anuranjita

B L O O M S B U R Y
NEW DELHI · LONDON · OXFORD · NEW YORK · SYDNEY

BLOOMSBURY INDIA
Bloomsbury Publishing India Pvt. Ltd.
Second Floor, LSC Building No. 4, DDA Complex, Pocket C – 6 & 7,
Vasant Kunj New Delhi 110070

BLOOMSBURY, BLOOMSBURY INDIA and the Diana logo are trademarks of
Bloomsbury Publishing Plc

First published in India 2019
This export edition published in 2019

ISBN:TPB: 978-93-89000-48-1; eBook: 978-93-89000-49-8

2 4 6 8 10 9 7 5 3 1

Bloomsbury Publishing Plc makes every effort to ensure that the papers used in the manufacture of our
books are natural, recyclable products made from wood grown in well-managed forests. Our
manufacturing processes conform to the environmental regulations of the country of origin

To find out more about our authors and books visit www.bloomsbury.com and
sign up for our newsletters

Printed in India by Replika Press Pvt. Ltd.

For Sid and Avni, as they fly away from home…

What was true then remains true today. Basic truths do not change. It is a truth that can be embraced by the English, and by the Indian, and by the Mexican, and by the Bantu, and by the Luo and by the American. It is a truth that lies at the heart of every world religion— that we should do unto others as we would have them do unto us. That we see ourselves in other people. That we can recognise common hopes and common dreams. And it is a truth that is incompatible with any form of discrimination based on race or religion or gender or sexual orientation. And it is a truth that, by the way, when embraced, actually delivers practical benefits, since it ensures that a society can draw upon the talents and energy and skill of all its people. And if you doubt that, just ask the French football team that just won the World Cup. Because not all of those folks look like Gauls to me. But they're French. They're French.

—Excerpt from former US President Barack Obama's speech at Nelson Mandela's birth centenary celebrations in South Africa, July 2018

Contents

Reflections   xi

1 **C**onnect   1
2 **O**penness   39
3 **L**ove   79
4 **O**bjectivity   118
5 **U**nderstanding   164
6 **R**esilience   200

Looking Ahead   235
Acknowledgements   260

Reflections

Ignorance and prejudice are the handmaidens of propaganda. Our mission, therefore, is to confront ignorance with knowledge, bigotry with tolerance, and isolation with the outstretched hand of generosity. Racism can, will, and must be defeated.
—**Kofi Annan**

As a child, I loved colours, all kinds of colours! I felt nature was so beautiful. It had given us such beautiful colours that it was difficult to find words to describe the magic. I felt speechless with joy every day, as my eyes tried to decipher the intriguing shades in the rising sun, in the gorgeous blue sky of the afternoon or in the sun-kissed twilight. Each changing season filled me with unnamed feelings—each colour evoked an emotion, slightly mixed, yet distinct. The bright sunshine of the summer drenched the flowers with its golden glow, when wildflowers blossomed on a velvet green carpet of tall grass—all to teach me the secret ingredient of happiness. The relentless winter brought with it a sort of reincarnation, when everything was covered with white snow and the pristine whiteness infused me with peace and calm. Colours draped me with compassion and tenderness, teaching me the essence of life.

Even the colourless water serenaded me with its crystal clear beauty. There was a sense of wonderment and I was mystically immersed in the very essence of water, which in its fluidity adopted any colour as if it were its own. An essence that wished to submit itself and dissolve itself in any hue. Various colours reflected their radiance on the water surface as if this was always their home.

This realisation also makes me think—are we all essentially colourless, spending our lives in the quest to be colourful?

In hindsight, I realise that this thought came to me from a marvellous epiphany—that nature is like a palette, a magnificent infusion of all the colours that exist in the universe.

I am very fond of two flowers—*tesu* and sunflower—one a flaming orange and the other a vibrant yellow. Their magnetism has touched me deeply and spurred me on to live with energy and vitality. Time and again, they helped me allay my momentary despondency and made me want to live life to the fullest. Both these colours play with my emotions, they make me feel happy and optimistic about the world.

My fondness for colours also led me to my interest in art. As a child, I drew almost everything I saw! I was never apprehensive of painting my raw, innocent thoughts on paper. I loved drawing trees, houses, rivers, flowers and my family. I would drape my mother in a yellow saree and my father in an orange shirt, while I stood between them donning both shades. I felt I could use all the colours that my eyes could see to paint my perception of the world on paper. However, as I played with the paint brush, trying to bring my picture to life, the colour of skin always made me feel unsure! I wondered if I could mix two colours and create a new one, or was the colour of the skin ordained to be a certain way? My imagination ran wild and I experimented with all kinds of colours that could adorn my skin. I felt art stimulated me to invest in the freedom to think the unthinkable and imagine the unimaginable! It made me fearless and bold.

One time in school, as I was pondering over my painting, my teacher, sensing some confusion, instructed me to mix pink with white to paint the skin of the figures I had sketched. I was quite befuddled with this statement and when I compared that pinkish white colour to my pale brown skin, something seemed amiss. I could not deceive myself into believing that I could paint everybody with the same colour and, indeed, the same brush! The moribund homogeneity of the human species provided room for evolution and that holds true even today as far as skin colour is concerned. For a long time, I believed that it was the pinkish white colour, which was 'supposed' to be the colour of the skin— of anybody's skin. However, I was compelled to reflect upon the uncomfortable suggestion imposed on me—why were the lighter shades used as 'skin colour' and the darker shades forcibly looked down upon as an aberrant? Over days, weeks and years, I learnt that the colours I loved so much did mean different things, even though people could not choose any of it for themselves at birth—black, brown or white!

I had no inclination or aversion to any colour in particular. However, over time, each colour started to represent a quality of a person—black was dangerous, brown was boring, white was beautiful. When we are guided by such views, we fail to understand the 'whole' person. We are so confined and constrained to see the world as we think we ought to see it that we sometimes accept our erroneous perception to be the reality. At a young age, I was fortunate enough to realise that the world is spectacularly occupied by various colours, but our minds were quick to judge them in black and white truths.

As I reminisce on my childhood, I am reminded of one of John Lennon's greatest compositions, where he sings:

> *...Imagine no possessions*
> *I wonder if you can*
> *No need for greed or hunger*
> *A brotherhood of man*
>
> *Imagine all the people*
> *Sharing all the world.*
>
> *You may say that I am a dreamer*
> *But I'm not the only one*
> *I hope someday you'll join us*
> *And the world will live as one*
> —John Winston Lennon; Imagine lyrics
> © Universal Music Publishing Group

The colour of the skin has occupied a crucial space in public discourse because colour is symbolic of a variety of beliefs that have evolved over a period of time. And so have our experiences with it—some good, others not so good! Human beings are largely driven by visual cues. Our initial response to one another is often based on how we look physically. The colour of the skin is an irrefutable visual fact that we cannot hide or ignore. It tends to portray an unspoken characteristic of the person rightly or wrongly. Hence, it occupies a place of prominence in private as well as public interactions. In fact, it has grown to become symbolic of a person's identity and values beyond what that individual may be.

When I played with my 'white' (read: beautiful) Barbie dolls as a child, they often left me wondering, 'Why don't they look like me? Or am I supposed to look like them? Why does she have light coloured skin? Why is the shade of my skin colour not matching with hers?' Once I asked my friend this baffling question and her answer was quite simple, 'But that's how they are supposed to look! So fair and pretty!' I was perplexed and bewildered at the definition of 'prettiness' and was forced to think that perhaps I could never be pretty as I did not possess the 'right' skin colour. For generations, dolls have projected the so-called perfect physical image that many little girls aspire for—slim, fair, tall—and that has been the definition of beauty, changing only in recent years as the world became more sensitive to the colour dynamic.

One size and one colour do not fit all. We are all different. We come from different climatic regions, ethnicities, geographies, and it is impossible to have one skin colour represent all different types of colours that exist in the world. I feel it is important for our 'Barbie' minds to realise that the physicality of all the women in this world cannot be the same because we are all genetically predisposed to look a certain way. Children from all over the world play with these dolls and they should not be fixated by the idea of white being the better or the prettier skin colour.

But then again, as I peek back into my childhood, everything about these dolls had to be white in some form to be 'right'. My dolls were all white-skinned, with bright blue glassy eyes that peered at me as soon as I woke up. Smiling through well-kept pink lips, they had cheeks that glowed with a natural blush. A look that was fresh with a soft and velvety finish, and nowhere close to my rough, unruly natural one. When I spied myself in the mirror, I pondered if I could be beautified to match my dolls.

Were we unconsciously growing up to think that if we were not like our beautiful dolls, we may not be good enough? I do see boys playing with superhero toys that look rough and tough with bronzed skin, sometimes, signifying ruggedness or toughness. Is that a symbol of brown or black? I was confused as a child.

I was graduating from the dreamy world of multiple colours to a black and white world of race! Our minds have been manoeuvred and cajoled to associate a particular colour with a way of being and even today it has not ventured much beyond the categories of black, white and brown. The conversation about race and colour is weighed down by the multihued and phenotypically diverse human population of this planet. The doll experience was only an introduction to the notion that, more often than not, light skin always stood for beauty and dark skin was invariably demonised. Skin colour, as it gradually dawned upon me, was used by many as the most obvious criterion in the process of evaluating and judging a person before really knowing their thoughts, minds and feelings.

I sit back and reflect on my journey—from my worries as a child and then later in life as a career woman—I have had my qualms. I tried hard to be noticed, to be heard, to get ahead in the corporate race in a multi-ethnic environment. I won some battles and I lost some while contending with skin colour. At times, happiness was defined by successfully overcoming the challenges thrown at me due to my skin colour. At other, more trying times, I had to salvage my respect and dignity through skin colour battles—this required challenging others and sometimes myself to not accept the status quo.

During the course of life, one is defined by a surname, a degree, a school, a job. However, for me, colour overarched in some ways across all these phases of life. And then magically, a moment arrived when those shackles liberated me as I began to discover my real self beyond my work, my relationships and past learning. I started to open up to the nuances of various ethnicities and how the world reacts to them.

Often when I watch the news on TV or flick through newspapers, the debates and conflicting perspectives on ethnicity sting me. A recent news item carried by CNN stated that in Britain, children are whitening their skin to avoid racism as hate crimes rise against minors. There was a study carried out by a child protection group. To quote from CNN[1]:

'... an average of 29 [racial crimes] a day—were recorded by police in 2017–18, the National Society for the Prevention of Cruelty to Children (NSPCC) found.... That number is now a fifth higher than it was just three years ago, and is growing at a rate of about 1,000 new crimes a year.'

The report, based on UK police records, displayed how rapidly hate crimes have soared in recent times, impacting our future generations. The group highlighted that many children, as young as ten years old, suffer verbal abuse publicly, which has impacted them deeply. Some excerpts from the NSPCC-CNN report[2]:

'I've been bullied ever since I started school. The bullies call me nasty names; it makes me feel so ashamed. My friends won't hang out with me anymore because people started asking why they were friends with someone who had dirty skin.'

'I was born in the UK but bullies tell me to go back to my own country. I don't understand because I'm from the UK. I've tried to make my face whiter [than] before using make up [sic] so that I can fit in. I just want to enjoy going to school.'

This conundrum and shame that is being sowed in these young minds need to be addressed through compassion that can help us ensure their future and ours.

---

1 'Children "Whitening Skin to Avoid Racism" as Hate Crimes Against Minors Rise'. *The CNN Wire.* 2019. https://www.msn.com/en-us/news/us/children-whitening-skin-to-avoid-racism-as-hate-crimes-against-minors-rise/ar-AACcSGh

2 Ibid.

Who really owns the planet?
Who really created these divisions in races?
Why are certain countries in a state of chaos
while others build their 'walls'?
I don't understand politics anywhere,
are human dynamics so hurtful?
Do we really understand each other across boundaries?
Is ethnicity and colour about comfort or power?

Going back to our origin, it is apparent that our mammalian brains have some reactions to the colour of the skin, which we may not always be conscious of. Black is the dangerous dark night and white is sunlight! Over generations, this may have taken shape in our reactions to people. In spite of intellectual debates, the preference for white colour has been well known among both fair and dark communities for generations. White is associated with a subtle sense of beauty or superiority that is handed down to us. It is this privileging of white skin over dark or black skin that is the fundamental reason behind the malaise, which afflicts society today—*racism*. Skin tone and racial features could, at some level, be a factor of who gets ahead and who does not, with all else being equal.

As I reflect on these issues, I am forced to think through my journey and contemplate upon deep-seated, systemic issues that encouraged me to ponder over how we draw distinctions between people. The discussion about skin colour, when punctuated with racism, assumes a powerful place in society and transcends into discussions of power and prejudice.

In my life's journey too, the most obvious attribute that attracted any initial reaction (or sometimes made me revel or suffer) was the rooted perception about the colour of my skin. The strange bit is that it never really mattered to my self-confidence or self-esteem, given my global exposure, but I had to learn to deal with it as it did matter to people around me. The question arises— *is this what we wish to hand over to our next generation? Or is there something we could start to change to help create more unison for fragmented minds?* Unfounded perceptions create distorted realities that we can actually help change.

Did any individual choose to be of a certain ethnicity or colour? If not, then why do we make people suffer for something in the web of unfounded views? Often I am reminded by some people about how '...there is a perception that I...' and I usually stop listening beyond this because perception is not reality. But, I am well conscious of how people's reaction towards individuals is driven by their 'impressions' of them. Perceptions are mindsets that people grow by observing or hearing anecdotes over a period of time. They may not be emanating from their repeated/extensive direct experience. Perceptions are fallacies that are potent enough to impact the lives of people for no fault of theirs. The colour conundrum is such a reality today that it implicitly, if not explicitly, becomes a part of our cognitive mechanism.

Race and racism—do we really need to contend with how we were created?

I take pride in having been born in India, in having worked across multiple countries over the years; and now being British with a child in the US, and another getting ready to get back to the UK. The whole world is my oyster and I truly feel I belong here. In my cross-cultural experience, I have learnt that different cultures have different ideologies and that in the culture map of the world, life is rather colourful. I would like to place myself right in the middle as someone who has had the good fortune to live, work and engage with people from different cultures and communities. I do cherish and preserve the 'global' part of me as it helps me see through the different races, making me somewhat 'colour-blind'. I feel the experience of living in different cultures across different continents has helped me tide over diverse and complex human interactions. With each diverse connect or conflict, my understanding of human dynamics grew. It made me think harder and look for signs, which did not include colour; one attempted to understand the individual from a different country or a different culture. I take pride in saying that I am a citizen of the world!

THE NORMALISATION OF RACISM

Why is it so difficult to talk about race, colour, caste or even ideologies? I have been a woman of colour, and have worked in different geographies. There have been many moments in this journey where I felt the urge to shout out when wronged, to be understood better, to be supported and not to be judged even before I spoke. I have had to hold myself back when I was in the minority group, lest someone brand me a troublemaker. I have kept quiet at times as thoughts of, 'why attract too much discomfort?', lingered on my mind. Although I have to admit that a few times, I did muster up the courage to seek support in a conflicting situation, there was someone to hold me together, someone to walk with me to cross the trenches, someone to open the doors. I learnt that this journey starts first with self-belief and courage. The external world could be dealt with only if this was addressed. I needed to be self-aware and confident of myself to be able to deal with colour associated biases before someone could help me. My own mind may have been 'coloured' too!

As we know, rules are only visible to the minorities in any environment. A tacit acceptance of discrimination leads to normalisation of race. People from the majority group rarely see the discrimination, while minorities accept it as their necessary fate that they must adapt to lest they are ostracised for raising it. Racism becomes the new normal in this case. I do believe that we have to learn and adapt to new environments with new people. But, adapting does not mean submission to biases and imposition. I have seen that happening often with minorities. Not all rules work for them, but there is a fear or discomfort that one may be lacking the power to raise one's voice or resolve such issues amicably— somewhere something gets lost and life goes on.

Minority people in any country often live with a double consciousness and wear different personas. This is not akin to being inauthentic in any way. I have lived liked this, wherein I belonged to two very different worlds, but loved them both. Why am I forced to make a choice when I can make peace with the two spectrums, no matter how far apart they may be? This is a wonderful phenomenon and is an experience worth going through. Once you stay outside your home country in a completely different environment, your adaptability quotient multiplies by wearing different hats. I recall that while I was in the West, I was fully immersed in its culture while preserving my core. You don't always have to give up who you are!

Most organisations have policies, processes and sensitisation interventions in this area; however, mindset changes are not easy to bring about. It is arduous and takes time, given that we are blinded by differences in colour over centuries. Intellectually, no one disagrees that workplaces have to be an equal opportunity employer. However, realities are not always as close. What happens in the corridors and within the four walls of an office environment, or even outside it, is driven by generations of learning through families and social groups. These are ingrained so heavily in our DNA that in reality, this underlying bias takes over any intervention or learning at the workplace.

The dungeons of colour are deep-seated in our minds. They continue to drive our actions, reactions, thoughts and world view. They have emerged triumphant in the past and present. Often skin colour leads to biases that force us to lose ourselves in dark alleys of isolation without us even realising it. A change of mindset can help us find our way back and connect with people better. It is only a conscious reset of our mindset that can set us free—a journey I've been on and continue to seek answers to.

Racism is fundamentally hollow, yet it has gained strength from the support it gets from 'coloured' minds. The social fabrication of society is woven in beautiful shades of emotions, connections and love that every individual carries in her/his heart. We are born with eyes, arms, feet, nose, hair and ears, but a race is ascribed to us. Is this really genetic or are people naturalised through socialisation to believe and behave in a certain way, depending upon where they belong? Race is a reality, and I wonder how we can make it an asset for ourselves. When flowers are gathered together in an orderly manner, the mesmerising bouquet brings joy to all. Is that possible with different ethnicities and races?

POWER AND SECURITY

Ethnicity debate could also be driven by a need for power and security. Our mammalian brains are always at work, driven by a deep-seated desire for power that forces actions and reactions! There is a sense of strong identity associated with power, providing us with a much-needed sense of security. It may come at the expense of others, without us even realising it.

Sometimes people find comfort when they feel, or are rather made to feel, 'greater than' others. This need to feel superior slowly transcends into the need to feel powerful and then people start deriving a sense of 'me' at the expense of defining the 'other'. For better or worse, stereotyping people according to the way they look, the way they talk and the way they behave is the easiest way of establishing individuality.

The feeling of 'better' is so intoxicating and addictive that an individual unconsciously pushes to 'feel that feeling'. This leads to forced judgement to find superiority, which is like a mirage in the desert. It is not real, but miraculously people find convenient comparisons, while excluding other key humane factors to quietly justify this. Unconsciously, individuals want to feel like a winner in the race of life and sometimes, people do what it takes to get to the victory line. They strive to do that, unconscious of the fact that winning and losing is just a part of life and *racing across at the expense of humanity may mean we collectively lose*. We lose both our power and our security.

In the good old days, people lived in tribes to derive a sense of security. Among tribes, people helped each other to seek food, protection and joy. There was a sense of security within the tribe as there was strength in unity, especially against any danger or adversity. The sense of security drove a sense of collective power. Over a period of time, these tribes grew and the stronger ones survived. Collective consciousness is also born out of homogeneous thinking, such that there is little room for debate and discussion. This search for identity and a sense of belonging could segregate and categorise the entire populace into identifiable and recognisable groups creating 'human boundaries'. It is these human boundaries that assist in the creation of geographical boundaries, which can only be traversed by empathy and love. In the modern world, such tribal behaviour may manifest itself in the form of racism at its worst, and as collective heterogeneous groups tied with a common purpose at its best.

Among the 2,017 immigration stories collected during the writing of this book, the tragic image of a small boy wearing a red T-shirt and blue shorts, lying with his face down on the shores of Europe, is symbolic of the devastating death of humanity. The lifeless body of the little Syrian boy shows the tragic plight of refugees who are taking huge risks in search of a safer and better life. The small boy was one of the few Syrian refugees trying to reach a Greek island. They were ironically washed ashore, a few kilometres away from Bodrum, one of Turkey's most fashionable resort towns. The three-year-old boy, identified as Alan Kurdi, would have scarcely known that in the quest of finding a life full of ebullience and joy, he would be washed away forever! We need to build a more secure future and leave behind a more humane legacy for our children.

The untimely demise of Alan Kurdi is representative of the apathy that human beings have developed for those who do not belong to their 'own'. It is catastrophic and devastating to witness three-year-olds with happy faces engrossed in playful activities, while a small bundle of joy in another part of the world does not even get an opportunity to live life. According to the United Nations High Commissioner for Refugees (UNHCR), around 2,500 people died in the summer of 2015, while making a futile attempt to cross the Mediterranean Sea to reach Europe.

Lately, I see debates on migrants across the world. As I see the anxious, yet hopeful faces of people on a ferry headed towards European shores, Bangladeshis towards India, Rohingyas or Filipinos towards Singapore or Hong Kong, Mexicans towards the US, it seems the only motive for all these people to leave home is to find a better life elsewhere. One wonders if that is an evil driver.

Today, we are aware that many migrants in Europe are employed in blue-collar jobs, which has contributed to prosperity there. We also know that borders are man-made. We know too that geopolitical problems in some key countries in Africa and Asia are politically motivated! Who is really responsible for people moving out from Africa and Asia to greener pastures? It's troubling to see shutters coming down on people who are simply looking to live, and our respective governments not supporting them for political reasons. We would rather let them die in the precarious seas or have them shot down by our security forces than give them a chance under the guise of economic affordability.

I feel humbled and privileged today to be able to afford myself a safe and secure life in the subcontinent, and perhaps even more fortunate to have provided the same to my children across different continents. I shudder to think that had I been born in a war-ravaged state, I could also have been one of them—stuck at sea, begging for food and shelter and, most important of all, acceptance from 'foreign' people on 'foreign' land. This urges me to help those who need this support.

Some individuals move across borders, away from their native homes, in search of security, livelihood and rightful recognition of their talent. One key aspect of this is how they adapt to the culture of a new country or how they are treated by different communities. It is also interesting to note the role colour plays in their lives, in success or in failure. Sometimes, it is a game changer of sorts in this so-called global, modernised world.

PERSEVERANCE AND PERSISTENCE

The definition of 'racism' has been evolving, but the perseverance to deal with these challenges and staying the course is what gives us hope. Challenges cannot be avoided when diverse sets of people come together, but the will to persevere supersedes all differences. It gives us the courage to persist and make the moment ours. It emboldens us to not only fight prejudices, but to be brave enough to show our real selves for others to do the same. Many times in my life, I have felt down and out when faced with a situation of preconceived biases. What kept me going was my belief and willpower, along with support from a few who believed in me. My persistence to change this, slowly and painfully, originates from my focus on building a world for our children in which they face far lesser of such challenges.

Oprah Winfrey rightly said that excellence is the best deterrent to racism.

I recently met the CEO of a global firm who is a person of colour. Given his impressive credentials, I had assumed he was one of the fortunate ones who had garnered a lot of support during his climb up, through his extraordinary talents. When we met in a meeting, I did ask him his mantra of leadership and he shared that through all odds, as a minority, he believed in what he could become. He invited himself to explore his possibilities in different and, sometimes, alien environments. This gave him the courage and conviction to go on. I was truly impressed by the number of crossroads and challenges he had faced due to unconscious biases against his colour yet he persisted with dogged determination to go on despite them. I also noted that the strong relationships he had built with people who mattered had helped him to get where he was today.

Persevering in the face of odds is an essential outlook for leaders who tread forward, setting the path for others, opening gates and inspiring many minds to join the journey to break these barriers.

Long back in 1880, a young black individual left the US and moved to Italy as he could not get acceptance as a student in his country then. He was born into slavery. His parents worked hard to get him some education, but local church revolts hampered their efforts. Racism continued to hinder his quest for learning. As a budding priest, he found it tough to get any American seminary to accept him. However, he persisted with his efforts in spite of all the prejudices he faced. He continued to support the local communities with messages of inclusion and social justice.

In Italy, he found his calling. His perseverance to become a priest with a purpose built a rich legacy for many. Recently, Pope Francis announced that this black priest, Tolton, was being recognised by the church for having lived a life of heroic virtue. He is the first black priest who could be declared a saint, posthumously.

In the times of Tolton, hardships were multiplied for people of colour; however, his focus, belief and will to go on ensured that the universe conjured to make things happen for him. The narrative that defines our identity needs an infusion of courage to make it a reality.

Take the recent sports news, 'Moise Kean [a black player] as the face of Italy', for the country's under-21 football team. Despite being subjected to racial abuse, he has stood tall all through his ordeal. He was abused through monkey boos and shouting throughout the match in Sardegna, but he defiantly continued to play the game. His deafening silence against other racist players and political figures was his best answer. He felt Italy was his home.

Kean's parents were Ivorian and divorced when he was four years old. He and his brother were raised by his mother, who made ends meet by taking up small jobs. To help himself, Kean used to collect a few euros every week and try and double it by playing a six-a-side match near a street church. He learnt his game on the streets, fighting all odds before being picked by a local club.

Having been through childhood hardships, he was ready to take on the battle both on and off the field to prove himself. No shade of colour could defy his perseverance.

In the interplay of colour, it is important to remember that individuals can also be discriminated against in the guise of protection for another community or ethnicity. There is also a phenomenon of reverse racism, wherein the intention to prevent, for example, black or brown people from being discriminated reaches such a point that unconsciously, or consciously, situations arise where white people are discriminated against in their own country.

Kevin Pietersen was a white South African who had to leave his country because he wanted to play international cricket. It is interesting to note that in 2006, he had accused Cricket South Africa (CSA) of 'racism' or rather 'reverse racism'. CSA has a quota system wherein each first-class team in South Africa is expected to contain at least four non-white players. Kevin Pietersen, after repeatedly being ignored and being made to sit on the bench despite continuously performing well, made an interesting decision. He packed his bags and relocated to England to realise his dream of playing international cricket.

This situation did provoke a debate about reverse racism and the policy trade-off that a policymaker had to make to 'reduce' as opposed to 'eliminate' discrimination against 'whites' and 'blacks'.

Pietersen had to wait for four years in England before he got a chance to represent the country in international cricket.

Each of us, who may have experienced being a minority at some stage in our life, face such challenges. The first step is to have clarity of our own goals and then set out on the path to achieve them with self-respect, self-belief and courage. No one can make one feel inferior apart from one's own self.

RACE AND ITS DIFFERENT HUES

I have changed my mind, or seen others change their minds, about a certain race or ethnicity. This came about with an openness to engage with someone different from oneself. Engagement helps us understand the 'other' beyond the colour of their skin. It is only when we are able to dwell on their thoughts objectively that we are able to empathise with their feelings without being affected by our own— and the 'connect' happens. And when that happens, inexplicable magic is created and 'colour' becomes invisible! You look at people in a colourless way. They become people like ourselves with feelings, emotions and thoughts. You can feel their joy, their pain, their fears. There is purely a human connect, wherein it does not matter how anyone looks or which part of the planet they come from!

I don't know if this debate on racism and ethnicity is human, political or economical, but what I do know is that it is somewhat primitive and driven by basic instincts of power. World history is strewn with diabolic debates about the 'superior race' with hate crimes or even genocides associated with it. Such events do not happen in isolation, there is usually a build-up of parochial perceptions that go ignored for a period of time before culminating in violence and wars. I do believe that as much as these dynamics are difficult to control, there is something equally fundamental that can bind us together—our simple love for humanity. Our openness to the world is jeopardised by the fear of losing out; and the associated power of feeling superior drives people in absolute opposite directions.

I don't have all the answers yet, but my search continues and perhaps in my search, I will find my calling!

The Flow of the Book

This book brings C-O-L-O-U-R alive. Each chapter starts with a theme based on the letters of the word 'colour'. The chapter unfolds a topic with related experiences and learnings from others like you and I. It attempts to enable you with thoughts and learnings from our everyday experiences of people around us. This unfolding of stories and thoughts in the book represents my ongoing search.

Each chapter commences with my views, as I share conversations with my children. As a family, we have regular conversations, like any other parent-child interaction, about the day gone by, about what made them happy, what bothered them or what made them afraid. Throughout our conversations, I think that I have learnt a lot. Ruminating on our interactions brings a few priceless nuggets to mind. These will serve as a prelude to each chapter of the book.

As a parent, I feel that since my children have had a global upbringing, they have evolved as world citizens. It is easy for children to connect, to empathise and appreciate different ethnicities and cultures at a young age, if we can help them keep an open mind. Sid, my son, goes to an international school, and Avni, my daughter, studies in the US. They, therefore, have friends from nations all over the world! It's interesting how young children can sometimes instantly connect with each other, no matter the differences in their colour or culture, in the language they speak or the food they eat!

If this book can motivate you to reflect on the topic in your own way, I would consider my efforts worthwhile.

Connect

Sid: 'Mom, there's this new boy, this term, in school; Jae-Bong from Korea, and he hardly talks! It's so hard to figure him out. My teacher wants me to be his buddy, but I don't know what to do with him!'

Avni (interrupting): 'Hey, he is new Sid, he may not be very comfortable with English yet, so go learn Korean!'

Mom: 'Hey, both of you! He is new to the school and the country. Sid, have you asked him how he is feeling? What does he like about being here and what does he find tough? If he doesn't talk, ask again!'

Sid (nodding his head): 'Well for that he needs to talk! I can try Mom, but why is it so difficult?!'

Mom: 'We all have to try and connect. The outcome is less important than the effort. He is away from home, away from his old friends, and he has to learn how a new place works. Remember how you felt when you returned to India from the UK?'

Sid: 'Well! Now that you say it, it was a bit weird. I recall a boy making fun of the way I spoke. The whole school seemed like an alien territory, and I was lost and scared. I just wanted to run back to London.'

Mom: 'Hmmm, so now you know what Jae-Bong may be going through!'

Sid: 'I think he is better behaved than I was. I can put myself in his shoes and feel the pain. I'll talk to him tomorrow and take him out for a game of football. Let's see if that works.'

Mom: 'Sounds good, Sid. Perhaps cricket might help too, since he's in India now!'

Today, Jae-Bong and Sid are great friends. Jae-Bong loves 'butter chicken' and *parantha* and Sid can have Korean for any meal! Magic happened.

True 'connect' is a state when a mere exchange of ideas, messaging and learning moves into a higher state of mutual understanding and deeper acceptance. Connect is an essential ingredient that helps us navigate through the cultural alleys and bridge any differences in ethnicity, race or religion. We are born with family ties, but the bonds of friendship that we create reflect our innate longing to extend beyond mere blood boundaries. The 'human connect', as it is called, is fundamental to our understanding of relationships and responses. These are formed when barriers disappear between individuals unrelated by blood, ethnicity or nationality. It is the glue that holds and builds a bond. It helps us peek into each other's hearts, feelings and thoughts. It helps us become 'colour-blind', which is not always a bad thing!

BOND BEYOND BARRIERS

'Sunita, let's go! Come play with me, it'll be lots of fun, na? Sunita, I am waiting, this new board game is so exciting!'

That is how I used to call Sunita every day after I came back from school. I used to wait for the evenings because I had gradually discovered how special that time was for me!

My parents were busy doctors and we resided in a hospital campus. As a six-year-old, my best friend was Sunita, a little girl of my age. We often hung around together, playing with our dolls (she had only one), playing in the house or running around the tall eucalyptus trees in the backyard. Our innocence and energy were in full bloom during that stage of life.

Although Sunita and I went to different schools, we would get together after school to catch up on the day and plan our adventures with toys and other friends. Strangely, she never ate at my house; her own house being smaller than mine, she would often come over to mine to play. I remember one evening, when she had not turned up at our usual play time, I went over to her house to investigate and found her unwell. Her mother had made some fresh bread. Very hungry myself, I had asked for some too. Strangely, her mother declined to serve me, and that too quite rudely! I remember feeling absolutely bruised and the stubborn child that I was, I insisted on fulfilling my demand. She conceded after much persuasion, but told me not to tell anyone at home that I had eaten at her house. I found that even more strange and queer. Anyway, I ate the food before heading home.

> **When minds meet, thoughts flow, words come alive, then magic of connections happen.**

I was confused by what Sunita's mother had said to me and could not comprehend what the issue was. After dinner that day, I remember telling my mother of all that had happened at Sunita's house. I asked her if she too thought that I should not have eaten with my best friend's family, and if so, why?

My mother was quiet for a few minutes and then she took a deep breath before gathering the right words. She started to explain to me the confounding situation in the simplest way she could to a six-year-old, although I could see her visible discomfort and embarrassment as she went along. She explained that the family we were born in, the work that we did and the profession we were in often defined who we were in the world. People were born in different families and did different kinds of work. Some studied and had great jobs, while some others did basic work. This determined their position in society. In India, it was not befitting for those from the higher strata of society to eat with people born in a lower stratum, who did basic work such as sweeping or cleaning. She was confusing me further and I had to quiz her with my multiple 'whys'. She patiently explained to me the caste concept in India and how some people were considered 'untouchables' and that most people thought that it was not desirable to mingle with them socially. But, she encouraged me to break all such social barriers and continue with my after-school conversations with Sunita. My mother made me feel that I had nothing to feel ashamed about visiting my friend's family as long as I was safe. That was an eye-opening moment for me; a new paradigm was understood.

My friend Sunita was the daughter of a hospital sweeper and the most beautiful soul I knew. I could sense that her parents were poor and that she stayed in a one-room house and the food they ate was very basic. But, despite our many differences, we understood each other and felt 'connected'.

A real connect emanates from love and compassion for others that encompasses everything else. I loved the serenity, the transparency and the purity of our relationship. We both respected each other and were oblivious to our social differences, concealing nothing. We led two different lives, but learnt to make our life even better by complementing our differences. I admired her tenacity and her will to go on, and she respected my humility and kindness. When there is mutual admiration, trust and understanding between two people, it automatically transcends into a bond, which is strong and durable. I also feel that this came from our own personal beliefs of being equals. The feeling of superiority and inferiority distorts a relationship and denigrates it to a superficial level. As children we do this so beautifully and unconditionally; however, we discard this as we learn more about life's social norms. What if we can keep this alive forever and let the magic unfold with connect?

Over the years, I have worked with all types of people—some kind to me and some not so kind. However, when I reflect back, it fills me with a sense of gratitude because each person touched my life in their own special way. They all came into my life for a reason and they were magically gone once their purpose was over. I have worked with people of different colours, but I now recollect that what had brought us closer was our humane connection that led to moments in which we understood each other at a deeper level. What surely helped in forging deep ties was tiding through tough times together at work rather than just the happy moments we shared.

I feel that every relationship gives you an insight and enriches you in its own unique way. Interacting with Sunita and spending time with her was a kind of sacred indulgence. For me, each one of us is different, in the way we think, in the way we behave, the way we look and the way we are brought up. The culture or society we grow up in has a long-lasting impact on the way we perceive relationships with people close to us as well as with 'strangers'. A stranger will always remain a stranger if we fail to understand them and envision a future where they can be our friends. The reluctance to engage with a person emotionally and psychologically leads to a lack of connect with that particular individual. This disconnect leads to gaps that may hinder the formation of a relationship because distrust, suspicion, insecurity and hatred are all liable to creep into that empty space.

The beauty about forming a connection is that it has no formula. Any relationship or connection unfolds on its own over time and connections convert into strong, unbreakable and intense bonds that last a lifetime. All one has to do is to keep one's presuppositions in check. If we do not allow individuals from different ethnicities to mingle with us and enmesh themselves into our culture, then how are we to appreciate the differences among ourselves? In some ways, we grow up accepting the norms of colour as established by society, classifying people around us in character boxes or on the basis of their physicality, rather than our direct experiences with them. It takes courage and will to be able to adopt a new mindset, challenge existing paradigms and accept the 'perceived unacceptable'.

As a child, like most others at that age, I was colour-blind when it came to people. I could not see the difference between social inequality, leave alone caste or religion. We should always be open to discovering ourselves, with another, irrespective of the strata of society that an individual comes from. My personal learning and growth from my friendship with Sunita have been immense, as I connected to the person in her and not to her background. We connected because we allowed ourselves to be vulnerable and innocent children. Neither of us was ashamed or awed by this connection, and this is what helped us to stay immersed in our own world of blissful humanity!

She remains a friend till date.

Costs of Casteism

Treating someone respectfully is a basic human courtesy, and starting with a positive intent makes a huge difference. For me, the feeling is reflected in an explicable sense of ease while interacting with anyone without making any assumptions basis their physicality. I feel that the warmth, tenderness and leniency that accompanies this kind of a connection assists the evolution of a bond over a longer period of time.

I think we should try to live with contradictions in how people around us are, be a little accepting of each other's cultural differences, try to find out the similarities and imbibe tolerance. I feel that whenever we take caste or race into consideration while connecting with a person, it automatically imparts a biased definition to the relationship, which makes it hollow. It induces a behaviour that hampers the formation of any deeper connection.

India, in particular, is a land of dichotomy where inequality coexists with the harmony of co-dependence. Even after centuries of evolution of progressive mindsets, especially in urban centres, it is still difficult to completely neutralise thoughts and views on the age-old caste system in India. This is reflective of how we perceive people from different social and regional backgrounds. There are very few countries in the world where your surname lets one identify the region of the country you come from, your social 'caste', possible food habits, dress codes, et al.

And yet, even in 2019, reservations continue to be the primary handout for the polity. Add to this the various Indian states that demand their own subsets of differentiators based on language and region. Today, when Indian society stands at the cusp of a revolutionary transformation, an open dialogue on caste, reigning in caste-based crimes and caste-based discrimination in the social, economic and political domain is an imperative need. The economic impacts of racism and regionalism in India continue, and visibly so. The inequity among various 'classes' of people in India is a result of the biases against the backward classes. It is interesting to note that the socio-economic condition within the backward classes and the various caste groups is not uniform even though the Indian constitution mandated the reservation of the Scheduled Castes (SCs) and the Scheduled Tribes (STs) more than half a century ago.

In the past, each social group was identified by the quality and the kind of work they did, hence, it was quite natural for the upper caste groups to occupy white-collar jobs as opposed to the lower caste groups. In fact, as most unskilled workers came from the lower castes, this indirectly led to the inequality in the distribution of income and wealth in the country. Therefore, a division in the social sphere also affects those from the lower castes economically. It is quite evident that the lack of connect between individuals from different castes led to the sustained division of people into various social groups. In rural India, especially, people from certain castes prefer to mingle, marry and associate within the same groups, and there is lesser inter-caste interaction or association outside of the urban centres.

Casteism prevents the mingling of people across societies and hinders the dissolution of mental barriers and fences. We seem to have lost the ability to use connections as an important way of redistributing wealth across different divisions of society. Our lack of connect with the lower castes has pushed them to the lowest end of the income pyramid for no fault of theirs. This segregation has led to the poor becoming poorer, and to the perception that the lower caste should engage in low-skilled jobs, leading to socio-economic divisions in the allocation of the quality of work. A real connection in such cases would help us harness the fresh energy, the talent and the skill of the nation's youth so that we develop much more equitably.

ROOTS MATTER!

Communities we grow up in give us life lessons and relationships that help us integrate and progress further. Being respectful of our roots, while evolving our perspectives will keep us on a strong foundation. Any loss of connect may lead to a lost identity.

The white privilege extends across the globe; time and again, the colonial era surfaces in the minds of people. Although I was born well after India had achieved independence, I have often found special treatment being meted out to fairer people by the local populace. They reserve a special status, as it were, for the Caucasian race, while unconsciously assuming a slightly subservient role for their own selves. I am unsure if white people actually expect such treatment, even though it is completely enjoyed by most. Indians are good at forgiving and forgetting. I think one can forgive, but should not forget history. There seems to be less awareness about the past, but it continues to subtly impact our relationships with the world even today.

It seems that the white populace, who have been beneficiaries of the 'white privilege' and have embraced it for centuries, may feel lost when they are compelled to envision a future where they are not entitled to that past privilege anymore. White privilege has been described by Paula Rothenberg as the other side of discrimination. It has been defined by experts (such as DG Hays, CY Chang, ML Manning and LG Baruth) as a 'combination of exclusive standards and opinions that are supported by whites in a way that continually reinforces social distance between groups on the basis of power, access, advantage, majority status, control, choice, autonomy, authority, possessions, wealth, opportunity, materialistic acquisition, connection, preferential treatment, entitlement and social standing'.

Preeti, a high potential employee working in a global financial services organisation in India, was keen to work in another country, ideally a developed market to gain some international exposure. Keeping in line with her development plan, her manager worked through her request with key stakeholders and sent her to Hong Kong for an assignment. First time out of the country, she initially felt quite unsettled working in a predominantly white environment (incidentally, the work group was largely British in Hong Kong). She could not adapt to cultural norms and was constantly in touch with her previous manager back home, a well-travelled, global individual. He took over as her mentor and coached her on understanding the cultural norms, honing her softer skills, modifying her communication style, to suit the host country.

Over a period of time, Preeti started feeling settled; in a year's time, things changed dramatically for her as she began experiencing a different life, the comforts of a developed market and the fun of working with white people. This was all good, except that she now started berating how India was such a tough place to be in. She became vocal about how India was not a great working environment with too much pressure, the streets were not clean, the list went on. Having been a global citizen himself who loved India, her earlier manager and some other colleagues back in India were amazed at her dramatic change. Preeti continued her rant about the working styles of Indians and how it was so much better overseas. Her accent changed and something in her was not recognisable anymore to her colleagues back home.

In fact, as she let other working groups in Hong Kong know about her newly found negative view of her country, it hampered preferences of inbound talent that were considering moving to India. This was indeed worrisome.

The company had sent Preeti overseas as a brand ambassador, but she had actually really hurt the Indian image by focusing on racial stereotypes rather than on the strengths and exposure to opportunities for learning. Every country and region has its pros and cons, and so does India. The team back in India was sure that for Preeti, being on the other side of the table meant distancing herself from her roots, which she probably perceived as being more beneficial with her new work group.

This individual had been born and brought up in India, and she came from a well-to-do family, so this reaction was triggered by reasons either unconsciously embedded in her psyche or were driven by other motives that were unfathomable.

Moreover, as the India team discussed a few open roles for other such high potential talents to move to Hong Kong, Preeti would not select the Indian candidates. Instead, she would prefer others for these open roles, citing frivolous reasons such as how she would be accused of taking her own, if she selected Indians, etc. Her condescension for fellow browns was evident as she worked diligently to ensure she was not seen as an Indian anymore. She was convinced that being closer to the local white people was more productive for her. This misplaced belief was so firm in her mind that she started to overlook who really had her back and well-being at heart.

She thought that distancing herself from her roots would give her professional advantage. Unfortunately, she had fallen prey to a misconceived hypothesis about the route to make those professional connections.

In a few years, a restructuring was carried out in Hong Kong and Preeti's unit was put at risk. She was the first to go, being on a sponsored work permit. When she made that call to India, asking people to bail her out, there was no one to take that call, except her earlier manager who obliged her for old times' sake. He decided to help her connect with the local network, but was clear about not having her back in the team, given that the relationship had been lost. She returned to the country unsure of where she belonged and who she could connect with! Her ambition to be someone else, to be somewhere faster than anyone else, had blinded her so much that she was now left lonely in this journey of life, bereft of friends.

Reflecting on Preeti's journey does beg the question—what prompted her to drift away? It would seem that the need to be accepted by the majority who may have carried biases about brown people may have triggered this behaviour. To be a part of this new group, Preeti may have felt the pressure to speak their language/ views, without realising how this may play out for her long-term relationships back home. Her drive to be successful in a foreign land at the expense of denouncing her roots seemed a compelling proposition among the group of people she worked with in Hong Kong. Rightly or wrongly, she chose a path with short-term benefits, but long-term consequences on friendships and belongings.

We have to be cautious of how our old connects are redefined when we make new ones. Old connects only get stronger with time, if we are truly vested in them. We need to be careful about our short-sighted and limited judgements when we live in diverse environments. Often it is not black and white, but shades of grey that have to be understood granularly. Engaging in the right conversations with ourselves helps clear clouds and misplaced perceptions. When we are shameful of who we are, we harbour a skewed view of the world. Connecting with one's own self, therefore, is more important before connecting with others.

In a new environment filled with good and not so good views about diverse people, it is imperative to form relationships with a new cohort on the basis of authenticity, sincerity and value addition. This may reap stronger connects in the long-term, as new people will understand you for who you really are. This may take more effort and patience, but if you are truly adding value to the team, it will help mitigate any biases leading to an inclusive environment. Adapting to new cultures does not imply that one needs to berate one's own. Each culture has its own strengths and nuances that can be brought together for making the best of both worlds, rather than rejecting one in favour of another.

THE MANIFESTATION OF 'CONNECT' THROUGH COLOUR

I have often wondered how our educated and enlightened minds harbour prejudices and often believe in it wholeheartedly, although never expressing it overtly. This is often a result of the environment in which we grow up, the people we connect with and the ones we do not connect with. This eventually drives our beliefs and our world view. We naturally tend to be much more comfortable among people from our own community and ethnicity. There lies an element of certainty and security in mingling with our 'own' and an element of ambiguity or threat in mingling with the 'other'.

Most relationships thrive on compassion. If you are in the majority in your home country, then displaying some warmth and tenderness would go a long way in making a foreign person feel inclusive anywhere. The feelings of isolation and loneliness are the most difficult emotions to deal with in an unfamiliar terrain. There is a lost sense of belonging. I believe that if each of us extended a helping hand in comforting an individual from a different ethnicity or nationality, it would go a long way in enriching their experiences within a new community.

I have always let my curiosity guide me in connecting with different kinds of people. It has been an eye-opening experience, traversing the world and letting myself go into different regions and learning different ways of being. Surprisingly, it was not very different across communities. I was touched by the same human emotions, just the triggers varied; communication, verbal or non-verbal, was disguised in different languages and forms. Simply put, in most cases, judgement had to be held back and diversity needed to be embraced.

The morning alarm went off at the usual time for a young executive, Seema, who had joined the London office of a leading advertising firm. It was a light and breezy summer morning. Happiness in the form of the rising sun and blue sky invited her to venture out some distance on foot. Usually, she was not a morning person, but this beautiful calling was hard to resist. She quickly got ready and started on a not-so-routine journey to her office.

Entering office that day felt like being captured inside a claustrophobic chamber. She managed to drag herself into an even smaller cubicle where Microsoft Outlook stared out angrily from her laptop screen. It almost yelled at her for being late for the day's very first meeting with a senior leader, Hannah James. As a new joinee, it was her first meeting with Ms James along with another colleague, Ella, a young Londoner who had also joined the agency at the same time. This was part of their induction meeting!

Seema collected a notepad and ran towards the elevator to make up for lost time. Getting off at the forty-second floor executive level, she fell in love with the view across the river. Hushing her mind, she fumbled around to find Ms James's office. As she entered the room, she saw her colleague already there. Apologising profusely for being late, she sat down next to Ella. Ms James greeted her tersely, looking over her specs balanced on the tip of her nose that reminded Seema of her strict boarding school matron.

The conversation started with how Ms James had joined the agency, and as Seema listened to her intently, she realised that her senior was not looking at her at all. As the conversation progressed, Seema felt invisible and that only Ella was being addressed. She felt she didn't even exist in the room for Hannah James, although she sat right across the table and was difficult to miss!

As Hannah James spoke to Ella, Seema noticed a soft expression on her face.

Seema coughed momentarily to catch her senior's attention, but she seemed too engrossed to notice anyone else in the room. Instead of asking Seema if she was fine or if she needed any water, the expression on Ms James's face was that of irritation, a look that questioned her very presence. Seema wasn't sure if it was just a figment of her imagination, but her feeling of discomfort grew exponentially. She felt left out and completely out of place in the room. Her biggest cause of perplexity was being unaware of the reason behind such rude and unwelcoming behaviour. But most likely, it was a reason that she did not want to accept!

As the conversation drew to a close, Ms James asked if there were any questions, looking pointedly at Ella, who asked a few. Although Seema raised her hand, she was ignored; but, when she persisted, Ms James snapped, 'Yes Seema, what is it that you want?' Before she could even begin to ask, 'I needed to know…', the curt rejoinder from Ms James was that she could go online and read about it. Seema thanked her and requested to be excused.

Seema's heart was sinking, something was hurting, the pain was excruciating.

What had just happened?

'Did I do anything wrong?' Seema asked herself, 'Why did Ms James ignore me? What was it about Ella that got her the attention?'

Plenty of questions confused her thoughts. She had been forewarned about Ms James's habitual rude behaviour, but had never believed this could happen to her!

A candid question arose in her mind, 'Was my colour so appalling?'

Who knows? She never found the answer, she never had the courage to ask, but deep down she believed that the colour of her skin was, in some way, responsible for the treatment, and that old hurt still haunts her to this day. More so as she felt she could have been more courageous to challenge it, but something held her back. What was it ?

Sometimes you just don't want to know the answers or you are not ready to face them. Sometimes such episodes upset you, but you do not always have the experience and the maturity to handle them and do something about them. You are scared about what challenging these issues may mean for you. Seema could have had an open conversation with Hannah that might have stopped her from suffering silently for weeks together in the aftermath of the episode. She was young, too naïve and lacked the courage to deal with such subtle discrimination headlong as she was a minority in that room; she felt vulnerable. She was unsure about what she could really do to tackle the situation in the best way possible.

Hannah made a lot of presumptions and judgements without making an effort to know Seema or witnessing her performance. It was disheartening for Seema that she could not do much to change her initial perception. This lack of connect between Hannah and Seema led to a situation where Hannah strongly believed in the 'single story', the prejudgements affected their equation and they could never share what could've mutually fructified into a successful working relationship. The absence of an intent and the quick judgement from Hannah led to the end of a relationship even before it began. In the fast-moving agency environment, this introduced an element of artificiality in their otherwise professional relationship. Since there was no connection, there was a severe gap and coldness between them, which eventually became very difficult for Seema to bear for too long. In fact, at a counselling session, she confessed that the fact that Hannah did not like her was difficult for her to deal with, especially because there was no concrete reason behind it apart from her colour.

Seema finally left that job.

What could she have done differently? Perhaps she could have persisted more to explore the nuances in a new culture and strengthen the relationship, but Hannah's attitude broke her confidence in the first instance. Therefore, that relationship remained in abeyance leading to misalignment, non-productive work environment and a greater loss of inclusion for Seema.

As I ponder on this episode, I think, perhaps judgement without information is the biggest barrier to connect with each other. People do need to leave behind social baggage or else it continues to drag into the future, pulling one back and not letting the past rest in peace. This blocks future growth. More importantly, one shouldn't take anyone's negative behaviour personally. Nobody can belittle us, but our own selves.

Self-belief and patience is the key to dealing with such situations in real time!

On further discussions with Seema's colleagues, it was evident that Hannah's presumption that browns were expected to behave in a certain way had forced her to perceive Seema in a certain way. It was a generalised interpretation of her mind, and Seema was expected to live with the tacit acceptance of these ethnicity norms. For Hannah, Seema did not behave like a conventional and seemingly quiet brown foreigner, because she was always asking questions, and was quite talkative and expressive. Perhaps that was the very fact that made Hannah uncomfortable. Seema broke the stereotype around 'brown behaviour' and Hannah was quite shocked to witness it because her interpretations of brown behaviour definitely did not match Seema's. Perhaps Hannah had had no exposure to people from other ethnicities and her own unfounded norms guided her on what was appropriate without any concessions to cross-cultural references.

These are exactly the instances when we need to reach a common ground of understanding each other because nobody indeed knows the rules of legitimate behaviour in a particular culture. Therefore, we need to have explicit conversations to connect and understand why and how one is expected to behave in a certain way in a certain country. This helps to better understand the context we are in.

It helps to brush aside stereotypes and make an endeavour to connect with a person at a deeper level. Magic happens only when we make an attempt to respect the individuality of the other 'different' person. It enables both individuals to reside in a safer psychological space, allowing them to seamlessly blend and get acquainted with each other's thought process and culture-backed ideologies. When we form new relationships with people of a different colour or a different ethnicity, it helps us to mould into a better version of ourselves and we grow with each and every relationship.

As is said, a journey of a thousand miles starts with a small step. My experiences have taught me that the first step we need to take is to break out of the caged mind that prevents us from saying that first 'hello' to someone we don't know, but want to or need to know. It seems to me that the problem often lies in our mind, which refuses to make an endeavour to go beyond colour, to go beyond the visuals and make that effort to extend a hand of friendship. It feels like hard work to open yourself and get to know another. Once we are free from the fetters of our self-imposed inertia, we are better positioned to connect with the 'differences' among people. The celluloid covering the populist ideologies of colour and race have somehow mollycoddled people into abandoning the truth that lies beneath every skin—the truth of mankind, of humanity and of pure human emotions. We need to remove this celluloid from our minds and open our doors to the humble beginnings of impossible or unfathomable relationships. This can be achieved simply through an open mind and holding judgements off for a while. Not always easy, but not impossible either. Make an honest start for yourself and see the magic unfold.

THE REAL CONNECTION

Competition is valued in certain cultures/races of Asia or the Americas, and shunned or expressed rather subtly in the EU or the UK. Dr Abraham Tesser, professor of psychology at the University of Georgia, US, discovered that when someone outperforms us in a task or activity that is relevant to us, it threatens our self-esteem in some way or the other. So we do not feel happy when some of our fellow colleagues do well. Unconsciously, we have a tendency to prove to the world that we excel at everything we do. The feeling of embarrassment at not doing as well as others, professionally or personally, sometimes makes us feel diminished and instils a sense of loss within us. This fear may push us to over-project ourselves when dealing with people who are different from us.

Dr Tesser feels that insecurities get the better of us, thereby projecting an unreal self-image. We forget that self-disclosure and vulnerability help us to form real connections. In 1997, the social psychologist, Arthur Aron from Stony Brook University, US, also conducted an experiment to prove that we must show our true selves to those with whom we wish to establish a lifelong connect. Results proved that disclosures do help in building and deepening human relationships.

Human experiences are not perfect and we must embrace our imperfections when we attempt to make connections. When you share your authentic thoughts with another person—that is when you form a deeper connect. The trick is to share our ups and downs with prospective connections and to break down the myths of any mistaken assumption.

(Fair and Lovely) > (Dark and Ugly)?

'I am a very very fair, slender, tall, good-looking woman, convent educated, aged 28 years, 5 feet 4 inches, Brahmin, Hindu, marketing professional and a caring, homely girl interested to marry a very very fair, tall, slender, good-looking man aged 30-35 years, height 6 feet, earning 6 digit salary, Brahmin, banking or financial professional settled in India or the US or the UK.'

I am surprised and highly amused to see these 'matrimonial advertisements' in the classifieds of one of the leading newspapers. It disrupts my neutral thought process on skin colour. The words 'very very fair' and 'good-looking' are annoying and amusing at the same time. The entire classifieds page is a comedy movie with still images and I wonder whether being good-looking and fair are the key requirements to connect with another individual. I wonder if mental wavelength, biological mappings, compatibility or blood group are even a consideration while choosing a partner here, although they certainly are for a divorce today!

I met my husband, Sandeep, in business school. One day, Sandeep decided to drop me home after a coffee meeting, and my parents happened to be there too! He entered our house after driving his bike in the warm winter sun for an hour. The warmth had turned his fair skin pink and rugged! I was a pillion rider with him and my brown skin probably looked more tanned under the same sunlight. My mother was instantly impressed with him, not just with his degrees, but also with his sun-kissed skin. I could see her expression change to a very welcoming one for Sandeep and an unsure one for me. In that moment, I felt like the foster or an evil stepdaughter. After a polite conversation, Sandeep left. My mother subtly let me know that my life's mission was accomplished because Sandeep seemed like a really good individual to marry. My thoughts, 'Really mother!!! How did you figure this one out in ten minutes?!' What had I missed thus far?

'Oh well, he was so qualified, he looks good, he is fair, you should marry him!'

Huh! *My* mother had fallen for the fair skin syndrome too as I was equally qualified. Even as a doctor she was not immune to it! My jumbled mind decided to filter this and go on with life as usual.

Sandeep and I were both away from home, living in our city of work, Mumbai, before our marriage. After a few months, I was visiting Sandeep's hometown and dropped by his home. As I walked through the door, his mother invited me to the living room for a cup of tea. She was warm and courteous, but I felt that she didn't smile enough or had I imagined it! Her gaze did not break and her laser eyes scanned me up and down, given that I was the potential girl to enter her son's life. Rightly or wrongly, at that time, reading from her expressions, I felt that I clearly did not meet the traditional norms of a demure daughter-in-law either in looks or my views on life and relationships. Conversations were short on both sides as we tried to gauge each other better. What was apparent was that she was totally unsure of how this was going to work between Sandeep and I. We looked different as I am brown, we came from different backgrounds, we had been brought up differently and various other things. I always suspected that the topic of not being the traditional *gora* (fair) *bahu* (daughter-in-law) came up with his parents. However, for the sake of world peace, my husband has refused to disclose such state secrets to me (till date)!

In some ways, it was evident for both our mothers that colour had some meaning or significance even though we were grateful that it was never imposed on us. The way society dictates norms around colours shapes the thinking of generations!

We were eventually married. In our three years of courtship, colour was never visible to either of us. We were two people connected at a much deeper level. We never planned our lives, we always went with the flow. We respected each other for who we were. We made each other's choices work in a way that it worked for 'us'. Our compatibility led to a marriage, a family and a global ride across four continents. We stayed separately in different countries, brought up our two children while spending more time on aircrafts. I think the beauty of human connections is that out of nowhere, two separate souls become one. When two people share a great bond and their fundamental values are the same, there are possibilities to evolve that relationship and strengthen it over the years, beyond all boundaries.

Colour, unfortunately, has a lot of implicit meaning in our society, which has framed our thought process leading to consequences for people. White is good, brown is poor, black is evil, pale is sick and so on. The fundamentals of our relationship were not based on our physicality, it was based on our compatibility and connect. It did not follow the quintessential conventions of marriage in those days, but it was based on a solid grounding of human emotions and shared thought architectures, which ran deep into the grooves of our hearts and our psyche. Sandeep and I have built this strong relationship together on mutual commitment because we chose to connect with an open mind when we met. And ever since, we have been discovering yet more of each other, evolving with every passing day.

When we are born, there is no sense of right and wrong, no view on skin colour—white, brown or black; the only felt sense is that of joy and pain, hunger and thirst, sleepiness or wakefulness. These needs are universal, irrespective of who we are, where we are from and what we look like. Then what changes as we grow up? The process of socialisation teaches us what is 'right' and 'wrong' within a certain norm. We are directly or indirectly taught how people of different colour are expected to be or could be. We learn what to expect on the basis of these mindsets that gradually take a seat in our heads and hearts.

However, a dilemma that was seeded within me since childhood kept coming back in different ways, diverse forms and with various people across countries. The colour of my skin often put me in a slightly different, and at times on a 'lesser' relative position in the eyes of others, as was evident from their reactions. There were subtle messages from elders about having more milk than tea. The rationale being that milk, which is white, will make me fairer (read: prettier). Fairer girls in India may be better liked and as a grown-up, be more marriageable, as is evident from the plethora of matrimonial advertisements even today.

More often than not, this was countered once I commenced the engagement or communication that either defied or changed the perception. I held on to my self-belief and continue to do so to this day. Growing up in small-town India, the reminder was subtle at times and more direct at other times. 'I am' as I think and feel about myself.

ASPIRE TO DESIRE

I have never stopped dreaming. Yes, I will, and I still have aspirations to touch the sky. This journey would not have progressed without the support of many.

I take this opportunity to express my gratitude to all my mentors, especially during my international assignments, who encouraged me to push myself harder and achieve my goals and aspirations. During my various stints, I developed some strong bonds with people who have remained a source of inspiration till date. They have been instrumental in shaping my thoughts, supporting me by removing any hurdles and believing in me when I did not believe in myself. This support energised me to invest my energy and expertise into fruitful pursuits that propelled me forward to do better each and every day. When we work in a new culture and space, such a supportive ecosystem at the workplace can galvanise your self-confidence and provide you with the necessary comfort to concentrate on your mission ahead.

The glue that supports this mentoring relationship is connect. Two people talk, get to know each other, find common values and mutual respect. One person in this mentoring relationship then supports the other with their experience and expertise. Mentoring may/may not always work through a formal programme, it is about mind alignment. Mentoring programme can open a door, but cannot result in the chemistry, which is only possible when people engage authentically with each other, deriving an implicit agreement on support. Chemistry and connect go hand in hand. Most of my mentors were found along the way, not because someone gave them to me, but because I chose them, searched for them and then engaged with them. It required effort at both ends!

During the course of my personal and professional associations, there were times when I intuitively knew that I had found the guide I was looking for. It emanated from a common thought process, working style, similar ways of working and a certain outlook in life. These connections then transformed into deeper and sustained associations through continued engagement. Each and every such relationship provided exposure, insight, inspiration and knowledge that I carry with me till date. I realised the power of these connections, they helped me navigate through a complicated spaghetti of life, which otherwise would have seemed quite gruelling and arduous.

Professionally, I have aspired to be audacious, but the complex ocean of skin colour had to be navigated. That was not always easy, as some of those around me did not let go of their unfounded thoughts and views. It played out subtly, but it did. However, for every such biased individual, there were others who helped me march on and affirm my belief that the world houses all kinds of individuals. I just held on to my faith and kept going.

I was engaged in a role in the UK, which was satisfying in terms of professional fulfilment. However, I knew I could do something more or take on a larger role to provide me with the needed stretch and progression. I was in my comfort zone. As it happened, unbeknownst to me, someone had been watching me at work. Peter was a senior British professional in the function. He had a strong professional pedigree in working with investment banking and was revered within the HR function for his fearless attitude. Peter was well regarded for his emotional and intellectual energy and possessed a sharp business acumen.

One day, I got a call from him for a meeting. Given our limited connect till then, I was curious. Additionally, given Peter's reputation of being a little short-fused, I was a bit concerned about having overstepped any boundaries with him. As the meeting commenced, it was obvious to me that he was a straightforward individual. After exchanging a few pleasantries, he came right to the point. He had a senior role open in his team and asked me why I had not applied. I was a bit stumped and told him that I was happy with what I was doing. At that time I was working for the regional HR head, who was Peter's manager too. This role with Peter was good, but it was structurally a level below my position at the time.

I recall Peter insisting that I consider the role, making an immense effort to explain to me the importance of a client-facing role. He painstakingly took me through the reasons, the development opportunity and what the future might look like if I took the 'road less travelled'. After an extensive conversation, it was evident to me that he had done his homework and had watched me closely at work, managing the ups and downs, taking tough decisions and handling the stakeholders. He was convinced that my skill sets matched the role perfectly. I was caught up with reporting levels and had missed focusing on building future skills through exposure to the right role at the right time.

He was probably much more convinced about my fit in the role, my performance and my potential than I was. It was not lost on me that investment banking was primarily a white, male-dominated work environment. It lacked women professionals and had very few people of colour. It was more of a 'white boys' club' in the UK. Often the reasons cited were that clients felt more comfortable with their own and that drove the business top line. Rightly or wrongly, it had some merit. I would have to deal with high-profile bankers in this role, and I was unsure of how acceptable a woman of colour, without any investment banking exposure, would be to them. A woman of colour with limited experience in the UK—was she really worth the attention? Perhaps my self-doubts such as these created unneeded dissonance.

I credit Peter with shaking me out of my stupor of contentment and pushing me to consider the opportunity. He challenged me to reflect and awaken the motivation and the conviction to take on the challenge—and I did! I conceded. I also realised that as a minority, the problem lay with me too for not breaking the self-imposed boundary. I was conditioned to self-doubt and I remember asking myself, 'Am I worthy of the role and its responsibilities?'

In retrospect, it was one of the most significant and fulfilling decisions I took professionally. Peter was around for about eight months to mentor me and then decided to move to other opportunities. In retrospect, I realise that he had identified me as his successor, and then worked through the plan by inviting me, supporting me and getting me ready for his role.

I remain grateful to him. It affirms my belief that there are people like him who can go beyond colour, ethnicity and gender and simply focus on capability. They connect at the core and can gauge someone's true potential and provide the requisite impetus, helping them become a better version of themselves. In my short time with Peter, I acquired plenty of learning and wisdom from his experience. He enlightened me about the various aspects of an individual's character, organisational dynamics and professional etiquettes. He taught me the importance of tenacity and how one always needs to hire better than themselves irrespective of any other variable. He had the ability to identify the right person for the right job. My gratitude stays as he believed and dug below the surface of the tangible aspect of colour and physicality into talents and professional abilities. It is quite evident that a man like him has a compassionate and holistic view of life that does not give any careless indulgence to baseless prejudices and biases. I indeed had a strong professional connect with him, one which was based on formal and informal interactions. We had mutual respect for each other. His ability to instil confidence in a brown person in an unfamiliar white land is a beautiful example that there are 'colour-blind' people in the world who make it a better place to live in.

Thanks to people like him, I continue to pay forward by building talent and supporting other people in unchartered territories. I think that's the best way to thank him.

My life lessons from him were:
1. Get to know people before you judge them in any way.
2. Keep an open mind to what life throws at you.
3. At the core, what matters is capability and the human connect.
4. Take bets on people.

Being selected to the senior HR head role, after Peter's departure, was just the beginning of my life lessons. The first few months, I found myself standing outside senior bankers' cabins who seemed a bit confused and curious about what I was doing there. I persisted and they resisted. However, as my path would cross with them every hour, I ensured I was fully prepared to engage, communicate and enable them at any task at work. I learnt the business, its language, its ways of working and the need to embed myself with the stakeholders. Gradually, we started to understand and speak the same language. This led to better understanding, thus helping us work seamlessly without any colour in between.

I loved this stretch at work. A few months of hard work paid off and I won the confidence and respect of the business head and COO. I hadn't had a formal induction since Peter left. Hence, one day, I requested the COO to send a message to all managing directors and bankers to ensure that I get easy access. He was a white British man.

I can never forget the look he gave me when he said, 'You are one of us, why send an email?' The statement left me perplexed as he had made an affirmation of inclusion, but yet was not willing to release a communication that would connect me with the wider management team. Then, suddenly, he got up and asked me to come along with him. Over the next hour, the COO took me to the office of each managing director across several floors and introduced me personally to every managing director with a statement that now I was their new HR head. I could sense that when the COO, a respected banker himself, walked door-to-door, a new sense of respect and credibility for me crept into the eyes of the bankers. I could see that every managing director was looking at me and thinking of connecting with me at some point of time now. It was surreal, and I was overwhelmed with nervousness. I asked myself whether I deserved all this attention and if I would be able to live up to everybody's expectations. The answer I got from myself was a resounding, 'YES!'

No self-doubt this time. Peter had left me with a great legacy. My mindset was transformed to conquer the world.

Nothing has changed me more, personally or professionally. The real change came in the way I had been inducted with the bankers, with a bold statement of inclusion. I did have a voice and now I had a credible opportunity with this introduction. This recognition, however, came with a lot of responsibility. Hard work, sincere commitment and great partnerships made the connections even stronger. Most of the bankers became personal friends and we all withstood the ups and downs of the financial crisis through thick and thin. Many of these relationships are still alive and are very precious to me.

As I reflect on my two working groups, what is obvious to me is that I effortlessly veered towards spaces where I found people to be more open-minded about doing things differently and appreciating a diverse perspective. There was a push and pull. It is usually not possible to establish meaningful connections with everyone all the time. Therefore, I nurtured and preserved the ones that were genuine, authentic, the ones that mattered to me and developed them into lifelong mentoring relationships. Through this experience, I also developed the ability to understand how people from different cultures thought, reacted and worked in teams. I was very conscious about expectation mismatches with diverse working styles that could be sorted by regular conversations enabling a deconstruction of stereotypes, if any.

When Colour Hurts

Sometimes I am lulled into numbness and left gasping with wonder when I see the kind of reactions that skin colour can evoke! We know that our physical appearance gives away much more than we think it does. It certainly can skew thoughts even before we speak. By the time we get down to a real interaction, people may have already etched out the outline of our character in their minds. As the prejudices that people harbour in their minds unfold, it becomes increasingly difficult to digest the negativity in some of them. It can be damaging and often it is difficult to manage the impact it has on innocent individuals who reel under its negative impact. I've always felt that sowing the colourless seeds of a relationship across racial boundaries was sometimes difficult, but not an impossible task. Ultimately, we are all human with emotions and although we might take time to understand each other, eventually our emotions 'feel' and 'connect'. We could smoothen out differences and start out positively.

It is perplexing that to some hard-coded people, skin colour can be indicative of a person's ulterior motives, and more so of a person's soul! Certain experiences in life have helped me reflect on my thoughts on this aspect. They have made me realise that sometimes fighting back an individual's biases, lack of maturity and sensibility to judge people correctly is not the right way to deal with engineered discrimination. Sometimes being too strong and forthright, especially with a person with whom you do not share a real connection, leads to a fertile breeding ground of negative emotions and backlash. I did not have this foresight earlier in my life to envision and manage such deep-seated negative emotions that could spiral into an incident which consequently could be grave and challenging for one's self-esteem. I could never fathom that the absence of a connect with a superior in the professional world would steadily brew into insecurity about the subordinate's strong disposition. The mind is unpredictable and sometimes what it can do may be incomprehensible to many. It is the mind, which is heavily involved in forming a connection or distorting it. Here is an instance when a subordinate failed to read his manager's mind and the manager's biased disposition created fissures and irreparable damage.

It is All in the Mind

It was January, usually a very busy time for Monica (a brown lady) as the year-end or compensation cycle is brought to a close, last year's performance review is finalised and new increments and bonuses are dispersed. Over her long career, she had realised that one should stop making an endeavour to please everyone with monetary rewards as one can never make anyone content with what they get paid. She was always told how underpaid an employee was, how employees felt that they worked hard and the reward was not commensurate and so demotivating! The list of such statements went on. Monica felt that the happy ones usually didn't talk lest it hurt them the next time, when HR paid them less, assuming that they were content. The unhappy ones talked endlessly. Sometimes the negative emotions manifested themselves in demotivation, sometimes in anger and sometimes in disengagement.

Monica was dealing with a multitude of these emotions throughout the day, when a lady from her Singapore office walked in. Monica looked at her work schedule and saw that she had a meeting with a member of the investigation team. The lady from the Singapore office politely introduced herself and clarified that she was indeed from the investigation team. Given Monica's senior role, it was usual for the investigation team to meet her regularly as various employee issues needed her thoughts and intervention, so no surprises there. She expected some mundane summary and a few questions from this investigator too and then assumed it would be done. She was quite distracted that day with all kinds of rewards and performance issues on her mind and was hoping the meeting would get over soon so that she could get back to the priorities of the day.

It was already 5:00 PM. Monica ordered some coffee for both of them and requested the investigator to get started. Her name was Sue and she explained her role in the investigation team. Then, she took out her notebook and began the interrogation. The conversation began with confirming Monica's name, what she did, how long she had been with the organisation, etc. Then, it went on to what she had been doing differently in her role over the last three months, any issues she had faced, and so on. Within fifteen minutes Monica realised that she was not being briefed about an investigation, but was being investigated herself!

An uncomfortable sense of anxiety, anger and confusion swept over Monica. She was less worried about the issues given that these multiple escalations were an occupational hazard in her role, however her real concern was being caught completely unaware with an interrogation. It felt like a sting operation without any respect to principles of natural justice. People need to be told what they're being put on trial for. In real life, when we sit on a hot seat we are often vulnerable to people pointing fingers at us or are subjected to reverse bullying. This unfortunately is the underbelly of a leadership role!

Monica's anguish emanated from the fact that no one had followed the basic protocol of briefing her; if not about the exact issue, then at least about an escalation and that she would be quizzed on it.

The investigator sensed her anger and confusion when Monica inquired whether her direct manager based outside the country was aware of this and the answer from Sue was affirmative. Hearing that, Monica requested her to step out for a few minutes so that she could talk to him. When she conceded, Monica called her manager, Stanley, in Singapore who was a few hours ahead of her time zone. He answered the phone, merry on a few glasses of wine in the evening. After a few pleasantries, she asked him about the investigation and anything that he could share with her. She informed him that she had an investigator in her room, without any heads up, and that it was not the usual protocol unless the breach was very serious, putting the bank at a high level of risk. Stanley told her that he was unaware and unsure of what was going on. Stanley was with his wife, Michelle, on the other side of the phone. Ignoring Monica's anxious inquiry, he asked her instead to first say hello to Michelle. Monica was really not in a mood to do so at that point, but did not have a choice.

Post the phone call, she called the investigator in and told her that her boss had said he wasn't aware of this proceeding and that it was against the protocol in the organisation. The investigator now looked visibly more concerned than Monica did. Sue categorically told Monica that her manager was made aware and she further shared an email that was addressed to him from the investigation team. Monica was now aware that her manager had a role to play in how this had turned out. She was acutely disappointed and sad. However, as a professional, she let the interrogation proceed on the allegations levelled at her. It was a gruelling one-hour conversation where she felt like a convict without really having been proven one. Monica felt her self-respect was being compromised in the process. They ended the conversation with Sue's request to meet a few other witnesses associated with the investigation. Monica was finally done that day by 10:00 PM and was absolutely exhausted.

She somehow dragged herself back home after the ordeal. Finally on her own in her own space, she paused in what felt like a vacuum as she lay on her bed. Being on the other side of the table with many such investigations, she knew she had to let it take its own course; however, she had felt completely set up here. She battled objective logic and intense emotion at the same time.

As Monica reflected on what may have transpired, the last few years flashed before her eyes.

A couple of years back, she had been spoken to about a role in the company that was her dream job. She was super excited and this discussion ensued over a few weeks; however, one day she got some feedback saying that the prospective manager, Stanley, was not aligned with the move. He had concerns about Monica, even though she hadn't worked with him or even in his team for a while. Gradually, he made it evident that he 'felt' she did not have the requisite experience or skills, and hence needed to go through an assessment process.

For her dream job, Monica was willing to go through any rightful assessment or scrutiny. However, there were debates at senior levels on how to staff it. Hence, to secure the role, Monica was initially brought into her manager's team at a slightly smaller role than what she was doing earlier. This was ostensibly to assimilate her with the team. She was apprised that this move would lead to the role she aspired to, but after a due process. Although Monica was unsure why the interim step was needed at all, she was driven by her passion and zeal to move forward and do what was asked of her. Many others told her that it was a foolish decision, but she took it up thinking that if it did not work out, she could always retrace her steps knowing that her dream was not ready to be fulfilled yet. What was the worst that could happen, she asked herself. If it did not work out, she would leave the organisation and find something else in the market. This was personally important for her and worth the risk, otherwise she would feel defeated for not having tried at all!

A few gruelling months and after a rigorous process, the role was accorded to her! Her faith was restored.

The first year in the role went by aligning with the direct manager who apparently had some concerns with a local in the role, but had reconciled to her selection. On the back of this context, Monica tried her best to adapt and align with his agenda. He had a reputation of working with a close coterie from his homeland in Europe. They were like family and in spite of some of the others striving to build a connect, they could never enter his inner circle. Monica contented herself with the proximity and her professional working relationship with him (as she thought it to be). Even though the countries she looked after were a large part of his portfolio, he always perceived that region as a problem child. She remembered once in Singapore, she was invited to dinner with him and a few others from his circle. Over dinner, jokes and imitations were made on different coloured people, till they turned their attention to a popular TV sitcom, which had a character called 'Monica'. Insensitively their joke got stretched to a point where it started to make her feel uncomfortable. The Asian accent was made fun of, and although Monica was not at a comedy show, it felt like blacks and browns were being targeted after a few bottles of wine. It went on for a while till it was past being funny and bordered on becoming disrespectful. Monica had to excuse herself, lest she said something inappropriate, given that she was the only brown person at that table and that too sober unlike many others.

Sometimes it is difficult to respond to such situations, especially when your response might have professional implications. She was shocked and felt that a verbal objection from her as a minority on the table would have earned her a distinguished title—that of a spoilsport! It would have further distanced her from the team.

In this senior team, there were clear distinctions on how Asians were perceived and treated. In some of the larger MNCs, there is an overt expression of sensitivity to cross-cultural dynamics, as it is subject to legal scrutiny, however underlying realities may be different for what minorities experience. Hence as a minority, you have to read subtle clues and focus on what is left unsaid to understand the real drivers and dynamics. Therein started Monica's journey of unpeeling the onion and understanding the unsaid. Even though her organisation had a clear policy with regard to equality and inclusion, the same was not necessarily practised in spirit by some senior individuals. Some people refused to change rigid mindsets about colour, no matter how inappropriate they may be. However, they continued in the organisation without being impacted.

Monica could sense this in her relationship with her manager. Over a period of time, she realised that she, as a progressive brown person, was not well regarded by her manager as she broke the stereotype. He let her skin colour, colour his views about her capability. Stanley was set in his old school thinking of Asians being pegged behind the people from developed markets. Given Monica was different and would fight back, he started to malign her for her forthright attitude in the guise of disrupting the 'standard operating procedure'. He often demanded that her teams should stay within their boundaries. Monica's aspirations began to threaten him. Her straightforward approach to life that was her strength, became her Achilles heel. The more she was pushed back, the harder she worked to move forward as that was her natural instinct.

Reflecting back, Monica realised that she could have done more to garner trust by engaging more. However, for that, she needed Stanley to reciprocate as well, which he was unwilling to do. She was destined to this hardship as Stanley had a negative view about brown people in particular and Monica created dissonance by being different. She felt that whatever she did was looked at with suspicion. She struggled and tried different strategies from mentoring to coaching, but it was not to be. In spite of all the odds, Monica survived as she was strong on relationship-building and had strong connects with other key stakeholders who continued to invest in her.

Back to the present. 'Trrriing!' Monica was woken up from her reflective stupor and brought back to reality. Her phone rang incessantly. She knew that she had to withstand this storm of biases by holding firmly to her unwavering belief that whatever she did was fair and honest from the heart. However, life is never simple and it is evident that a lack of connect could lead to undue politics and stress at the workplace, even though it may not be of one's own making. Monica was stressed from the previous evening, had a chequered sleep and got up the next morning with a heavy head. Somehow, she managed to get herself into office. Just as she finished checking her emails, she got a call from a trusted colleague asking how she was, as he had noticed that she wasn't looking too well that morning. That was when Monica could not hold back any longer, she just let herself go with all the anguish rolling down as tears from her eyes. She told him what she had been going through. She shared how she had pulled each piece together with authenticity in her professional journey to be who she was. She felt proud of it. However, her manager was passive-aggressive towards her. Perhaps he was getting back for not being able to accord the role to someone else. She struggled to fathom what she could do about this.

When you don't know what you have done wrong, it is difficult for you to commit any action.

The colleague heard her and advised her to stay calm. Then, he connected with the key stakeholders who helped her navigate through the situation by ensuring that she was treated fairly and appropriately. Monica's manager tried hard to nail her during this case by pushing it to a disciplinary committee; however, it was vetoed by some other senior members, given that the facts demonstrated appropriate work ethics on her part.

After a few weeks, it all got sorted. Monica was declared innocent. During the process, it had become evident that her manager had not played a constructive role. Finally, her manager called to close the matter, but the relationship had really gone underwater by then.

He had bruised her self-respect and compromised her trust. After much pondering, she actually felt sadder for him. He was ignorant, and perhaps not strong enough. Monica wanted to be constructive, but found it difficult to simply forgive and forget. She sought support from her mentors to heal from this experience and move on, learning that stronger connects help you through the adversity of dysfunctional associations. Through her global experience, she learnt that confronting someone, as was her natural style, did not work in every culture and that she had to simply wait for her time to either give feedback, retort or to move on, and she chose the latter!

Each of these experiences had a lesson in them. The anxious, hurtful feeling of one's dignity being compromised is brutally humiliating. Most young people just starting out do not know how to handle these situations in the early years; and so to keep the peace, they tend to either ignore them or politely pass it on as a light conversation, not taking it personally. That is a big mistake as it encourages more such behaviour.

The experience of this investigation made Monica feel hollow and empty as she went through it and yet, when it was concluded, she felt calm and grateful for the learning. The emotion was the kind that one feels when one has fought a huge war persistently for a long period of time. It was infuriating and exasperating to go through an ordeal when she had done nothing wrong. In her choked desolation, she did everything that she felt she did not deserve to be put through—answered questions she should not have answered, sat calmly while she heard accusations being levelled against her value system and her unblemished character. It did require a lot of courage and dogged determination to deal with the situation, and an element of despondency had surreptitiously crept in. Later, it felt as if there had been a storm in her life, but it had actually destroyed nothing, and instead provided her with more strength. She realised that it had emboldened her to face other hurdles in life. The incident invigorated her to continue her corporate journey with renewed vigour and zeal.

As I ponder over Peter and Stanley, what is apparent is that the colour did not matter, but the mindset did. Both were white, and in some ways, both had enough cross-cultural exposure, yet, they both responded to a brown person differently. Their values, the securities and insecurities that drove their leadership behaviour were different. One was a direction setter who built confidence in others, while the other started out with a preconceived and distorted view that had to be contended with by others.

Peter and I never ever saw any colour in our working relationship. We appreciated our individual strengths and maximised value for the organisation and our teams collectively. He had the uncanny ability of connecting at a deeper level with his efforts and positive intent. I have to admit he was selective, as this level of investment requires time and energy, which he was willing to give to the ones he considered deserving. When you connect with someone like that, you get motivated to reciprocate in equal measure with authenticity and sincerity. A common purpose is found and success is collective. There is no insecurity as there is no competition, there is instead a genuine collaboration. For me, there was a sense of security working with him even though he was tough and task-driven when it came to work delivery.

Peter as a leader was an evolved human being who thought about collective well-being. You cannot be a leader without being a good human in the first place. It is so simple, but so often missed by people in their obsession for the power that comes with leadership roles. There is no real power if you can't hold yourself accountable to do the right thing. Being too soft or too tough is not ideal as we know, but the balancing act is difficult. Peter got this right. There was never a free ride, you learnt, you delivered, you were trusted and you grew. It was fair play all around. Working for him, I would go into a battlefront fully committed and engaged, as I knew he had my back then and always.

I think when we are absolute strangers to each other's colour, cultures and identities, we can try to connect at a level of ingrained shared values and thoughts born out of our intellectual capabilities. We need not adhere to social or cultural prescriptions to carve out a cultural archetype. Peter and I connected because we had a similar value system and work ethics, we were both passionate about our corporate work life and we were keen on delivering value to our clients. His humane attitude helped our team navigate through unchartered territories, professionally and personally.

Where do I start with Stanley? A person with a narrow view about who are deserving and who are not on the basis of their colour, not merit. He surrounded himself largely with his own community. They were usually in the key positions of responsibility and that seemed to have worked for him. The rest of the team, who were locals, were not in his trusted circle. Monica happened to be the odd one out, with a desire to grow and push the boundaries, and that was his issue with her. He would have preferred that she had sat quietly like the others, but that would not have been the real Monica! She tried to adapt to his unreasonable expectations, but found it difficult to be what he wanted her to be and stay reconciled to it.

When you are faced with such a situation, it is best to strengthen and multiply your connections with others. Expand your network so that it helps you garner the support that you may need in such situations.

As a first step in any new working relationship, especially across cultures, find a common purpose to align and then agree on the 'how'. The work issues crop up usually on disagreements on 'how' not on 'what'. The 'how' is often driven by differing working styles and local norms. Different ways of working are sometimes perceived as wrong ways of working and the only thing that can resolve this is communication or 'engagement' leading to a better connect.

As is evident that Monica tried really hard when she worked with people like Stanley (and their tribe are aplenty), but the deep-rooted bias and lack of exposure led to gaps and made it difficult for him to change his views. He was her manager and in a position of power, so she was the vulnerable one in this relationship. She tried to work around it by tweaking her working style, but the feeling of not being authentic did not sit comfortably with her. The good part of any MNC is that you always have multiple matrix managers and she took solace in other professional relationships that worked well and kept her going to the extent possible with Stanley. Her patience level grew and her ability to find creative ways of doing things increased. She survived and her learnings of 'what not to do when faced with a diverse team' were:

1. Understand before you judge. You are dealing with someone's emotions.
2. Be respectful of a divergent view as a leader. Don't impose.
3. Hold people accountable for their behaviour once you know the context.
4. Connect and get to their heart, and not their head.
5. Different coloured people may work differently. Being different is not being wrong.
6. Raise awareness levels about human potential that is beyond colour stereotypes.

ARE WE NATURALLY AND BIOLOGICALLY WIRED TO CONNECT?

Long ago, Aristotle had written in his critically acclaimed, *Politics*: 'Man is by nature a social animal... anyone who either cannot lead the common life or is so self-sufficient as not to need to, and therefore does not partake of society, is either a beast or a god.'

Matthew Lieberman, in his book, *Social: Why Our Brains Are Wired to Connect*, reveals why relationships are essential for a fulfilling life and that more than anything else, they form a very integral part of our being. Lieberman borrows a lot from neuroscience and psychology to assert and confirm Aristotle's statement and much more in his book. Apart from the basic needs of food and shelter, human beings have this innate desire to form relationships and, more than anything, to form groups.

The primary purpose of the brain, according to Lieberman, is social thinking because he conceptualises the brain as the centre of our social self. Most human beings harbour a lot of desires and one of them is to be in a loving relationship with an individual or make a natural attempt to share one's happiness and melancholy with a loved one. The human species also wants to avoid rejection or loss and has a general tendency to make an endeavour to fit into the crowd. Humans also love caring and want to be cared for.

Neuroscientists have gone a long way in explaining the mechanism of the human brain. They have discovered what is known as the 'default network', which is the social neural configuration that the brain falls into after it ceases to engage itself in any active work. Therefore, neuroscientists have emerged with the most exciting findings, which basically proclaim that the brain has an inherently social nature.

Whenever the brain has a free moment, the default network induces it to think about other people and their minds. Thus, the brain, whenever it is at rest or is not engaged in any active work, tends to transcend itself into social thinking, so that it can make sense of other people and their feelings, thoughts and goals. The human brain has evolved to recognise what to expect next in social terms effortlessly and unconsciously. The need for love and affection is another reason why human beings feel it necessary to connect. Lieberman, in his book, has proven through various experiments that social loss or rejection almost feels like physical pain. Therefore, the social rejection felt by blacks or browns in a very white environment causes mental distress and anguish. It is basically indicative of the fact that when we refuse to live with an open mind and fail to connect with people due to the colour of their skin, we are making coloured individuals experience social pain of being alone and vulnerable. Hence, the desire to rekindle old connections or form new ones is born out of our innate need to relieve all those who experience social pain. We just need rewiring of our perspective on colour from time to time.

Social connections are powerful because they can help us in connecting one single thread across different cultures and ethnicities.

Summary

1. Align your thoughts; focus on the content and the character and not on the visual appearance of a person.

2. Don't forget your connections with your roots. Learn from your roots and evolve, remain grateful and build on it. It is the fundamental reason behind your being.

3. Don't judge on the basis of misguided information and prejudices. They break connections and perhaps damage relationships even before they are formed. In a professional space, judgements about colleagues should not be misguided by biases and prejudices.

4. It is important to get to the heart and not to the head of a person first! We should be able to accept divergent views and live with life's contradictions. It is important to connect with people at a deeper level to know and understand an individual.

5. A connection is only possible when we break our mind's walls to initiate a conversation with another.

Openness

Mom: 'So what are both of you planning for this spring break? You should utilise the time well! I so wish I could get one long break too.'

Avni: 'It is a busy first semester in my US college mom! The break is to do something different from studies. My college has asked me to consider going to Puerto Rico to work for an NGO during the spring break! I am excited, but also a bit anxious! I hear it is not always safe and can be a bit rough!'

Sid: 'Whoa, sounds cool Avni di! Mamma, I am going camping to Darjeeling. I hear it is beautiful, but different. Great momos, lots of greens and some decent weather and very different people.'

Mom: 'Hmm, so both of you are off to places you have never been to before, to meet people you have never interacted with before! Start familiarising yourself children!'

Avni and **Sid** (together): 'How?'

Mom: 'Well, read and explore a bit, talk to friends who are from those places or talk to people who have been there. Do some research and just make sure you have the right information about the place and people. This will help open your mind to different possibilities.'

Sid: 'Mom, that sounds like you are asking us to study again!'

Mom: 'I am suggesting you to learn about different people rather than walking into places and meeting people without knowing anything about them. That may feel confusing and won't be enjoyable.'

Avni: 'But mom, Puerto Rico is so different, I hear that it's a bit chaotic.'

Mom: 'Avni, it is an emerging market like India. Every place and set of people have their own characteristics. You need to be open-minded to embrace it. And, your Spanish should help you connect better. Language opens the gateways to the heart. You feel anxious because you may not know enough—so just find out what you truly need to know to feel comfortable. It is that simple! Keep yourself open to new ideas, thoughts and people. When you turn receptive to accept, assimilate and draw in learnings from another person or experience into your own life and circumstances, then you know you have opened up for anything and everything!'

Start each day as if it was the first day of your life, let the wonderment of knowing each other arise every day, let the curiosity of searching life in every interaction unfold every day, let yourself open to live this life fully every day!

WHAT'S MY FAULT?

'Hey Anu, I will be coming to India soon, I will be working there now. I am so excited. Just can't wait anymore!'

This was the message from my ever optimistic, always enthusiastic friend, James. He had been promoted to a larger role with a move to India from France. His organisation was collaborating with a construction company in India. He loved Asia and in particular had been curious about exploring secular India with its variety of religions, colours and, of course, the food! He simply could not control his excitement at this news.

James was a highly qualified engineer and had some good diverse international experiences. He had worked in the US prior to this assignment, and that's where we had met when I was working there. He had never worked in an emerging market apart from South Africa. He was born and brought up in France. I got a call from him before his arrival here. In a really happy voice and with childlike excitement, he made all kinds of enquiries—about the country, its people, its culture, history, places to visit, cuisines and so on. He was really delighted about his upcoming professional and personal journey in this diverse country.

As for me, a native Indian, it felt wonderful to see James's global attitude and his openness to embrace any country and culture.

He harboured a constant eagerness to learn more about this country and its people. Although he had no experience of working in India, he was willing to lower his guards and let the Indian tricolour seep in, as he mingled with the local people and lived the Indian life. There was a lot of written material in the public domain about India and 'Indianness', but he chose to get an idea of what India really is by experiencing how Indians live their life here. He did not form his opinion on the basis of what others thought about the land back home in France. He wanted his experience to define India for him.

There was a sense of human dignity when I witnessed James offering so much respect to Indian ethnicities and cultures. It made me respect James more. As I looked out of the window, sitting in my office cabin after his call, I realised that the openness of another person propels you to reciprocate with receptivity, immense love and warmth. It brings in positivity, and makes you feel good about the fact that irrespective of black or white, human relationships are truly born when there is openness and the willingness to connect and know more about each other!

I missed out one element in James's introduction, he was black.

He arrived in due course and commenced his induction into the company. The work was good and interesting, his team had a good mix of international employees and he loved the diversity. He took a house close to the office. It was about twenty to twenty-five minutes on foot or a few minutes by car, depending on the traffic. James loved the Indian seasons, the temples and even the traffic chaos. He enjoyed the multiple cuisines and the warmth that people bestowed upon him in the office. I was not surprised, given he was ready and open to be steeped in it all.

James was a compassionate individual and loved working 'for' the people. He always took a seat in the middle of the table with his team (never at the head) at any meeting, remembered every person's name (even the long Indian ones) and gave equal respect to everyone, whether it was the boy who got his *masala chai* or the junior team member who he was mentoring. He was open to making friends with all of them if they were willing too. The true test of cross-cultural collaboration is how you enmesh and blend yourself into a new culture, in a new country amid a new work environment with new people. The gates of his mind and his heart were wide open, there was no lock, no key and anybody could get in at any time of the day. In fact, you did not even have to knock! He was also equally reciprocated by most.

On one fateful morning, I was flicking through the channels on TV, when I heard something that caught my attention. One of the newsreaders spoke about an incident in the city, where a Nigerian gang was caught with drugs. There had been a few such incidents over the last year and Indian law enforcement teams were quite vigilant over the months gone by. The news channel flashed photographs of the criminals and the victims, which were rather worrying and left one with an eerie feeling of discomfort. Local politicians were tapping into the issue and berating the current government for unchecked migration. After a few moments, I brushed it off as one of the many chaotic news of the day, but that day changed James's Indian sojourn forever.

It was a regular morning for James as he got ready to go to the office. He decided to walk instead of driving down as the weather was pleasant, and the sunshine was inviting! He did not realise that this beauty was ominous. Even in his wildest dreams, James could not anticipate what was in store for him that day. James went through his diary that felt light so he was happy about spending time with colleagues informally. He packed a birthday gift for a colleague and baked a cake for the team. He packed it all and was looking forward to a friendly day at work. He was an eternal optimist and saw the glass half full. He always started with a potion of trust with people.

The first stage of openness is trusting people with your feelings, which may evoke some vulnerability but also garners support. James believed that to step forward and connect to an unknown individual, one had to expose oneself to the possibility of being harmed or hurt. Therein lay his strength in vulnerability. He believed that one had to learn to share, at the risk of being intruded. One had to learn to give, at the risk of being exploited. And one had to learn to trust, at the risk of being betrayed! Therefore, one had to have the courage to be open. James surrounded himself with similar broad-minded people that evoked a need in him to reciprocate. It was positively infectious.

I learnt from him that if one embraces this vulnerability, if one can immerse oneself in a sea of risk, with the hope of discovering pearls of relationships, the probability is higher to be able to find them. This makes this effort worth it!

As James got out of his residence and started to walk towards his office, he noticed a few young men looking at him in a strange manner. He felt a bit uncomfortable, but kept walking calmly. James was known to respond and not to react. As he walked further on, he realised that a few other people were looking at him with a mix of fear and disdain. This left James perplexed. Some chatter in Hindi was heard, which he could not fully comprehend. Some people gathered at the pavement as he passed by. He sensed that something was not right and for the first time, fear crept into his mind. His heart started beating faster, as now he could not gauge what was coming his way, but his sense was that it was not something good. He quickened his pace, but when he turned back, to his horror, he discovered that the crowd had paced up behind him too.

Out of sheer fear, he started running and they too ran after him. He was about ten minutes away from the office. He ran for his life, his chest was pounding, breathing really fast. Suddenly, a man caught him by his jacket and punched him hard in his stomach. James fell and groaned in pain. His office bag was snapped away from him, the cake stepped upon and the gift shattered as did his confidence at that moment. A man kicked him harder, another pelted a few stones, and then they all began bashing him till James started to bleed profusely. He could not cope with his ordeal and his vision started to blur. He took the blows and pain as it came and became numb with the intense beating and hurt. He was unsure what he was being punished for!

His God was watching over him. Fortunately for him, two of his office colleagues who had taken the same path saw the crowd and ran over to help him. They covered his tattered clothes and bleeding wounds with their jackets and tried to calm the crowd. When they questioned the few angry men for the reason for their deeds, the reply they received was quite astonishing, 'These black people are all criminals; they are scary, they take drugs and spoil our country. They are spoiling our children. All these people come from witchcraft backgrounds and scare us!'

Really, which world did we live in! James could not believe his ears. He was shell-shocked beyond words. He reasoned, even in that state, why him? There was no evidence behind their statements why was he particularly connected to drugs and criminality when he was an ally? This statement pierced through his self-dignity, his love for India and deeply hurt his sentiments. He was more qualified and diverse in his experience than many surrounding him there.

He was here to contribute and support India in his own away and not destroy its people.

At that moment, he wanted to shout out loud, defend himself and proclaim to the world emphatically and vehemently that he did not do any of the things that he was accused of doing. He wanted to reaffirm the fact that all black people were not drug addicts and criminals. In a foreign land, his ethnicity was being brutally disrespected and ridiculed, which infuriated him beyond any threshold of acceptance. The indignation and extreme annoyance were so overwhelming that it rendered him speechless. He failed to understand why they were talking about him with such disdain. He could not believe that the colour of his skin could trigger such torment and lead to distorted beliefs by brown people who were just a shade lighter than he was!

James was safely escorted to a hospital for medical care by his colleagues, and then sent home, after a few days of recovery. He met me after this incident and narrated the entire episode, which had left him with a severely scarred experience for life.

I was shocked, angry and disappointed with what had transpired. I apologised on behalf of the people who lacked empathy, lacked humanity and were driven by savage motives. It was really unfortunate. As I saw him writhing in this emotional bruise, it was evident that this incident had impaired his relationship with India forever. The physical wounds would heal, but the emotional scars would remain. It hurt. It really did and it probably always will.

James's comfort and confidence was shaken after this incident. He cut short his stint in India. At some level, this incident made me question how open were we in India towards integrating people, who might be different from us, into our lives. Perception and bias trigger anxieties leading to closed minds. It is entirely our loss when open-minded individuals like James become victims of a boxed thinking. Ignorant minds lead to bad judgements and humanity loses out.

> *'Thinking is difficult, that's why most people judge.'*
> *—CG Jung*

I wasn't surprised when James decided to leave India. We did not deserve him. His life was dear to me and that superseded every other lesson on racial inequity. I did not make any effort to stop him because his discomposure made me realise that he was nervous and scared. In spite of that he attributed his hardship to a few ignorant people and not the entire nation. The joy of living in this country had not diminished entirely, he still loved the colours and the food here, but he felt unsafe thanks to a few.

James was indeed an unfortunate victim of unfounded perceptions and biases. But, we must remember that perceptions are not reality and we should make an endeavour to gather adequate information before letting them become realities. This helps understand the context and the real person. James's relationship with India and his professional journey here had been damaged, but the good soul in him never spoke badly about the country he felt he had learnt a lot from. He attributed the harsh incident to mob mentality and its prejudiced mindset thanks to the media. He observed how vices sown by a few people take a life of their own and assume the collective thought process for a large number of people. But, it could still not touch the open-mindedness of James!

This incident demonstrates that misguided information can wreak havoc in a person's life and dismantle one's confidence. James was positively disposed to India and Indians, but some Indians were not, at least not the ones on the road. Certain misplaced notions about black people and a crowd mentality had driven the local people on that road to commit such a grievous crime. The closed windows of their small minds drove out a talented professional and a kind individual from the country.

Openness is about letting balanced and informed thoughts guide our feelings. Experimentation, testing, learning and practising with social realities is a good way to do this. When we meet different people, we may want to cling on to our socially driven views about them, which start forming as soon as we see them, much before we even engage in a conversation. It needs 'willpower' to hold back judgements, which creep into our thoughts quietly and start to filter our reactions to people. I have observed that the less time I spend on these cues, the more dependent I am on the physical features.

CLIQUE AND CASTE: TO BE OR NOT TO BE?

In spite of seventy-two years of our independence, the colonial hangover has not yet been obliterated from India. We often observe that in most emerging markets, white people are treated with more positive bias irrespective of their backgrounds, whereas a qualified black or brown person in the same country could be looked upon with fear and disdain in its extreme form. The psyche of human beings is consumed by the fact that white populace had ruled over them for a few centuries. This creates an unconscious bias of 'white implies superiority' in the minds of the masses, which continues to be passed down across different generations.

An example of this is found in a couple of Commonwealth countries, wherein the British way of living has assumed a sense of superiority because of history. The whites were perceived as the elite in the country and confirmed to the narrative that the colour 'white' equals power and prosperity and only the privileged few get to adorn this colour on their skin. When the image of an individual and what it represents is persistently fixated in the minds of people for several generations, it becomes a norm. Some people, especially those who derive benefits from it, refuse to wheedle themselves out of it!

Some people have their own conscious or unconscious interpretation of different people of colour with no concrete reasoning or logic. Some deny the presence of any kind of caste prejudice, while others justify it. In India, the incident in which Nigerian students were attacked at a Delhi suburb or the discrimination faced by north-eastern students has not been able to do enough to convince the political administration to make a public acceptance of the presence of cultural intolerance in this country. Take the classic *Amar Chitra Katha* comic books, which were the first introduction to mythology and core Indian principles for children of an earlier generation. They drew an explicit difference between non-Aryan dark-skinned creatures and Aryan light-skinned individuals. As they say, prejudices drawn earlier in life often tend to stick on. Cultural bias is not only a matter of colour, but rather of discrimination faced by anyone on the basis of physical differences such as hair, the shape of their lips, their eyes or other physical parts of the body.

Ever since the eighteenth century, skin colour has become the dominant index for discrimination simply because some of the colonists in emerging markets wanted to justify the enslavement of the African people. The link between skin colour and racism has been sustainable and efficacious. The word 'caste' in India is derived from the Portuguese word 'casta' which means lineage, breed or race. The first users of this term were Iberians, implying that they were the Spanish and the Portuguese living in the Iberian Peninsula, and then in the Americas and Asia. The 'normatively endogamous' communities in southern Asia have a long history and have been labelled with the word *jati* (which is a Sanskrit term), by the word *quam* (which is an Arabic term) and by *zat* (which is a Persian term). A large number of Jews had to convert to Christianity during the 1300s because the Iberian kingdoms had started religious oppression against the Jews. The 'Old Christians' swore by the doctrine of the 'purity of blood' and the idea that only they deserved to get favours in the Portuguese and Spanish societies.

When I meet new people, I find that I need to hold my thoughts in check and let their words, images and views simply seep in. In a way that creates a more accurate picture of the individual. Often I tend to dwell on simple things like what makes them happy or unhappy. A lot of this information flows from the words people use, non-verbal cues and ways of expression. Often when we are fully present with an individual, this process takes place fairly naturally. We need to go beyond what the eyes can see, so that the mind can process what the ears can hear and what the heart can feel. Sometimes a silent conversation is enough to sense a person's vibe and to understand their core.

THE DESIGNATED 'COLOURED' JOB!

A few years back, I was being mentored by a senior business head, who was well respected for his commercial acumen across the globe. He was from Harvard University, had worked in blue-chip financial services companies throughout his career before our paths crossed in the workplace. I recall him sharing with me that in his early Wall Street days, he wasn't sure if he was respected and thought of as competent in the trading room, because he was a tall, lanky black guy. When I asked him how he coped with this, he replied that he retorted through his actions and performances. Further, at some point, he navigated through certain senior mentors to stop this practice not just for himself, but for a few others. However, it took self-belief and courage to tell people to view him and others in the cohort with an open mind.

Most often during breaks, senior bankers would send him to fetch tea for other traders on the floor. I was disappointed to hear this. It was discomforting to see educated people behave in this manner. It was heartening to note that he did not accept it and worked his way to a deserving position. The insensitivity or favouritism shown to any ethnicity in the workplace creates divisions that impact engagement and productivity.

He was humble enough to give me some life lessons:

1. Our self-dignity and respect should never be compromised. You have to keep an open mindset to the ignorant lot too. First respect yourself for others to respect you.

2. Each person around you is fighting a battle and some are fighting demons. Help them. Be compassionate, even as you fight back for yourself. Being open and sensitive help to manage emotions.

3. Gauge the environment and acquire a legitimate status through capability and communication to make an impact.

My mentor impressed upon me that self-belief and courage are important to make oneself comfortable in a new work culture and to address the ethnic diversity debate at the workplace. Conversations assist in opening closed minds and a new perspective may challenge certain beliefs, which may have been unfounded. However, the first step is to be bold and believe that you are an equal partner to people around you; otherwise people will sense your hesitation and behave with you in the manner you invite them to. We need to respect ourselves for who we are and what we do. Consequently, we will be in a better position to ensure that the same is accorded to us by others. His experience told me that well-informed minds naturally tend to swerve towards openness.

Knowing the 'whys' and 'hows' of a cultural landscape
Doing groundwork on the ethnic deficit,
Analysing the socio-ethnic mindsets
Enlightens and prepares us
To manage the unknown and the unexpected

Openness of the mind is an invitation for others to be a part of our journey. It is about nurturing our curious need for discovering the unique nature of people who cross our paths. The physical being of an individual is a limiting factor and can never appropriately predict what lies beneath. Just as the curtain on the stage can never tell us what lies behind it, just as the calm surface of an ocean might not reveal the turbulence beneath. It is the quality time we spend with people, it is the quality of our interactions that help us develop a deep sense of their real worth and shape our way of thinking authentically. We can reach this level only when we allow ourselves to go beyond the colour and the physicality of the individual and more. This requires us to unlearn and relearn about people we engage with, while relishing our interactions.

SECURITY IN HOMOGENEITY?

James F Byrnes, a US judge and a member of the Democratic Party, had correctly said that people seem to be afraid of life more than death because they are thinking of the security and not the opportunity.

The usual visual homogeneity among many individuals beguiles people into thinking that they are indeed more compatible and secure with their 'own'. Additionally, they may be misled to believe that venturing outside their 'groups' to meet people may be fraught with risk apart from the extra effort to engage and understand the unknown. The mysterious sense of security, which is created by being with people of their 'own tribe' cajoles them into thinking that if a slightly different individual enters the group, it might disturb the sense of serenity and security. Their different outlook in life may threaten the way of being of the people in the group. Hence, people choose to keep the doors of inclusion closed to a minority. Multiple research data indicates that emotional well-being improves when one has been exposed to diverse cultures and ethnicities. It expands the mind to a different world and improvises the understanding of human dynamics by making one stronger and more secure emotionally.

In September 1986, a statement by the Japanese Prime Minister, Yasuhiro Nakasone, created quite a stir in the US. He said that due to the presence of a large Hispanic and black populace, the level of education and intellect in the US is low. As most of the Japanese in 1986 were made to understand, Nakasone was implying that ethnic diversity creates dissension and uncertainty. He was trying to state that societies function best when its inmates (people) act, think and look alike, as in Japan. He was affirming that there is a disposition in human beings to unconsciously prefer to be with those who are familiar and relatable, as being different may be discomforting and the unknown intimidating. We prefer to be with someone who has the same way of looking at life, the same values and similar looks and, in some cases, a similar ideology. It is just so much easier. This is an affinity bias and has the potential to cloud our judgement, keeping us in our comfort zones and thereby stagnating growth.

Japan did not have to deal with a demographic bomb then and the government did not foresee one coming in the near future, although it had employed some of the best development economists. At that time, Tadashi Yamamoto, president of the Japan Centre for International Exchange, had remarked, 'We are not accustomed to living together with other races. We do not have the basic training.' This begs the question whether recognising each other's differences and embracing them can be achieved through learning or not!

Being open-minded is about opening ourselves to ideas beyond our deeply embedded views, which were handed down to us by our family or other social groups. In essence, they are largely assumptions that are not always fully tested or validated with experience. They are beliefs that have been built on the actions of others from the past yet guide our reactions to people or situations today. In the context of dealing with colour or race, this factor forces us to operate within a boundary constraining our actions to form real bonds. We learn to love or hate some communities because we believe the known person who told us good or bad things about them. This may change if we were to explore the reality on our own. Just spending time with different kinds of people often helps with sensitisation, learning and better understanding of each other. We can learn to respond to people differently if we are able to change our lens through engagement and conversations. Simple questions like why someone does what they do? What do these actions mean to them vis-à-vis to me? Do they understand me? This could help us know them for who they are rather than expect them to be someone who we believe they should be.

Navigating Multicultural Landscapes

While I was working in Europe, my organisation ran a powerful programme for multicultural teams across Indians, British, Americans, Dutch and the Chinese. As a part of their simulated training, the participants were provided with a case study. In short, the case stated an incident putting each individual in the programme in the centre.

It started with a request: 'Imagine you are travelling with your significant other who you dearly love. You are returning from a late night winter party and it is about 2:00 AM in the morning. Both of you have had more than a glass of wine. Even though under permissible limits, you know that your loved one cannot handle more than a glass and it is easy to fall into a blissful inebriated state of mind with that! You are both happy and your significant other is on the wheel, driving the car at that hour with no one else on the road. In a rush to get home, the car speeds at 40 miles/hour, way above the city speed limit of 20 miles/hour. It is pitch dark on a winter night and the cold is ready to engulf you if you stepped out of the vehicle. You are both sharing jokes and reminiscing about the great food at the party. Both of you are looking forward to the warm fireside and maybe a good cup of coffee as soon as you reach home!

'There is a pedestrian crossing coming up. It has blinkers on, which requires you to go slow, watch for pedestrians on the road and then drive on. In your merriment, you are both racing through the road. It is too late in the cold night for anyone to venture out and you have not seen a soul on the road so far. And so the driver continues at a high speed.

'Suddenly there is an old woman who comes running through the crossing, possibly cold and rushing through to get home too!

BANG! A head-on collision! The driver is inebriated and the car speed is so high that even the emergency brakes are not enough to stop the car on that icy, slippery road. The old lady is badly injured, lying in a pool of blood on the road. Both of you come out of the car to help her as she battles for life! You are very shocked and scared.

'The police arrives on the scene. The old lady is taken to the hospital right away. The initial diagnosis indicates that she is critical with grim chances of survival. Investigation and cross-examination commence on the spot. Now the police officer turns to you as your significant other seems to be in complete shock and is unable to talk coherently. He asks you, "What happened? Was this a simple accident and the woman ran across suddenly? Was he driving within the speed limit?"

'You are the only eye witness and what you say, will be held against your loved one. You can decide the fate of the case. You are really torn.'

Pause: As you read this, I would like you to ask this question to yourself and ponder on what you would say. If you have the answer for yourself, then read on.

As we asked each person in the room this question, we had the following observations across different ethnic groups. I would like to put a disclaimer here that this is representative of the view of the sample attending the programme only and hence inferences are limited to that:

1. **Dutch:** They were extremely regretful of what had happened, but would call out that the driver was above the speed limit and it was his/her fault. They were in control of their emotions and any struggles in making a facts-based communication were less apparent.

   They shared that the relationship drivers for the Dutch are authenticity, being objective and straightforward.

2. **Asians:** They were traumatised with the dilemma. They clearly felt sad for the lady, but were equally distressed about putting their dear ones at risk by giving the honest answer to the police.

Most of them said they would rather give themselves in if needed, not their loved ones, and their statement would hinge on partial disclosures, mitigating risk for their loved ones.

They shared that the drivers for Asian relationships and family bonds are sacred. Asians are fiercely protective of them. They will do whatever it takes to ensure no harm comes by, even at their own personal cost. Emotional intensity and commitment were quite high towards these relationships.

3. **British:** They agreed that it was a really unfortunate situation and wanted to be seen doing the right thing as God is watching. However, they would try and find the right way of stating the facts to salvage the loved ones if possible. They would not give themselves in. They felt really caught in the dilemma.

They shared that they were driven to achieve a fair result that did not make them feel guilty (if not appropriate) and yet achieved the desired outcome. Hence, more debate was needed in decision-making.

4. **Americans:** The jury was divided among people reflecting the true diversity of thinking in the US. Some said they will protect the loved ones while others stated that they will disclose the truth. Their focus was on what made sense today and in the future. The lady was not going to survive, it was unintentional, so why risk the person?

Their driver was being future forward. A big focus was to remain objective in times of stress and think on your feet quickly. Relationships were important but so was a sense of self.

Now let's pull these cultural drivers together at the work place. Here is what may happen:

If we have Dutch and Asians working together and something goes wrong unintentionally, Asians would expect the managers to protect them and have their back, while the Dutch will do what they think is 'right', even if it means disrupting the team. Asians will be unlikely to respect a manager like this, while the Dutch would be aghast that anyone could expect them to even disclose an issue partially and manage it more subtly, which could be a compromise that they are uncomfortable with.

The Asian is wondering about the Dutch—if they can't protect their own spouse—how can they ever be trusted to look after us? The Dutch is wondering about the Asian—if their answer can change on the basis of the people involved, how can I ever trust them to play fair?

Let's get British and Americans together. The British would like to move things thoughtfully, in a process at a certain pace. The process of managing conflicts is subtle and consensus on approach is important. Sometimes the process becomes more important than the end. While Americans are clear on target and may wish to get it over as quickly as possible. The approach is important, but the process it not a goal in itself and will be changed if it interferes with the achievement of the goal.

The list goes on. It is evident that inter-team dynamics are strongly impacted by these cultural and racial nuances. What may feel appropriate in one culture may not feel right in another and vice versa. I see the perils of this lack of understanding and openness in every day team dynamics at work. The simplicity of this is evident, but people find it so difficult to practise as they are programmed to be blinded and behave in a certain way. When under stress in relationships, when trying to prove right and wrong, people easily fall back into cultural archetypes, attributing blame or generating negativity for each other.

The Asians expect their managers to protect them because most Asians come from a culture where the families are supposed to protect each other. Providing a sense of security is an expected duty of the family. The Asian concept of family is that of a closely knit set of individuals who stand up for each other as and when required, emotionally or otherwise. The family members are usually dependent on each other for support and fulfilment. This may be slightly different than the western family system that is more about independence, and letting each find their foothold in the world. Most American adults become financially independent at an early age and so it is important for them to become emotionally, financially and psychologically independent as well.

The Dutch, on the other hand, are more straightforward and they believe in calling a spade, a spade! Therefore, they do not believe in a protectionist attitude and believe in being ruthlessly honest and impartial to what a situation demands of them. It is the difference in the social systems that we need to be a little more accepting of. Each and every ethnicity, culture or country has had a certain system of conducting themselves in social terms and there is a reason behind every kind of behaviour.

Therefore, we need to strike a balance among ways of being and connect to individuals from other ethnicities and cultures professionally and personally. There are some cultures that value the process over the goal and there are some who do vice versa. There is nothing right or wrong about this. We need to leverage the benefits of both these views and reach a common ground in multi-ethnic contexts. We need to go beyond perceived demeanours and insipid norms to decode a 'common culture code' so that we can all assimilate the best of every ethnicity.

The way we are brought up plays an important role in how we perceive the concept of social inclusion and openness. If we grow up in a community which naturally is averse to opening up to different communities, then closed-mindedness becomes a way of life. The lack of exposure to unfamiliar cultures instils confusion and discomfort when we come into contact with them. Likewise open-minded nations that embrace different kind of people and thinking evolve to a new social system of the future. They are the beneficiary of diverse learning leading to a possibly better social evolution for the world.

Us versus Them

Colour, and its associated racism, is a complex and a persistent social issue, which has not been addressed adequately by a number of countries around the world. The dilemma that most nationalist governments face is that openness to multiple races or ethnicity may lead to a situation that eventually drowns the local population with foreign ideology, culture and people. This obviously creates anxiety and insecurity.

The concept of 'Progressive Dilemma', which says that higher levels of ethnic immigration seem to make voters support redistributive policies even lesser, points to the fact that when it comes to sharing public goods and public services and the overall prosperity of the nation, most individuals across the world want to share it with people who are like themselves, who face the same difficulties that they face or will face in the future. We associate with individuals who have similar experiences, where empathy for each other is mutual. The willingness to share resources, especially public resources, diminishes as society becomes more diverse because the consumption pattern and the ideology of each ethnicity are different. The general thought process behind the idea of redistribution is: 'Why should I pay for them when they are doing things that I would not do?'

The reality is that the prosperity of some is built on the services of others. Certain ethnicities and migrants do work in more developed nations as they have opportunities to contribute and add value where there may be a lack of local talent. Taxes are paid by them for any services provided or shared in the host countries. There may be a few bad experiences, but generalising those to all may lead to gaps in coexistence and continuity of services. To assume there is a homogeneous social cohort in any country is a myth. The fact is that in any race or ethnicity, there is diversity of thinking among the people as they may be brought up differently or in different circumstances. Opening the mindset to embrace people of different colour helps people find different sources of support for themselves and their nation.

The need for psychological and emotional security for an individual, who is duly satisfied by being among those who share the same skin colour or the same race, is mainly born out of natural human affinity. The social conditioning that children receive from an early age involves the 'calculus of affinity', which provides them with a natural preference to be in familiar surroundings to feel safe.

In 1943, the American psychologist Abraham Maslow, in his influential paper, 'A Theory of Human Motivation', proposed that human beings have a certain number of needs. His paper implied that human actions are driven by motivations. Maslow's five-tier model of human needs classified all the needs below self-actualisation as basic needs or deficient needs, which are essential for survival. The need for security is the second-most-important need for humans, and it is this need that prevents humans from being open to the idea of cross-cultural or multicoloured relationships. It is this psychological and emotional security that has sometimes led to 'strangers' turning into enemies or friends.

It is the discomfort and the sense of insecurity from the presence of 'strangers' (read: people of different colour or ethnicity) felt by the secure majority, which manifests itself into aggression and 'closed walls'. This, in turn, formulates conflicts in relationships. We are taught to trust and nurture emotional affection for familiar members and be wary of strangers. Perhaps, this is why we fail to embrace an open mind as it requires us to be secure in an insecure environment of people who are unlike us. Is there a possibility to find security by keeping our minds open to who people actually are? There is enough and more infighting within same communities, however that seems to go unnoticed. Family feuds, riots, homicide do take place across the world, and not always by 'strangers'.

A child is taught words like 'ours' and 'theirs'. These two words then drive how they relate to the world.

When I was born, I came unto this world,
I didn't know who is 'mine' and who is 'theirs'
I didn't know who is 'black' and who is 'white'
I didn't know who was 'us' and who was 'them'
But,
I did know the source of love
I did know the cradle of affection
I did know the degree of fondness
I did know the human chemistry and intimacy
But mine and theirs still blinds me!

In the rhetoric of the modern liberal state, the glue of ethnicity ('people who look and talk like us') has been replaced by the glue of values ('people who think and behave like us'). The need to be secure among people who do and think alike is born out of a peculiar kind of fear. The fear of giving up power, livelihoods and various other things to those from a different ethnicity or different thought architecture. Most sociologists and psychologists feel that the fear of domination by 'strangers' give rise to the resistance to inclusion, leading to a defence for false sense of security. This hinders the ability of people to integrate with other communities. Sometimes, the prejudices that people have against a particular skin colour are unconsciously intertwined with their emotions, which makes the bias so potent that the 'presumptions' (prejudices and emotion) instigate an individual to undesirable reactions and behaviours. Repeated behaviour leads to permanence of this bias that locks the corridors of the mind such that they do not open up at all.

The inbuilt desire to be with those who look like us and talk like us propels us to stay away from the perceived 'other'. But in doing this, we are missing out much that will be left undiscovered and unearthed. We abstain from trying out new dishes because we are unsure about the palatability of the dish for our own taste buds. There is a certain risk involved in trying out something new! It is this risk factor, which stops us from experiencing the new and the unknown. Pessimism associated with such risk factors discourages us to move beyond established conventions, to go ahead and experience a persona irrespective of the skin colour or nationality. Are we really living our life fully this way?

ARE WE SCARED OF MUSLIMS OR ISLAM?

Shabeena's relationship with Islam and with being American has troubled her for a fairly long time. It's like when someone asks you, who are you more attached to, your dad or your mom? Shabeena Khan is a sixteen-year-old college student in the US. Her parents are from Pakistan and both Shabeena and her sister live with their parents in the US, which has been her home since her birth. In the US, it seemed to her that her dark hair, her brown skin and her body structure had done enough to differentiate her from the crowd. Her *niqaab*, which hid her face, seemed to have given her a different identity altogether. It had literally segregated her from the mainstream.

Of late, it had made Shabeena and her sister, Rasheeda, feel that if they had been born in a different body, with blonde hair, light eyes and pink cheeks, things would have been different. The earth-shattering events of the 9/11 attacks and other incidents that followed, only made her life more difficult in the US. Since then, Shabeena said that she failed to understand what exactly has come under sheer mammoth criticism, Islam or Muslims?

As a child, in her new home country, every time she looked in the mirror she felt that she was imperfect, given she was brown. The leaves of the nearby tree rustled and it felt as if they were laughing at her as they saw her skin colour. There was a myriad mixture of light, dark and brown leaves beautifully intertwined with each other. It boasted of a sea of different shades of green. These colours had always fascinated Shabeena, but never really had they created divisions in her mind. Then, her eyes rolled down to the bark of the tree. It was dark brown and alternated between light and dark, according to the reflection of the sunlight. She wondered that if nature could accommodate for the inclusion of all kinds of colours without discrimination, why couldn't mankind?

While growing up with brown skin, Shabeena had contemplated plastic surgery; she thought she did not get romantic proposals because she was not as beautiful as her white counterparts. She thought her nose was quite strange. She did not hate it, but she disliked her facial features because it prevented her from feeling a sense of belonging with her homeland, which was not Pakistan but the US! She grew up in a country, which had a larger number of whites and she was quite overwhelmed and influenced by their ways of living.

She resented everything that made her look dissimilar to her purely white American neighbours, with a few black and brown people thrown in. She had begun to have aspirations, which involved moulding herself physically and mentally to be a part of the general populace of her country. She also thought of changing her name and surname, because it had instilled fear in the minds of most Americans she knew. She wanted to change everything about herself to escape the hate and the abhorred racism, which consumed and killed her emotionally.

This internal dissonance had left her puzzled. She cried herself to sleep almost every day, only to wake up with puffy eyes the next day, feeling bad about her ethnicity. *She felt that she was being racist towards herself.*

The cultural riptide and the racial profiling of Muslims as brown-coloured individuals, terrorists, unwanted migrants, as those who could only do harm and no good to anybody, was something that Shabeena refused to identify with. She was a brown Muslim and an American and had done no harm to anyone. In school, Shabeena would give away her lunch every day to some of her white classmates, because they found her food quite delicious. That was the only time they would ever engage with her—willingly and happily. That made her feel included and at home, something that she craved for; but as a result, she remained hungry for days together in school. She tried very hard to mingle with a crowd that she considered to be a part of her own, because she was residing there!

Shabeena's perplexities got the better of her as she continued to be befuddled with a large number of open-ended questions with no answers in sight—how would she reconcile and live with two identities, one defining her nationality and the other her ethnicity?

As the number of ritualistic bombings grew in the US, whenever Shabeena went to school, none of her classmates would speak to her. She could see the hate on their faces, because those from 'her' religion, 'her' race had killed many from 'their' religion and 'their' race. She was at the receiving end of silent and idiosyncratic euphemisms, which pierced her heart and she was thrown off balance.

It caused a lot of emotional upheaval that cannot be expressed, but only felt. Her heart sank at the narration of the dreadful stories that her ears heard and she developed a subtle hatred for herself. As days passed by, the sheer hatred for brown people (more for Muslims) grew. It hurt her even more when she lost her friendship with Rosy, her white best friend, to the anti-Muslim rhetoric that filled the public discourse. Once this news was circulated, some average bigots in school laughed at her and made snide remarks. If she wanted, Shabeena could silence the bullies and pull them up for taking advantage of the misinformation, which was spreading like wildfire, but she did not do it. She was scared.

She continued to walk through the corridors of racism in deep contemplation—is this how it was supposed to be now? Were all of them against us? Will not a single non-Muslim or white person open up to us, innocent ones? Bigots take advantage of the fragile emotional state of those who have lost their near and dear ones to spread hate; and once emotion gets mixed up with a manufactured and distorted narrative, it is difficult to make people see the truth behind the veneer of manipulated fiction.

A lack of openness is a consequence of the fact that there is a malaise, which afflicts society—most people have more opinions than information and this can be quite dangerous for social dynamics.

As a child, Shabeena was taught the Koran, because it is the religious text book of Islam, her religion. She was also taught to wear the *niqaab* because that was how Muslim women dressed in public. But should all of this, including her roots, make her feel alien in this country, even though she identifies with its purpose, ways of being and was even willing to give her life for this country?

At times, Shabeena felt like an object of ridicule and sometimes she felt no longer alive. How better could her family deal with the hate? The anti-Muslim sentiment gained strength and the Muslims earned a new definition for themselves. She could comprehend the hate, but she could not fathom the generalisations and absolute abandonment of openness as humans. She thought she lived in a progressive country with open-minded people, which had for years embraced good talent irrespective of the diverse race of the people. It was home to a huge number of immigrants who came from various countries of the world. Why had they suddenly closed their minds?

An article in *The Guardian* newspaper in May 2018 revealed that according to a study, half the British Muslim population live in 10% of the most deprived places in the UK; 31% of young children in the UK feel that Muslims are taking over while 37% of the British would support a political party which would reduce the number of Muslims in the UK and so on and so forth. The question this study raises is how Islamophobia will impact the future generations of this world. Is there a way to manage this more constructively through better integration of diverse people? If we continue on this path, where will it lead us? A lot of this is rhetoric, but with geopolitical dynamics this has instilled fear in many minds. Love begets love. And hate generates hate. Simply starting an interaction with a positive intent, not judging character till we really know someone, may be a step in the right direction.

During all the turmoil in Shabeena's life, she happened to connect online with an American girl on Facebook. Sara was one of her previous classmates' friend and had heard about her research project. She was working on a similar project and wanted some help. She was surprised that a white American had connected to a brown Muslim online to gain assistance for a project. It was quite unheard of at that point, but somehow the feeling was quite sublime. In the midst of all the hatred, there was a sweet spot of acceptance and she held onto it for dear life. The emotional connect was so overwhelming that physical proximity did not matter at all.

She was hugely grateful for the openness Sara had shown. It was evident that Sara was trying to get to know Shabeena, without being judgemental and this propelled Shabeena to reciprocate in equal measure. The most wonderful feature of the friendship was that Sara did not try to think too much about Shabeena's origin, her lineage and her brown skin. She was not influenced by the anti-Muslim rhetoric because she was confident about her beliefs and her sense of reasoning.

The two girls spoke for an hour every day, but they never met. They stayed in two different states, yet were very close. The bright sunlight traversed through the darkness in Shabeena's world when Sara came into her life. Sara was the fresh wind and the new fragrance, which added a new gush of rainbow colours to her drab life. Shabeena became more open to people, more open to life; she regained her consciousness, and she came back to open the door of her house to everybody, irrespective of colour. Sara became Shabeena's new lifeline. When just one person can transform a life so completely, imagine the power of many.

Shabeena had been living with two identities and had been trapped into a sense of double consciousness. She believed in doing everything with a sense of dual consciousness, which created a lot of internal conflict. On meeting Sara, she realised that one needs to balance between the two identities and decide to what extent one needs to belong to each other.

Reneging on the Inclusion Agenda

The preference for a certain kind of populace is born out of the preferences of our families and neighbourhoods. The rising trend of nationalism and the continuous efforts to fuel the racist or anti-immigration rant has once again established that we still find security among 'people like us'. The nationalists have always asked their countrymen to resist the false song of globalism, but in doing so they are being quite disrespectful and ignorant of the composition of their own 'countrymen'.

Social psychologists have argued that the propensity to perceive in-groups and out-groups is innate among human beings. Burkeans (the populace supporting the political philosopher, Edmund Burke's school of thought, which is known as Burkean Conservatism) have shared that we are most comfortable with and are ever ready to share and sacrifice for those with whom we share histories and values. The extent of our obligations to those with whom we are not connected by race, blood, kinship or nationality is at best described as a purely private decision. Sometimes natives of most homogeneous communities believe that the needs of desperate outsiders are in conflict with their own.

The human mind gets caught in a quandary of local inhabitants and outsiders. When we create such concepts, we are deliberately creating a breeding ground for frictional and divisive ideas. This reduces our ability to think beyond what is said and heard, and we tend to submit ourselves to the 'group think', which manifest sometimes in dysfunctional ways. Further, factors such as security and safety intertwined with the earlier-mentioned concepts create fear or plant the idea that outsiders may encroach upon the resources and territories of the local population. This is where some fight the race battle, but humanity loses the war.

Some misinformed ideas and narratives assume such a significant space in our minds that we tend to visualise them as facts and fail to see the fiction in it. It closes the mind and opens fragmentation.

The reality is that in most places there are majorities, not complete homogeneity. It is the interplay of diverse mindsets and of thinking that moves groups and nations ahead. Together they are able to look at problems of life in different ways, yielding to better solutions. An openness of mental borders can create richness in our hearts; a legacy we may wish to leave for our next generations. Being inclusive makes all of us stronger and better versions of ourselves as we don't mirror each other, but complement each other instead.

DISCOVERING IDENTITIES: WORK-IN-PROGRESS

Laxmi was born in India and raised in Singapore. Her name was quite long, Laxmi Venkateswaran and she had seen many instances of her classmates struggling to pronounce her name properly. Her father was from India and her mother from Russia, but she had lived in Singapore as a child. So where was home? It was difficult for her to search for one and she had to dig deeper to find the answer. Her extended families stayed in two countries and she stayed in a third country. Her expat friends were as confused about her identity and often asked, 'But where are you actually from?' and her retort had always been, 'From nowhere, yet everywhere!'

Sometimes Laxmi begrudged the fact that her answers to simple questions were always complicated. She resented the question, 'Where are you from?', for years together because there was an inherent perplexity that always got the better of her. She often felt the need to prove herself through her various origins, because of her brown skin, her Singapore accent and a preference for Russian food. To avoid an awkward reaction, she would streamline her story to make it palatable for an individual by deleting some aspects of it and keeping some of it to make it sound believable enough! It was confusing.

As a person of colour living outside her native country, she suffered from the existential question of who she was and where she belonged. A strange and unusual mix of autocorrect cultures had altered her cultural DNA and formed a puzzle inside her. But she found comfort in the fact that there were others who were trying to understand the idea of identity in her international school in Singapore. She was among a number of students who were bicultural or multinational and were unable to find that one place where they could belong to completely. Laxmi used to discuss with her school friends if home felt like a place full of memories and emotions, a likely place one could honestly belong to. She did feel a bit Indian (thanks to her father's fascination for Hindi songs, which were always playing in the background), and a little bit Russian. She had not been able to understand what being a Singaporean was really like, apart from being cosmopolitan (which she loved). In Singapore, she still felt like a happy outsider in spite of being a citizen. She loved the friendly people and the infectious energy of that country.

Laxmi went to the US for her undergraduate studies, only to discover that the culture there was even more alien to her. It was somewhat unsettling in Iowa, where she struggled to come to terms with the isolation and the differentiation. It was too individualistic for her or perhaps she thought she was not as adaptable. She stayed in a rented apartment with a few Americans and the chemistry did not work out well for her. One day, she used an extra loaf of bread from her roommate, Mariana's food tub, because she was very hungry and too ill to go out and get one. Mariana came back and was quite furious to discover that Laxmi had taken 'one extra loaf of bread'! It made a world of difference to her monthly budget and her food stock, she said. In her weak and disturbed state, Laxmi stepped out to get an extra loaf of bread. She felt humiliated and lonely.

Relative to Asia, the relationships in the US were quite transactional, quite matter of fact.

For the first time, she saw the implications of racial profiling behind closed doors, when in her apartment, she had to put up with some distanced interaction for almost two years. Jane and Mariana were both on one side of the line of control and Laxmi on the other. Even an extrovert like Laxmi struggled to make friends as the two roommates were not open to embracing someone who was different in looks and mannerisms than them. Iowa was one of the smaller, less cosmopolitan cities relative to New York or Washington DC and she definitely did not feel that she was welcome there. The upbringing of a person reflects in a person's attitude and Laxmi felt that most people there were engaged inwardly. Her Asian orientation sometimes conflicted with this ideology.

As she graduated, it dawned on her that the documentation required in the US on a student visa, especially for brown people from Asia, was quite cumbersome, which automatically made her feel a little unwanted, unlike Europeans in the US! Even in the professional environment, there was reduced openness for browns or blacks as opposed to whites.

After Iowa, she went to California, where she felt much better and very different, despite being in the same country. There was immense openness and inclusion of diverse people in that part of the US. She formed a diverse group of friends—two Russians, one French, one African and one Italian. It was quite refreshing to be surrounded by people who made you feel a part of them. She chose to stay alone in an apartment this time. She noticed that people were much more straightforward and missed no opportunity to help others, whether an outsider or otherwise. The warm reception in California, as opposed to the rude culture shock in Iowa, made her aware of the paradoxes that exist in this world. She felt a little safer and much more secure in the West Coast, perhaps because emotionally she was in a good space. She stepped out to have fun; going for drinks and a few parties made her feel good, and almost made her feel at home.

This experience across continents taught her to be more patient with people. Laxmi learnt not to react or berate any race or nationality (in this case Americans) as no two people are the same. She began to think differently and was much more comfortable in a diverse environment. She learnt not to give up but to adopt the culture of a certain country without losing her originality. She believed that she had the freedom to wear different masks, in different societies and cultures and live a different life every time she changed a country, whether for education or otherwise. She felt that since she had no official roots, she could wander around and choose to wear the 'colour' that she wanted to. She learnt not to generalise people on the basis of a particular incident or event, but rather to take an aggregated view of the entire episode to come to a conclusion. She realised that she could choose to belong to many places as she had the exposure to understand the emotional and psychological fabric of multiple ethnicities or cultures.

'Life gave me the opportunity to surrender my prejudiced mind, to pry open and consider the thoughts, the feelings and emotions of my fellow beings and I discovered a new sense of belonging that came out of that openness,' she shared. Laxmi continues to live in the US.

LESSONS FROM THE PAST

Historical imperial interventions might have sown the seeds of racism in the eastern world. Europeans brought with them their technical inventions, ideas and institution to the region. Their aim was to create an ethnicity-centred cultural void that the imperial powers could utilise to step in under the guise of being saviours or protectors of the populace and hide their strategic interests. *Those who are subordinated under imperialism are perceived as being submissive, refugees and helpless victims and not as independent individuals with a face and a self-sufficient voice.*

Some imperialists also prevented the formation of any social organisation in the victim's country. The sole motive of the colonial powers was to control every aspect of the captured nation— economic, social and political. This explains how the British 'tea' came to India, along with the belief that 'fairer is better and superior'. European linguistics, culture and institutions have unabashedly seeped into modern day institutional systems of most countries around the world.

Colonisation and imperialism tend to create this mirage that certain colonising powers and the products they use are superior in terms of their quality. When it came to socially accepted norms of mannerisms as well, the imperial powers set the stage to ensure that they established all such behaviours and their standards! Their ultimate aim was to emerge as a powerful force, both financially and more so socially, so that they could also conquer the social space of the colonised land.

History tells us that imperialism paved the way for the creation of superior and inferior cultures. Once we reflect on this, we understand the careful creation of structures that favoured those with a particular skin colour and belittled others. Such biased structures cannot assist in the creation of a society that is fair and equitable. The far-reaching hangover of this exists till today in closed minds. Unless we are able to open our inner wisdom to break the shackles of this doctrine, it will continue to subtly govern our behaviour.

DEFYING WELL-DEFINED PERCEPTIONS!

International students studying in the UK always look for work to earn some money to help them to tide over their expenses in a foreign country. UK rules for students do permit a few work hours after college time. This acts as a good source of pocket money for the students in a country where the cost of living is quite high. There are options galore for such students—from working in call centres, department stores to shopping malls or even working in restaurants as waiters.

Raj, a young student, was excited to find out that there was an opening for an event manager at a nearby pub. He eagerly waited to be interviewed on the back of his application. He had been studying in London for a few months and had been exploring an opportunity like this that suited his interests and could also get him some money. In fact, he had worked with a few event management companies in India and had managed some high-profile events with aplomb. Therefore, managing an event in a pub was quite a cakewalk for him, given his experience in his home country.

He was requested to present his CV again in person. He reached the venue at an off-peak time. The English manager of the pub met him at a table and without batting an eyelid asked him to join immediately as a bartender or a waiter instead of an event manager. 'We have enough Asians in serving roles doing a great job and you can join them too,' he said, without giving a single glance to the CV Raj had presented him.

Raj was quite stunned at the unexpected turn of events. He was further infuriated with the stereotyping. The event manager had assumed that just because Raj looked Asian, he could be nothing better than a waiter. He just kept the CV on the shelf in his office, without any consideration. Raj felt belittled. The manager gave Raj a cheeky look and told him, 'Go on gentleman, now that's enough of a conversation. You can start working right away! Now have a look at your attire and change.' Raj looked at the waiters working around and shuddered in dismay as that was not in line with his interest. He shook his head in disbelief and continued to writhe in anger. A waiter earns around £4.5 an hour and the event manager's job would get Raj £12.5 for the same amount of time!

Finally Raj found his words, 'Sir, I would prefer to work where I can produce value for you. That lies in creating events, that's my passion and your need.' He insisted how this made more commercial sense for the pub too as they would pay him a student rate. Raj shared a number of events that he had managed in India, including a show on MTV. He requested the English manager, Mike, to interview him so that he could contribute with his prior rich experience that would make a difference to the guest experience at the pub. But the English manager chuckled, only to move his hand in the air and tell his colleague, 'These fellows, these Asians, I tell you, really gone! Haha! Okay, you have two minutes to make your case.'

Raj started to mimic the manager in a really funny way that attracted the attention of the guests in the pub, who guffawed with laughter and offered him drinks and requested for more comic performances! Rounds of applause followed Raj's act. As he finished his show and started to walk out, Mike took him aside and literally scolded him politely, 'Hang on! Do not create a scene. I will have a look. Just have some patience young man!'

Subsequently, Raj asked Mike to let him manage the events at the pub for about a week free of cost. Raj wanted to prove to Mike that he was indeed talented and that he was being truthful about his credentials. In spite of this, he was hired on paper as a waiter so that the other formalities could be taken care of far more easily than would have been otherwise. Mike told him that he 'would assess' if he could hire Raj as a manager later.

Pub sales went up that week due to the shows that Raj conducted. In a week's time, more people visited the pub to be entertained by Raj. His simple jokes, his self-deprecating demeanour and his wonderment of life in the UK kept people in fits of laughter. He became a sought-after entertainer on the high street.

A week later, Raj was hired with more money than he had asked for by the owner of the pub! The local newspaper could not stop writing about his 'Punjabi Fusion' night and the 'Gujarati Razmatazz', which witnessed record footfalls. Raj was praised for his managerial skills and his innovative ideas. The owner of the pub was so impressed with his performance that he was also paid the whole month's salary of an event manager. The weekend nights would be jam-packed in the pub, thanks to Raj's persistent innovation. The

English manager, Mike, tried to remove Raj from the pub by bullying him and making his work environment difficult, but the pub owner saved him each time as he was truly impressed with his dedication and sincerity. He was quite open to Raj's diverse way of thinking and working. He gave him the freedom to try out new things and was quite supportive. This gave Raj the confidence to not only survive, but thrive in the pub for close to three years while he pursued his college degree. He assumed a fan following among the other staff at the pub and Mike finally gave up and moved out of his way!

Raj had steered his way around a difficult environment, where he was initially looked down with contempt. But, he was determined and kept his optimism, not letting any negativity touch him. He also quickly changed his strategy to focus on the key stakeholders—guests at the pub. He mobilised his energies with his positive and forward-looking attitude. Then, slowly and steadily, he tried to win over the owner and staff at the pub, leading to a lifetime of friendships!

Raj was assertive and level-headed enough to navigate through the racial stereotype that a few carry. In fact, he was open-minded to put himself out there and prove to those very colleagues who had indulged in racial profiling that he could reset their perceptions. The best part of it was that when it came to addressing his humiliation or hurt to his self-dignity, he sublimated it through his work, which was emphatically appreciated by all. Raj helped the manager learn, in a constructive manner, that the process of stereotyping may lead people to make gross errors about others and their abilities. Raj's advice to his friends was that when faced with adversity, persist and persist and bang the door open! The world is yours too, but you need to stake your claim sometimes.

ARE BIASES CARRIED ACROSS GENERATIONS HURTING THIS GENERATION?

At present, we are faced with colour related issues, courtesy the biases, ideologies and other notions that have been passed down through generations. Noreena Hertz has successfully interviewed 2,000 teenagers during 2015–2016 and has come to the conclusion that the present generation is under a lot of stress and anxiety. In fact, young adults are quite suspicious of their surroundings and are quite mistrustful of diverse people! This generation is grappling with a number of problems such as economic instability, financial pessimism, income inequality and job insecurity. Almost 70% of the generation is worried about uncertain threats such as terrorism.

The most alarming revelation of the survey is the fact that youth today do not feel that successes and achievements in life are based on merit.

According to the survey, none of the students agreed with the fact that society is fair or that there is equal opportunity for all. The teenagers shared that a number of uncontrollable factors determine their future such as their socio-economic status, the colour of their skin, their gender and their parents' economic status. This further elucidates the fact that the youth of today thinks that society does not reward merit alone, but many other factors that one inherits at birth, like ethnicity and nationality, have a significant impact. How does one get to a neutral starting point in a mixed-race environment? No one selects their skin colour, family or country, and yet they determine our life in every way.

Dr Herron from Harvard University has revealed that racial ideology has existed in history and in our culture for several generations. Our identities are connected to race and, hence, our thought processes related to colour continue to be relevant and in practice even today. Many scientists and anthropologists from earlier generations had supported and validated such ideologies, which is why a lot of people believed in it. Dr Herron says that anthropology was almost viewed as a science, which was based on racial thinking for almost a hundred years because a lot of racism was purported to show that indeed these racial differences were born out of biological differences between human beings. This is a refuted theory today. Just being conscious of it and wanting to change this dynamic is a constructive start.

Looking at it from a futuristic perspective, it has impacts on the way our children develop, positively or otherwise. Shared values, common interests and traditions have been upheld as the hallmark of society and have become the standard that should be adhered to in different communities. Their relevance is not challenged even though they may not serve any purpose any more. This results in misleading myths, such as black people are great at pop music, untouchables in India are 'dirty', brown people and Indians are loud, Koreans are introverted, certain white communities are more skilled than others. The list goes on.

Presumptions to Reaction—Through the Shades of Colour

I have never been able to fathom how coloured individuals are perceived to commit particular crimes or are expected to behave in a certain way by some people. For example, in India, blacks are 'perceived' to take drugs and apparently lead 'dark' and 'notorious' lives by the uninformed. Browns are perceived to be 'thieves' by some in certain countries, and the narration of a personal experience will only prove my claim. Often the lack of openness towards each other leads to the formation of misconceptions, which are impossible to eliminate if both parties do not make an attempt to have an open, honest and candid conversation.

In fact, a dialogue can be effective in not only opening up to a person at an individual level, but can also assist in clearing misunderstandings whilst removing any room for negative perceptions for future interactions. If we stick to the generalisations that exist in the public domain, we will never be able to understand what lies beneath the surface. Generalisations are visible to the naked eye, but reality will surface when one spends time and is tolerant emotionally and with coloured people to get a deeper insight into who they actually are!

During our early days in Europe, we fell in love with the beauty of the European landscape and a better work-life balance that gave us time to pursue other interests. Often we would take short holidays from London to the continent to explore different countries. One such sojourn was to Switzerland in the spring school mid-term break. It was a slightly cold April day, when my husband and I landed in Zurich with our young children. We had booked a hotel in the city centre, making it easier for us to walk around with the children around the lake, which was surrounded by purple mountains and luscious gardens serenading us to leave our worries behind. Cheese and wine added to the magic and we were truly enjoying our family time.

On our last day at the hotel, we packed our bags and my husband went to the check-out counter to settle the bills. As he browsed through the itemised costs, he realised that he had been billed for certain in-house movies, which we had not watched. We checked with the children just in case they may have used the service and the answer was a negative. As we requested the hotel to relook at it, the receptionist insisted someone had pressed the buttons on the remote and the duration may have been a few seconds, but it had to be billed.

As we discussed this with the reception staff, a stout manager walked in. He seemed quite nonchalant and rudely told my husband, 'You Indians, you are always looking for a bargain, you are thugs and thieves, not sure why we even gave you the room here! Not sure how you could even afford it!'

Suddenly a discussion that was going well so far, turned uncomfortable and hostile. The manager went on with his rant about Indians, almost accusing us of stealing the service for which we were seeking clarifications. As my husband tried to reason with him calmly, anger began to take me over. I firmly told him that he could not behave like this with us and that he could be taken to court for that statement. Again, he nonchalantly replied, 'Do what you want! Here is the cop's number. Call them and I will tell them you are all thieves!'

I just could not comprehend what to say to him, apart from holding myself from socking him. A violent shouting match ensued between us, as I was not one to take this lying down. Soon the hotel staff and my husband intervened to calm down emotions. My husband, visibly upset, settled the bill, tipped another €100 to the receptionist just to prove a point and left the receipt for the racist white manager to stare at. However, the experience left us very bitter. My children were scared and my daughter started crying, 'Mama, we can't go to jail. What have we done wrong?' I did not have the heart to tell her that the manager wanted to send us to jail because he thought all our countrymen were thieves. More importantly, he assumed we were Indians because we were brown. We were British, but he was simply guided by the colour of our skin. The deep-seated animosity and racist views that they witnessed during this holiday left a lasting impression on the young minds of my children.

Reflecting back, I wonder if in the heat of the moment, I could have done something differently. The manager probably carried his view on the basis of some experience, but will he ever change it? Was it passed down to him?

Some of these questions will never get answered, but what was obvious to me was that no one would get away by violating our dignity and self-respect. The €100 tip was to teach him that brown people could afford more than he thought. Further, I launched a complaint campaign against the hotel and took it up with the European hotel association that it was linked to. I flew down at my expense, spent my time, recorded witnesses to make them realise what had happened and finally an action was taken to terminate the manager and a notice was issued to the hotel management. However, the deep-seated scar it left on my children (albeit they laugh about it now) could never really be wiped away. I was surprised at their recall even after fifteen years of the episode. Seeds of how they can be treated differently due to the country they look to be from (in spite of residing in England) were sowed then. The soft whisper to be cautious when not with familiar looking people was known. I would not have liked to have it this way for them.

I remember this incident because of the humiliation we were subjected to by a stranger in another country without doing anything wrong. Further, this incident spoiled the fun-filled family holiday we had at Zurich. This incident taught me that being rigid and being fixated on a certain character sketch of individuals from a certain community can be so dysfunctional. These thoughts are not based on evidence, but born out of a lack of openness of their small hearts. The narrow-mindedness of the manager had led to a situation where we were reduced to thieves, because the manager was overconfident about his presumptions. His overconfidence led him to be unwilling to think of us as just normal happy tourists. He basked in his ignorance and baseless notions that created hurt and pain for all.

This incident taught me that uninformed reactions to someone's physical appearance can lead to toxic consequences. Some people live in their small cocoons of misinformation and ill-founded notions. They find it very comfortable to be there! Unfamiliarity can lead to such misleading connotations about individuals. An open mind and a kind heart are all that is required to live in peace and tranquillity.

The water flowing through a river assumes the direction imparted to it by nature. If the direction is changed through man-made interventions, the ecosystem of the river is disturbed. When we come into contact with strangers, we must allow our interactions to take their own course, their own life. We should not try to control it or steer it forcefully in a particular direction. We should give it the time it deserves and embolden ourselves to be open to new discoveries of interactions across human race.

SUMMARY

1. Don't compromise with your self-respect. Each individual should learn to respect herself or himself, before others can respect them.
2. Persist in a tough and closed environment. Be open to the various cultural mindsets that exist in society so that you can understand reactions and behaviours across different ethnicities and nationalities. Don't give up even if people do not open up to you.
3. Reciprocate the goodness bestowed upon you and think of coexistence as a way of life. Firstly, be open to the idea of altruism! The warmth and the kindness that we affectionately display to those who are our own can also be displayed for those who are not.
4. Empathise with individuals from different ethnicities. Get a sense of how they think and ideate. Make an attempt to understand their histories and their values and find a way to align their values with your own to reach a common ground. Don't make assumptions on the basis of established perceptions.
5. Hold back your snap judgements. Let the conversation take place, let yourself into the individual's thought process, let the words and the images seep into your mind so that you can arrive at a better conclusion.

Love

Sid: 'This year I have so many new students in my class! Everything is a bit unsettled!'

Mom (retorts with a question to his question): 'Why is it unsettling for you? You have been in this school for a few years now!'

Sid: 'Oh mom! You don't understand. As the vice-captain, I am now a part of the student council. I am responsible for the new students; I have to take them around and make sure they get to meet other students, help them understand how things work here, etc. Honestly, the new ones are so lost! Some of them are in this country for the first time. But, some common sense things like how to greet, meet and talk should be evident irrespective, right?'

Mom: 'Well, not really! Remember the time you went to Japan and called me, shrieking, that you were finding it difficult to get your way around! You loved the food and that's where your love for the place stopped. Their language and social manners were not known to you. You shared that people looked at you strangely, and that it felt lonely. Do you recall how that felt?'

Sid (ecstatic): 'Yes! Not good, but then I am more adaptable. I figured my way around with my friends.' (He gives a naughty wink.)

Avni (mockingly): 'I am not sure that those kids adapted to you! I think you were lucky to find a couple of friends in the exchange programme. They helped you with the place, mannerisms and even a bit of Japanese.'

Mom: 'So how did the magic happen, Sid? Think about yourself in Japan, and now think about these new children in your school!'

Sid: 'Oh! That must be scary. I need to help them get a hold of this place!'

Mom: 'Yes, that will be good. They will appreciate it. Learn to love their newness and help them see from a new life lens too. It will create that magic of respect and love. It is the friendship that arises out of a sincere accepting heart that helps all of us cherish life and coexist!'

Sid looks at me curiously.

Avni: 'So mom, would you be okay if I married someone who was very different from us?'

Sid (retorting to Avni): 'I am sure she would be okay, so long as he is dumb enough to marry you!'

Avni throws a pillow at Sid and he throws a book back at her. Before World War III breaks out, I step in!

Mom: 'Hey stop! Any friendship or bond is about the colour of love and if you find it, grab it. It is mutual understanding, respect for each other's thoughts and a will to coexist in spite of each other's differences. We learn from each other's perspective, thereby contributing something together, which is even more meaningful and magical. Being comfortable with who you are also helps others be comfortable with you.'

The moment when it stopped being just about me, and it became about others, their feelings, their joys and the exuberance, the world became a better place to live in.

Love, a universal feeling of respect and understanding, can exist between a mother and a daughter, between two friends and also between a husband and a wife. Needless to say, it knows no colour, it just takes shape over time through time spent together, various shades of emotional exchanges and through appreciation and veneration. When two people relate and identify with each other, when they share their happiness, anxieties and their sorrows, when there is mutual trust and regard for each other, that is when friendships that last forever are formed. The indissoluble force in any relationship, which blossoms into friendship, partnership or a bond is undeniably love and this beautiful emotion is cherished by one and all, irrespective of the colour of the skin, caste, creed or religion.

LOVING v. VIRGINIA: CHANGED THE FUTURE FOREVER!

Three armed policemen burst into the room of the newlyweds, Richard and Mildred Loving on 11 July 1958. Mr and Mrs Loving were arrested and put in jail for the crime of miscegenation.

In 1958, in the US, twenty-four states in the country had laws that strictly prohibited interracial marriage. Would anyone in this day and age have wondered that this kind of a law could be allowed to exist?

It was actually illegal to marry someone from a different race. Virginia, in those days, had severely strict laws to prevent interracial marriages. Five weeks prior to the wedding, the couple had learnt that Mildred was pregnant and both had decided to get married in defiance of the law. The couple had to travel to Washington DC for the ceremony because they wanted to evade Virginia's Racial Integrity Act. Upon their arrival in Virginia, they were found guilty of defying the act and arrested by the police. The judge told Mildred that as long as Mildred lived, she would be known as a felon. The Lovings were compelled to move to Washington for a safer life, but they were desperate to return to Virginia. They approached the American Civil Liberties Union to fight their case in court in 1963.

After a nail-biting and a nerve-racking battle, the Supreme Court of the United States declared all laws prohibiting interracial marriage unconstitutional. The Supreme Court of the United States took nine years to quash all the laws, which barred interracial marriages in a landmark ruling handed down on 12 June 1967. It is a widely celebrated case, which witnessed the law cede to the power of love and it also officially put an end to the bigotry and the astounding harassment faced by interracial couples. 'Love conquers all' was the redemptive trope born out of the judgement in the Loving versus Virginia case. Virginia's dual passage of the Sterilisation Act and the Racial Integrity Act in 1924 highlighted the twin concerns of interracial love and the popular public perception that the white race was in infinite danger of being weakened by inferior traits of the 'coloured' races.

The decision of the Loving versus Virginia case further strengthens and reaffirms the belief that love knows no racial boundaries. It is relevant, even today, for contemporary discussions on racial proximity. It helps us to refute the illogical political and economic justifications of the highest authorities around the world about who belongs to a region and who doesn't, who should remain on the sea and who should set foot on native land, who is weak and who is strong, and who deserves to live and who should perish. After more than fifty years, the Loving decision emboldens us to pursue a more inclusive, diverse and equitable society, and essentially that is what honest love is all about.

The Loving versus Virginia case is appreciated for fostering multiracial relationships and multicultural ecosystems that have made communities stronger and have brought happiness and joy to many families. The political rhetoric that guides government proposals aimed at banning immigrants from ravaged countries (which are ravaged in the first place due to political and power plays in developed countries), restricting permissions to asylum seekers and reserving social services and civil rights programmes only for the local communities leads us to one question:

'Who gave anybody the right to obstruct human mobility across the world and on what basis can anybody claim to have the power to make such decisions?' The planet certainly does not belong to a few human races alone. Boundaries have been drawn artificially that have divided some humans irreparably.

Today, it is unimaginable to think that once upon a time in this world, there were laws, which prevented the formation of biracial relationships. But, that changed, and hence, there is hope. Multiracial interactions need to be nurtured for strengthening and formation of such relationships. Where love follows, prosperity flourishes.

In this day and age, interracial marriages and relationships would have been impossible in the US had it not been for this landmark judgement. Certain events in history have changed the course of human interactions and associations and, therefore, the evolution of humankind itself. The subject of cross-border migration or rising interracial affinity or animosity would fail to be a subject of debate, if this law had existed today. Such legal events and steps are extremely important to liberate mankind and allow us to explore and discover ourselves anywhere and with anyone on this earth.

DIFFERENT AND YET ONE!

Jagruti was a new director in the banking team. She had recently moved to New York from Singapore and was figuring her way out in the new city. The culture and the professional environment of the new office were a bit alien and confusing for her. She was excited, yet nervous about being there and what success meant in New York. There were a few people she was beginning to feel comfortable with, whilst discovering and experimenting different styles of interacting with others. She was focused on collaboration with peers; respect for authority dominated her conduct. However, she pushed herself to reassess how this needed to be moulded to the uber competitive world of the East Coast.

On the professional front, clients and their expectations were quite different in New York than what she had experienced in Asia, where she was used to a more tolerant style of working. Good or bad news was not put forth in a direct manner. She pushed herself to adapt to the new place of work, as it was critical for her desired success. She had worked across other countries in the past and understood the importance of adapting to a new culture. Given her brilliant track record, she was given a few high profile accounts, which would soon be undergoing a merger. These were key accounts with high returns and she knew she had to put her best foot forward on behalf of the bank.

A client call was due the next day. The pitch books were ready with some incredible research. A group of bankers were pulled together by Jagruti for the client presentation. Next morning at 8:00 AM, the group led by Jagruti entered the conference room and began their presentation to senior managing directors. Ten minutes into the discussion, the mergers and acquisition head, William, raised an objection to the financial structuring for the client portfolio. He was direct and to the point with a killer instinct. No frills, no niceties, just straight talk. Time was money in these transactions. His objections further raised questions from the risk team on the proposal that Jagruti and her team had put forward. Within a few minutes, the pitch was unilaterally declined by the senior managing directors.

Jagruti was shattered. She was extremely disappointed and brought the meeting to a close. Then, she wearily walked back to her office to relook at the pitch. She was very upset with William and had found his conduct insensitive and appalling, especially in the way he had given his feedback so curtly. Even though the points William had raised were appropriate, but the way he had communicated it made her feel like it was a public shame. She was overwhelmed with the meeting and tried to think through other options, when she saw William walk into her office. Her instinctive feeling was to throw something at him and ask him to get out. A German in the US, how would he ever think beyond himself was her take away from him, in the brief interaction in the last hour!

William had sensed Jagruti's discomfort during the meeting. He did not know how else to express his opinions in the meeting apart from being direct. For him, it was just work and they were professionals. He was oblivious to how it landed and realised that something may not have gone right when he found Jagruti all by herself in her office late in the evening, looking lonely and dismal!

He tried to make polite conversation. Jagruti mumbled curtly. William asked if he could help. Jagruti's eyes welled up. Unable to handle the situation, William offered to take her out for coffee. Jagruti agreed and over coffee they talked about life in general and then veered towards the day's meeting. William shared his perspective on the proposal in detail. As the discussion progressed, Jagruti realised that had they gone ahead with the client as planned, it may have been a disaster for the bank, the client and her professional journey. In her emotional reaction to the way she was provided feedback in the meeting, she had overlooked the content of the feedback, which was quite appropriate and relevant. She understood that direct feedback was not an evaluation of her capabilities, it was information being imparted by William in his own way. Perhaps this was his best way!

Now she began to feel comforted in William's steer and after their coffee, they decided to carry on the discussion over dinner. As the days passed by, they started to enjoy each other's company. Drinks led to dinners and more interaction, culminating into a beautiful relationship and a bond of love. On Christmas that year, William proposed to Jagruti and she conceded unflinchingly.

William was a German native and fairly objective and pacey in his interactions, whilst Jagruti was an Asian with different nuances of subtlety and tolerance. In some ways, the two complimented each other. However, it was a little confusing to people around them, given that they seemed quite different in their ways. The seriousness of the relationship demanded the involvement of parents, and extended family, as they set out to get married. Jagruti told her parents about her decision with immense joy. She had expected the first reaction would be fairly anxious and muted, and it was. They struggled to reconcile that their daughter was marrying a German native in the US. In some of the Asian communities, marriage is not simply about two individuals coming together to spend their life, but about two families coming together for a deeper and sustainable lifetime association. Jagruti's parents had not lived outside their home country hence, they truly struggled to understand this. They were confused and uncomfortable about how they would adapt to their future son-in-law or how he would react to them, their religion, their way of being, especially their strictly vegetarian orientation!

They had never been associated with a white person, hence their perception about them was based on what they had seen in the media or read in books. They carried a perception of white people being arrogant, intolerant and that they lacked any appreciation for

Asian values and culture. This led to an unspoken uneasiness and tension between Jagruti and her parents when she disclosed her relationship.

William's parents were Germans and had extremely limited interactions with Asians. They seemed ignorant and nervous about what was in store. They were unsure about how Jagruti and William would really adjust with each other given the diversity and 'perceived gap' in their upbringing. There was a sense of nervousness in them too as they perceived Asians significantly different in behaviour. They had been to Asia as tourists and found it not so clean and organised, except for a few countries. The lack of knowledge and awareness regarding a culture created a feeling of insecurity and fear in them.

Jagruti and William, however, bonded at a deeper level where their colour or cultural differences had become invisible to them. They had simply accepted each other just as they were. The love between the two had overtaken any such differences and had cemented them together with compassion and care. The couple, having spent enough time with each other, knew that they shared similar values, beliefs and love for life that was far more significant than the colour of their skin. Although love has a generic definition, it is a rather subjective concept. It has a different meaning for each and every individual.

Jagruti started to learn about German upbringing whilst William learnt about Indian history. He did not warm up to Indian curries easily because they were rather spicy for him, but Jagruti loved the bratwurst. However, her Asian parents found it tough to accept such a big cultural upheaval in their life. They continued to feel that William was far too alien for their culture, and far beyond their mental wavelength. Hence, they could not warm up to the association. On the other hand, William's extended family was not as well conversant with Asians and kept a distance from Jagruti. Initially the language kept the communication patchy as most of the family spoke only German. In their minds, India was still a land of snake charmers, elephants, the Taj Mahal and little else. They presumed that Jagruti would be a cultural misfit and were not willing to give her the opportunity to get close to them. As a result, she often felt somewhat excluded from the social events in the family.

The two individuals directly involved in the relationship tried their best to make things work by getting their parents together from time to time, so that they get to know each other better, but the families somehow could not relate to one another. Jagruti and William struggled!

Sometimes we need to wait for that miraculous right moment and the right time.

In spite of all these odds, William and Jagruti decided to marry and stay in the US, slightly away from all the family tensions and controversies. They were trying their best to ensure that the love between them acts as an anchor that binds them together in a strong, compassionate relationship. As years passed by, they graduated to becoming the parents of a beautiful daughter. She was the precious love of their life. Little Samaira was a bundle of joy, a symbol of pure love and her arrival transformed the equation between the German and the Indian families. Both families were connected by this little German-Indian prodigy.

A child is a magical gift
A beautiful coming together of two lives and one thought
A beautiful combination of two hearts and one love
Blended hues of feeling enmeshed in a new emotion
A child is a symbol of unison of two different worlds
Of two different cultures
Of different thought and ideas
Can make relationships your world
Can turn foes into friends
Can give new identities to relationships
Embed unrealised love in the hearts forever!

Samaira evoked a miraculous and an unexpected change in her grandparents. Suddenly they started reaching out to Jagruti and William together. They felt a sense of connection with the new addition to the family, who in some ways was their own blood, even though the spouse of their own child was seen in a different light. It is intriguing to note that both the grandparents felt a high ownership over the child even though they never fully accepted the partner of their children. Beautiful magic unfolded when the small child brought the two families together. It was love that the grandparents had for the child that enabled them to dissolve all their differences and move forward. The child was biracial and an amalgamation of German and Indian genes and this statement itself explains the power of love!

As I heard Jagruti narrate this story, I could see her deeply in love with William and it really did not matter where they came from and how they looked. It was a bond of minds and thoughts that kept their relationship together and made it stronger in the face of how the world saw it. Together, they overcame the resistance and the difficulties in fitting in each other's social norms. Jagruti's association with her husband was based on mutual respect and they cherished their life together. Their respect for each other blossomed into romance because they were deeply impacted by each other's being. The sobriety of the relationship was evident when neither Jagruti nor William forced either of the families to accept each other's cultures. Their child helped them bond with their families further.

The trust and respect for people can transcend into love for humanity. It is the driver of understanding, which brings about friendships, relationships and alliances.

Love is an antidote to mindsets
When people connect, there is respect
Where we comfort, we understand, in almost every case
It is at this inflexion point
The curvature of the mind changes
We become colour-blind
We embrace humanity in a real way
The connection is there
The wavelength flows from one heart to another

Thoughts start to resonate
Remember, this is when love of humanity has taken over!

Love is a pure and universal emotion in our lives. It is about mutual understanding, connect and giving each other the freedom to be themselves in any relationship, not just a romantic one. Love is our soul manifesting itself to express its life's longing. Our soul is a part of the larger universe and is constantly looking to merge with other souls. When we love someone, then our perspective and feelings predispose us to behave in an accepting way that strengthens the bond. The question is how do we positively channel this emotion of love when we deal with people who are not like us? For some people the learned response to people different than us is to keep away from them, whilst for others it may be curiosity that may lead to deeper interaction and that discovery may lead to the ignition of love, respect and compassion for the person.

The definition of Love is unknown to me
The colour of Love we seek, only to find is colourless
The nature of Love we wish to fathom is boundless
Love travels here, there and everywhere
Love is respect, Love is understanding, Love is connect
It is this opportunity I take
To make this earnest appeal
Spread Love to all. It is free!

THE RISE AND RISE OF INTERRACIAL MARRIAGES

Interracial and interethnic partnerships and marriages in the US rose from 5% in 1970 to 18% in 2015. According to the data collected by IPUMS International at the Minnesota Population Centre and the analysis by *The Economist*, 400,000 interracial marriages took place in 2015. Even though white people account for 65% of US's adult population, around 82% of 400,000 marriages involved a white spouse. The increase in the rate of interracial marriages can be attributed to the presence of immigrants in that country. Marriages between members of different racial minorities, for example between Asians and blacks are not as common as they make up only 1.4% of the total number of interracial marriages. This is partly because they do not coexist in any country as extensively. It is interesting to note that four-fifths of the women, who are recent immigrants in the US from five South East Asian countries, constitute one in ten of all interracial marriages to white men.

The following figure gives a comprehensive view of the rise of interracial marriages in the US.

Figure 3.1 Fifty years of loving

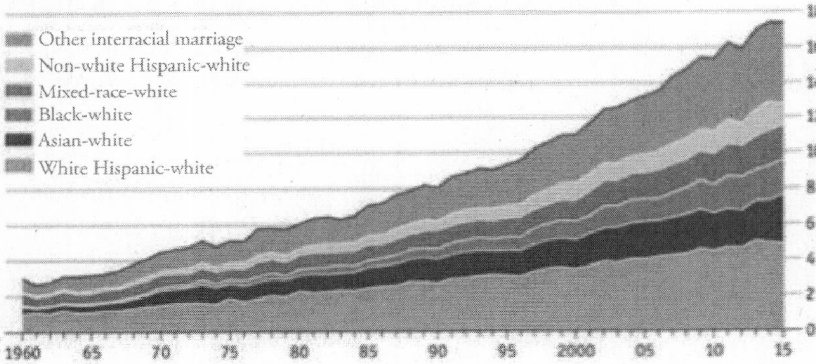

Source: Census. IPUMS US. The Economist. June 2017

The Economist reports, 'Blacks and whites tie the knot with each other far more than they once did: they made up to 14% of all marriages in 2015, seven times higher than their share in 1979.'

In 2010, white-black couples constituted 8% of interracial associations, while white-Asian couples made up 14% of such associations.

A survey by the Pew Research Center found that 63% of Hispanic respondents said that they would be fine if a family member chose to get married to someone outside their racial or ethnic group, 72% of the blacks and 61% of the whites gave the same response. The survey found that the acceptance of out-marriages to blacks was the lowest at 66% and to whites was the highest at 81%. The acceptance of out-marriages to Asians at 75% was marginally higher when compared to Hispanics at 73%. People with higher educational qualifications were more likely to marry outside their racial or ethnic group. Therefore, areas with people with higher educational attainments were more likely to have a higher number of interracial couples. Some countries like the UK, and in some cases India, were stratified by class and region too.

Compassion and empathy for each other's thoughts and feelings can create that magical sense of love that can open doors of any closed mind to let waves of friendships enter.

When Italy meets 'Bangla'!

The tall, fair lady got out of her car and glanced at the typical Old Kolkata house in the northern part of the city. The neighbourhood clearly noticed this lovely 'white' lady who was in boots, a leather jacket, shades and leather pants. She was astounded by the crowd, which stared at her. It was one of those early Sunday mornings when a lady from Italy had set foot in the neighbourhood only to discover that she was the news of the town. It was still the Kolkata with its Raj mindset, and anybody who was white was considered to be close to a movie star! This was in the 90s.

Renate, a young Italian designer, had fallen in love with an engineer from West Bengal whilst they were both working in Germany. Satrajit, the Bengali engineer who worked in Volkswagen was struggling to learn the role of working in a foreign land, in those days. He found it difficult to converse with the workers in the plant till he met Renate at a boutique in Munich, who taught him local ways. Satrajit was quite impressed with her ability to explain design to a man who had hardly any interest in it. Also, she had offered to speak in English with him and explain everything about local culture, with oodles of patience.

Renate and Satrajit started to meet each other after the short boutique rendezvous. Satrajit wanted to learn German from the lady. Under the pretext of German language classes, Satrajit continued to meet Renate for over a year leading to a deeper connect with each other. This propelled them to take the relationship forward and tie the knot. Renate was an independent woman and had lost her father very early in her life. She had taken up a course in apparel design after she finished school and had started working while she was in college. It was quite a struggle for her to manage classes and her work, but she had to do those extra hours so that she could pay her college fees and assist her mother in running the house.

Renate had a mind of her own and Satrajit was yet to figure out how she would adapt to an unapologetically Bengali household. But, he chose to disclose his decision before tying the knot to his mother. The reply from the other end was not very positive and his mother expressed her concern about a white daughter-in-law from a foreign country. But Satrajit was determined and chose to tie the knot in a church with Renate against his parents' wishes. Renate was six feet three inches tall and her husband was a few inches shorter than her. That day when she arrived in Kolkata at her *shoshurbari* (in-laws house), there was nothing in her attire that made her look like a bride, as per Indian standards. Almost all the relatives of the Mukherjee family had dropped in to see the first white daughter-in-law of the house. It was an event in the history of Indo-European marriages and that too in Old Kolkata where such possibilities could not even be imagined. Renate was already uncomfortable with the undue attention she was getting. So she chose to enter the house to escape all the unwarranted looks that she seemed to garner on the streets.

As she entered through the door, the mother-in-law stared at her from top to bottom—no sari, no *shakha-pola* (bangles married Bengali women wear) no *sindoor* and no *alta* (a red liquid that married Bengali women wear on their feet)! Satrajit was trying hard to make the encounter easy for both women, while the rest of the family was too stunned and awed by Renate and the overwhelming impact she had on the inmates of the house. They could not clearly foresee the future domestic life of a couple wherein the husband was visibly shorter than the wife. Renate was not groomed to touch anybody's feet (a sign of respect in Indian households). She did not understand such customs or practices. But she greeted everyone lovingly and bestowed gifts on everyone that she had chosen carefully and brought from Italy. The father-in-law was quite surprised at her behaviour, but he chose to keep quiet because his silent annoyance was with his son, who had defied him.

Renate did not know how to cook. She only knew how to make simple European dishes. Therefore, the white *bahu* could not make the first meal of the house as per Indian rituals. All the children of the house surrounded her and asked her a dozen questions. Renate patiently answered them, but surely she could not fathom the curiosity and the 'in awe' countenance on each person's face. The relatives were all taking their turns to speak to the lady, and she did nothing to behave as the demure *bahu* of the house. The maid in the house was quite fascinated by her skin colour too and one of them dared to ask her if they could touch her finger. She had never seen a white person before. Renate was visibly surprised with the demand, but she allowed her to do it. The maid was so enamoured by the reality of Renate's complexion and aura that she covered her mouth with her hands. It was as if she had touched God. The maid had made the other daughters-in-law conscious of their not-so-good 'brown' skin colour and their visual appeal. They certainly did not stand a chance against the *mem* (shortened from the colonial address for white women as the *memsahib*) daughter-in-law. A lot of invisible insecurities crept in, but there were no external manifestations yet. The other daughters-in-law of the house could see what was coming their way. It seemed that they had vanished into oblivion for all the good reasons.

Over the next fifteen days, Renate tried her best to adjust to the household, but her assertive and independent demeanour did not really go down very well with the mother-in-law. She made all possible efforts to talk to the other members of the house and even went to the extent of making some 'bland' Italian food. After she gave birth to a son, the grandmother in the mother-in-law softened to her a little, but not much. She was happy that the child was *phorsha* (fair), unlike the dad who was *kaalo* (dark), but she still felt that Renate lacked the wife-like qualities (according to Indian standards). The silent banter (there was a language problem because the mother-in-law did not know English or Italian) formed the exquisite feature of the relationship that was shared by Renate and her mother-in-law and she h=ad learnt to live with it. The rest of the family had warmed up to her, to the extent that they took fashion advice and health tips from her whenever she came over.

After eighteen months, Renate and Satrajit moved overseas as his work took them away. Renate was sad and relieved at the same time. It had been tough to adapt to India, yet just when she was becoming a part of the fabric, they had to move out. Her husband's undying support made her persevere and understand the people better, thereby keeping the family ties intact. In some way, it had helped Renate tide over her engagement with the family. Her love for her husband drove her to enmesh in a new and perhaps discomforting experience for her. Satrajit was by her side and he was with his family too, doing his best to get all of them together.

Love acts as a powerful force and converts impossibilities into possibilities. Satrajit was one of the few Indian men in those days, who had the gumption to go against his parents' wishes and marry a white girl. But that is what love can do. It merges boundaries and removes any lines of division. It was love, which brought Renate from the Mediterranean shores to the Indian subcontinent. She was quite firm about what she thought and spoke and had none of the features of a submissive Indian *bahu*. Satrajit, having been born and brought up in a country where the culture was for women to follow and not lead, was quite fascinated by Renate's way of being. It is quite interesting to note Satrajit's choice of woman given the fact that he was brought up in a country where aggressiveness or assertiveness might not be a desired trait in a woman. Renate did not even bother to think that Satrajit was brown and she was just enamoured by his intellect. Their love for each other was born out of the respect that they had for each other, for the difficult lives they had led in childhood as both the people in question here, were self-made individuals.

Skin colour indicates the origin of a person, but not their predisposition in life. Love is an emotion, which allows people to know each other at a deeper level and learn from each other's experiences. Learning to let someone you care for be who they truly are helps foster a strong bond. It reduces the psychological distance between people and sometimes families, helping to live whilst enjoying the contradictions.

ROYALS AND RACE

Germany Kent, the famous American journalist, once made an accurate observation:

'Prince Harry marrying Meghan Markle says more about him than any historian could ever write.'

Meghan Markle's 'inclusive' wedding with Prince Harry generated a warm enthusiasm on the streets of Brixton, which is one of the most multicultural locations in South London. Prince Harry and Meghan Markle's courtship has been referred to as 'a modern royal romance' and some non-English British citizens feel that it represents modern Britain.

Romance is in the air,
Harry, the royal man, has fallen for the dusky lady
By the name of Meghan Markle
The white man has shown the world that dark is beautiful
His choice has revealed that modern day royalty,
Knows no race,
Knows no colour,
Together as they walked the aisle after exchanging wedding vows
They created history
Although, I am sure, they did not realise!
There was a lot of colour in the royal nuptial
As black American culture made its first appearance inside the church
An African American had just been married to an English Royal
The African-American-English marriage
Has brought together races and countries

To celebrate their inter-continental union
As love pierces through the royal white traditions
This coloured royal marriage
Has propelled the advent of a new dawn
A new beginning
When the royalty in England
Has welcomed a coloured woman
With open arms and accepted her, as one of their 'own'
And of course the rest, as they say, is history!

Some citizens of England come from mixed-race families and Meghan Markle's entry, they feel, has changed the face of the royal family. As mentioned by an Ethiopian, whose mother is English and father Ethiopian, 'The family is not purely white anymore.' Meghan has given hope to coloured men and women who have always been marginalised in society, and they believe that she has brought diversity to the royal family.

A lady who has been staying in London for over thirty years exclaims that everyone in Britain is witnessing a generational shift in terms of cultural outlook and thought process. The royal couple visiting Brixton, which is home to Britain's largest African-Caribbean community, evidently signifies the fact that the new generation of royals is coming closer to the people of all colours. The blacks in London feel that Meghan's harmonious marriage with Harry shows how integrated the royal family is as opposed to popular perception. The royals have embraced a different culture and colour and they have progressed with time. They think in the present and are not afraid to face the future. The blacks in London foresee that the world tomorrow will be more integrated and inclusive. Just imagine such a transformative change in the way people think, all because of one biracial wedding!

The Americans in England look upon this union as a sort of change because they identify with Meghan's biracial and American identity. The royals are perceived by some to be rigid in their ways. In fact, they are one of the main symbols of colonial times, bloodlines, empire and 'pure whiteness', but the 'happy' addition of

Markle into the royal family is a sign of progressive change. Britain's royal wedding was indeed intensely infused with black American symbolism.

Speaking of the ceremony, the presiding bishop of the American Episcopal Church, Reverend Michael Bruce Curry, made a mark with his powerful sermon that beautifully and cleverly wove black American culture throughout. Curry also made intermittent references to poverty, slavery and colonialism, standing in the heart of the British Empire. The bishop started his address as well as ended it by preaching for the power of love and by quoting Martin Luther King: 'We must discover the power of love, the power, the redemptive power of love. And when we discover that, we will be able to make this old world, a new world.' The Kingdom Choir was a predominantly black gospel group with around twenty members. It was almost akin to witnessing a drastic change in the royal taste when the sermon by Curry was followed by Karen Gibson and The Kingdom Choir's rendition of 'Stand by Me'. This song is a powerful rallying call for racial unity and justice and was performed originally by an American singer.

Another interesting factor in the ceremony was the presence of Sheku Kanneh-Mason. This young nineteen-year-old boy was the first black artist to win BBC's Young Musician of the Year award and he had also earlier made appeals for classical music to be more inclusive of black people. The most significant deviation from the traditional royal past is the bride Meghan Markle, who is essentially a divorcee, an American and a Catholic woman of colour, and all these categorical features technically fall out of the British royal family tree. Markle's mother is African American and her father is a white man. Meghan's position on racial relations and inequality are fairly open and public and sometimes it also pushes her royal husband to take a stand. The cross-racial romance has been accompanied by global curiosity and admiration for both the bride and the groom. The biracial American actress's ascendance from a celebrity in the world of entertainment to a place of universal impact as the Duchess of Sussex has been meteoric and metamorphic.

Black women feel that the wedding of Meghan and Harry will lead to greater acceptance of African-American women in business. The Markle Effect, as it is called, will have a positive impact on improved opportunities for African-American women at the workplace. The acceptance by the royal family to include a divorcee and a biracial woman into the family the world hopes and trusts, will herald the initiation of developing an unbiased attitude towards blacks and Hispanic women at the workplace. It is interesting to note that this biracial wedding in the family in England can do so much in the way people perceive the future of cross-racial relationships and reposition perceptions of coloured women. Such a wedding sends a strong message of tolerance and broad-mindedness. Love, indeed, knows no boundaries or racial barriers and the modern royal wedding is the living proof of that very statement. But we must look into an important event in history, which made many others see the light of the day!

Meghan Markle and Prince Harry's courage to go ahead with this relationship deserves thumbs up. It has given hope to a large number of people caught up in the racial battle. Such events are symbolic and provide an opportunity for us to accept the differences between us. Meghan and Harry's marriage is not only a marriage of two individuals, but a marriage of two different cultures and nationalities, along with their ethos. This is indeed a great illustration of how love indeed has naturally and subtly propelled the royal family to be a leading example of open mindsets that drive inclusion. The love between Harry and Meghan has quite beautifully laid the path for a coloured woman's entry into the house, which perhaps was forced to delete all the lines between the different colours of skin. This breakaway from convention has sent an important message. This marriage is the new oxygen, which will allow cross-border relationships to breathe. Time will tell how this bond survives the test of time as this is just the beginning, but it is a good beginning.

The Possibility of Impossible Friendships

Jesse Owens and Luz Long's lifelong friendship proves that brotherly love can surmount any divisions and overcome racial barriers.

James Cleveland 'Jesse' Owens is the most remembered athlete in Olympic history because of his stunning achievement of four gold medals at the 1936 Olympic Games in Berlin. Jesse Owens was the son of a sharecropper and the grandson of a slave and he had accomplished a feat which no Olympian before him had achieved. Jesse's achievements were his unique sequence of collecting his fourth gold medal at the 1936 Berlin Olympics, as a member of the US 4X100 relay team. In his twelfth event as an athlete, he proved Hitler wrong, and that too within a span of seven days.

The racist ideology of the Nazi regime, championed by Hitler, was gathering momentum. Growing negative intensity of the Nazis had started to portray 'negroes' as 'black auxiliaries'. The 22-year-old young, black man was competing in the most intimidating environment in Berlin where Hitler was a regular at the stands. Hitler's team had spread the myth that a black man could never be successful, as they had already proclaimed only one ethnic group to be superior. Owens's courage and determination helped him to reach the peak of his performance in an extremely degraded moral environment in Germany at that time.

Germany's war armaments minister, Albert Speer, recalled in his memoirs, *Inside the Third Reich*, that Hitler was annoyed by Owens's series of victories. In fact, he went on to say that people whose antecedents came from the jungle were primitive and hence their physique was stronger than those of the whites. According to Hitler, the 'superior' race was civilised, and hence such 'primitives' should be excluded from the games in the future.

Despite some formidable opposition, Owens won the 100m and 200m track events with effortless ease. Then he set a sprint relay world record, which could not be broken for twenty years and this also gave him his 'final track gold'. The racist Nazis in Germany did their best to poison the proceedings of the Olympics, but sport bodies fought hard to maintain neutrality even then.

On 4 August 1936, Owens won the most cherished Olympic prize of his life—he won the comradeship of Luz Long. The German long jumper was fair-skinned, blonde, tall and blue-eyed, the ideal Aryan symbol of the Nazi ideology. At first glance, Owens was wary of Long's prodigious leaps.

During the track event, Owens failed to see the judges raising their flags to indicate to the participants that the competition had started and by mistake took a practice run down the approach only to be told by the officials that it would be counted as one of his three efforts. To add to his dismay, he fouled on his second attempt and this added to the embarrassment of a man who had won his morning 200m qualifying round in the Olympics in a record time of 21.1 seconds.

David Wallechinsky, in his outstanding work, *The Complete Book of the Olympics*, reports a conversation that Owens had with Long, after the white young man sauntered up to him.

'Glad to meet you,' said Owens, in a tentative manner and asked Long, 'How are you?'

'I am fine,' replied Long, 'The question is how are you?'

'What do you mean?' asked Owens.

'Something must be eating you,' said Long, proud, the way foreigners are when they have mastered the American slang.

Long further added, 'You should be able to qualify with your eyes closed.'

For the next few minutes, Long and Owens spoke about various things. Long's tall, lean and muscular frame and a strikingly handsome, chiselled face threw Owens a little off-kilter. Then Long suggested that since the qualifying distance was only 7.15m, Owens should ideally shift his mark back to ensure that he takes off well short of the board and does not foul again. Long added that he would qualify easily in this scenario and it did not matter if he did not come first in the trials. Owens accepted his advice and retracted the initial marker for his run-up by a foot and a half and he qualified easily with a centimetre to spare.

When the finals took place that afternoon, in the first few rounds, Long matched Owens' performance. Owens, in his final attempt, landed at 8.06m and Long in his concluding attempt, could not improve upon his best performance. Among the jubilation, Hitler rose from his seat and left the stadium because he could not see his 'white supremacy' theory falling to pieces. Long was the first person to congratulate Owens in his moment of triumph.

Owens later wrote, 'The business with Hitler did not bother me.'

He said that he did not go to the Olympics to shake hands with Hitler. The most memorable segment of the Berlin Olympics for Owens was the friendship he struck with Luz Long. The German was a formidable rival and the strongest one in the Olympics, but it was this very man who had helped Owens win the finals by giving him critical advice.

Owens's victory in the long jump event was largely due to Long's intervening and encouraging suggestion, which proved to be fruitful for Owens. The two men of significantly different colour corresponded regularly through letters till Hitler invaded Poland. Luz Long was killed in a British military hospital after receiving fatal wounds in the Battle of St. Pietro in 1943. After which Owens continued corresponding with his son to preserve his friendship with Long. The camaraderie shared by Owens and Long is indeed a symbol of hope of sports being a powerful force in bringing people of all colours together and celebrating humanity.

'You can melt down all the medals and the cups I have,' Owens wrote later, 'And there couldn't be a plating on the 24-carat friendship I felt for Luz Long at that moment.'

Such a beautiful relationship forming on the Olympic track and field between a black and a white only goes to show that love knows no colour—neither black nor white! It shows that the spirit of sportsmanship and mutual love and respect can go a long way in forming long-lasting relationships. Both these individuals revered each other for the talent and the sporting skill that each of them possessed in their own right. They made an attempt to learn from someone who was better than themselves and the relationship between these two Olympic participants had originated out of their common love for sport. These two individuals in question were sporting personalities with distinct identities in their own right yet they did submit themselves to the power of friendship and cherished the moments they had spent together. They had no unreasonable expectations from each other and were just looking to share and give more than take from others. Their profession as a sportsman had brought them together, but their mutual admiration for each other had helped them stay together. Their bond is symbolic of the simple fact that human emotions like love and respect have the power to transform human history.

> *'No one is born hating another person because of the colour of his skin, or his background or his religion. People learn to hate, and if they can learn to hate, they can be taught to love, for love comes more naturally to the human heart than its opposite.'*
>
> **—Nelson Mandela**

Love is a unique feeling that can transcend the melancholy of beliefs and smoke screens of mistrusts. It is the effervescence that has the ability to rise to the top and provide the necessary zing to life itself. It can open closed minds, it can bring families, societies and countries together. All we need to do is start with a positive intent, without malice, prejudice or expectations and this is when the transformational power of love engulfs you! This serenading power is a force of unity that can dissolve other opposing divisive forces such that it provides us with the opportunity to create a bond between individuals. Love is a pure feeling of bliss, which helps people to reach a place of authentic communication with each other thereby breaking walls of colour.

Courage, Compassion and Camaraderie

I have always treasured my autonomy and have usually worked better with managers who have provided me space and empowerment, whilst stepping in timely to coach and guide me as appropriate. Very close supervision and micro-management bring out the rebel in me and I may not be as productive. Self-awareness had helped me mould my style as I worked with different people and teams.

While I was working in London, we were three seniors in the banking HR team, facing off the front-end business. Two white ladies—one American, the other English—and myself, visibly brown and Asian. We came from different backgrounds and our upbringings instilled in us the varied paradigms of how we related to life and authority.

Jenny was English, very polite, possessed a high need to preserve her individuality and loved her space too with two decades of experience behind her.

Susan was American and a little more direct, with a higher bias for action than Jenny.

I was a cross between Asian, American and European values. I was straightforward (a bit too much I think) and preferred my manager to coach me without interfering, if that was possible. To clarify, I did not suffer from an identity crisis and loved every bit of being a global citizen, but it was always confusing for others who would assume certain behaviours and demeanours associated with the colour of my skin!

We had our circle of friends and 'people to hang around' with, hence, apart from social pleasantries, the three of us probably did not feel the need to spend more time than what our work required of us.

During one of those years during the financial crisis, our teams were restructured and reorganised. There was plenty of stress across the organisation and as we worked through the upheaval, we lost our senior leader in the function who kept us together as a team. With his exit, we were lost and sensed chaos in our office life.

There was an existential anxiety in the team, about which leader to approach and where to go for resolutions; who would represent us and where did we belong. In a few months, a new leader, Thomas, assumed the vacant position. He seemed diametrically opposite to our earlier manager in terms of connect with the team and the management of business stakeholders. This started to gradually create a distance between us and the business leadership whilst also impacting our client delivery. We often found ourselves at the receiving end of issues and yet could not individually gather our voices to the leadership table. Thomas was representing us. It was evident to all of us in the team of thirty-two people that he was disengaged from our well-being as well as with that of the business. He was self-centred and wanted to be seen as creditworthy for our delivery. He had clear views on colour and as a brown individual, I certainly was not deserving of his time. Honestly, I did not feel I was missing anything. I just tried to ensure that work was done appropriately. Gradually, the team started losing clarity and motivation.

One evening, I shut down my computer at 6:00 PM and was wearily dragging myself to go home. As I stepped out of the office, I saw Susan coming out of the next office wearing the same expression and Jenny walking across the floor looking more dejected than both of us. There was an unsaid code that started emanating among us, creating a sense of much needed belonging. It was unspoken, but commonly felt by all three of us. Without much thinking, I found myself saying, 'Hey, perhaps the three of us should get a drink today, what say?'

It seemed I had uncannily expressed the desire of the other two! With instant and unanimous agreement, the three of us headed to a nearby pub, ordered a bottle of wine, then another bottle of wine, then another and before we knew it, we were at our fourth bottle.

Jenny shared that she had been in a foul mood after having managed a business crisis since morning with no support from Thomas. Susan had run with a regulatory issue, and despite flagging it to Thomas a few times, not much escalation had taken place and the path forward was unclear with the accountability of timely closure still resting with Susan. I was all over the place; Thomas wanted to attend a few of my stakeholder meetings, which were denied by the business heads and Thomas held me accountable for his lack of entry to these meetings. As a result, I was not permitted in the senior HR forums with him to present projects that I had been working on.

By talking and debating, we found solutions for all the problems that each one of us was facing. Alcohol helps, but honestly nothing is more therapeutic than letting off steam with work colleagues. It always has a calming impact as it did that evening on the three of us. We complained, cried and laughed about the situation, trying to evaporate the negative emotion out of us. In spite of our differences, there was something common that connected us. It was an inexplicable bond; clearly what a lot of diversity training had been unable to achieve, Thomas had magically done with one master stroke of mismanagement. The common cause was a bad manager and resultant struggles to sort at the workplace. A heady combination of good wine and candid conversation went beyond differences of how we looked, spoke or behaved. We felt so safe and so connected that our collective care for each other made us feel better and stronger.

A glass of stem-winding wine
Helped us to unwind
When the magic potion
Emboldened us to laugh, cry, complain and whine
The minutes passed by fast
The honest conversation got longer and better
There were three different colours at one table
Love, care, affection had smoothened all the differences
Such that a passerby wondered,
'How colours had meshed together?'
I tell you it was that night, that beautiful night,
When new friendships were born!

Next day we all walked into office feeling much better. A lovely smile of new-found friendship donned our faces. There was lightness and ease as we approached each other and sought support from our new-found bond. We now had a sense of security with each other. Our relationship was born out of a kind and authentic camaraderie and genuine friendly love. Sometimes tough times make the bond stronger. If a friendship can weather the storm, then it is there to stay forever. Each and every relationship grows with time and with it you grow too. We had not realised till then what we were in for!

A few days passed by and one afternoon, whilst Susan and I were munching our sandwich lunch in my office, we saw a really harried Jenny walk by. As we dusted off the breadcrumbs from the table, she barged into our office feverishly. She told us with a tense expression on her face, how a bonus-planning budget from last year with incorrect entries had been provided to the finance department. She was concerned that this could have some serious implications on whether bonus may be paid or not.

In investment banking, if you get bonuses wrong, it could be your doomsday. It required her to escalate the matter to her senior, Thomas (which she admitted was done); however, he needed to urgently appraise the global teams in HQ to have this sorted as soon as possible to avert any disasters. But instead of helping Jenny work through this, he had not only pulled her up harshly, but made her a scapegoat for an issue that was not her fault. He had then asked her to get it sorted with the global teams first before he intervened. Jenny did not enjoy a good network with the global senior team to approach the right people. We calmed her down and I asked her to be patient till I called a few people who I knew from my experience of working in the HQ.

Jenny went to her room. Susan and I discussed the situation, made a few calls to our contacts and went over to Jenny's office. What we saw melted our hearts. Jenny was sitting under the table, sobbing. She had a breakdown. We tried to calm her down, but she was inconsolable. As I hugged her, I could feel her stress seep out of her body. The power of human touch! Sometimes a warm hug can take away all the pain, the pressure and the stress. It did not matter if it was a brown arm around a white person or a white arm around a black person. What mattered was the genuine feeling behind the gesture, the fact that there was a shoulder that Jenny could cry on.

That moment is unforgettable for me. Apart from Jenny, I went through a volley of emotions. There was no white or black between us, there was sheer compassion and empathy for not only a colleague, but a good friend. Susan and I were both sensitive to what Jenny was going through. Even though there was silence and very little was said between us in that moment, a lot was felt and understood. It was a human to human connection that needed compassion, not words.

That afternoon, Jenny poured her heart out…

Susan realised that Jenny needed emotional support and took over the conversation, while I called up her business stakeholder to sort the situation at work. They fortunately valued Jenny's contribution enough to deploy extra time and resources behind the issue so that we could push for timely resolution with the seniors in HQ. As we worked through Jenny's situation, Thomas walked in to check what was going on between the three of us.

I really wanted to publicly give him a piece of my mind, but my upbringing forced me to take him to a nearby office and do that privately. Susan and I were so affected by the entire incident that Jenny's issues had become ours. Thomas refused to acknowledge us even after this. He blamed us for the mess.

The issue had not only become bigger for us, but also for the entire team due to Jenny's breakdown. We finally garnered the courage to speak collectively to the senior HR head and expressed our desire to be better led. Finally, the structure was changed and we had a new manager.

Sometimes a crisis dissipates the division of colour, especially when there is a collective and common purpose. Jenny, Susan and I had found our friendship whilst dealing with a bad manager. Our colour and differences had melted to make us one. Thomas was too self-centred and lacked empathy. He lost the opportunity to act as a compassionate leader. He was beguiled by his preconceived notions and incorrect judgements about his team, which ultimately led to his exit from the organisation. Compassion and sensitivity go a long way in motivating a team to work harder and better.

The inexplicable camaraderie that I shared with Susan and Jenny was born out of a sense of mutual trust and understanding. Our skin colours did not come in the way of our sentiments and the regard that we had for each other. Some friendships are accidental, but they are for lifetime. Such a relationship creates a safe environment to share, to give and to assist in whatever way possible. Two important ingredients in the friendships of virtue are time and trust. Tough times bring people together and it is the moment of vulnerability, the weak moments, which sometimes bind people together in sustainable relationships. Jenny's moment of weakness and lack of support from the manager brought us together. Friendships require due time and attention. They grow and blossom with respect, love and trust. Such genuine relationships bring with them the sweetest joys that life has to offer.

Racism is a complex and a persistent social issue, which has not been addressed adequately by a number of countries in the world. Psychological security refers to a number of things like stability, dependency, predictability, the need for law and order and most importantly emotional safety. We feel strong when we know someone has our back and we have their support not because of our looks or colour but because they truly appreciate who we are.

Love transcends these boundaries, but it requires a sense of empathy and compassion. It can help you overcome fears and provide you a sense of security when you know there is someone you can rely on and trust. These are provided by friendships that last forever and love keeps them glued together. Jenny, Susan and I are still good friends.

LOVE AN ANTIDOTE TO COLOUR DILEMMA?

Love helps us to dissolve our differences and mesh with others, and appreciate their unique propositions. When there is no love in a relationship, there may be a lack of real understanding. The absence of self-disclosure leads to the inability to connect. Love generates the willingness in a human being to give more and beget more in return from the other. It provides the necessary fuel to embrace humanity and abandon coloured minds. Building relationships is a lifelong process of discovery that may be bitter or sweet but progresses us in bonds that provide support when faced with a diverse coloured environment. Love for self is equally important. At a young age, children tend to pick up the perils of colour from their social environment, leading to love or shame for self.

At a playground experiment in a Denver summer camp, conducted in a playschool, it was observed over a period of one month that the white children aged between two and three years, generally preferred to play with light-skinned lookalikes, whereas the small minority of black children were found to play among themselves.

Mahzarin Banaji, a renowned Harvard University psychologist and physical prejudice expert, conducted an experiment to showcase the fact that children exposed to racism tend to accept it and embrace it even at a very young age within a short period of time. He said that the experiment proved that three to four-year-olds display the same type of bias as adults. In a study, about 263 white children between the ages of three and fourteen were shown a number of graphically drawn facial images. These images were drawn in different skin tones varying from light tan to brown and the children were instructed to describe them as happy or angry. In some parts of the test, children were shown an 'inconclusive' light tan colour that could represent a white coloured person or a black person. In brown, black and this segment, most of the children, without any prompting, described the faces as black and angry, irrespective of the facial expression. Whenever the children identified some faces as white, irrespective of the expression on the face, they would describe them as happy.

Then, in another segment of the experiment, white children were asked to compare white faces with Asian faces. The outcome in this case was the same because the faces that the white children perceived to be Asian were described as angry with no exceptions and the faces perceived to be white were almost always described as happy. The black children showed no pro-black or pro-white bias when they were tested in the study. Hence, this experiment proved that children also develop racial biases at a very young age. It gets unconsciously embedded in tender minds, possibly through social observations. This seems to play out from childhood to adulthood and people accept this to be how life is meant to be.

Sujata Saha, a chemical scientist, narrates her journey of being brown in a 'white' land as a child and as an adult. She was born in London after her father shifted to the British capital immediately after his marriage. He worked with a leading foreign bank at that point in time and was posted in London for an international assignment. The struggle to be British for her mother was quite stressful, as she was a native Asian, with dusky skin colour, and felt like a misfit among the British. Her father took to the British ways quite comfortably and quickly, though. Their mannerisms became quite different. As Sujata sat at the dinner table every night, she observed that her mother would eat with her hands and her father would eat with his fork and knife. Irrespective, they both enjoyed their dinner equally. She was always in a dilemma with regards to which parent's mannerism she should follow. Eventually, she started eating with a fork and knife as well. Her mother was thrown into an unfamiliar city and culture. She found her surroundings a bit strange, for she could not simply knock on a neighbour's door to have quick chat or walk across the road freely. Places like super marts confused her. Much to her mother's anguish, Sujata's father ultimately decided to make UK his home as he had been deputed in London for a long period of time.

As Sujata joined her new school in London, she noticed the difference, for the first time, between white, black and brown children. Some of the Sikh and Gujarati children were fairly light-skinned, but she was dark-brown, to be more specific. Some of her schoolmates were polite yet distanced, while some called her hurtful names. It was upsetting for her to realise that some white children found her strange and did not allow her to join their games.

One day, two white children found Sujata sobbing after school. They approached her to have a conversation. She shared with them that she was upset because she had no friends to play with. Thanks to her disclosure, Sujata found these two white friends who gave her chocolates every alternate day to make her feel at home. Yet they would not play with her openly lest they got alienated by the other white classmates. Language was also a slight problem for her in school as Sujata was not fluent in UK English. Her mother only spoke to her in Bengali at home; she was very apprehensive that Sujata would forget her mother tongue. Her father used to keep away from home due to long working hours and business travels, hence her spoken English was a little weak. The family did not have many British visitors at home initially.

Her childhood curiosity gradually came to the realisation of how colour can impact her life in a new country. She finally found one white British friend who sat next to her in class. Frequent interactions with her led to the understanding of common interests, toys and games. More interaction bloomed into a closer friendship. Her name was Margaret. She helped Sujata hone her language and was partially responsible for her acquired British accent. Margaret's mother fell in love with Sujata's mother's beautiful sarees and her culinary skills, for she could whip up any dish from any part of her native country. Margaret would teach Sujata the acceptable English mannerisms, whilst she learnt about Indian culture from Sujata, braving the wrath of a few scornful white students who seemed to look flabbergasted by this 'coloured' or cross-racial friendship.

The class teacher sensed the reason behind Sujata's improved comfort and performance in school as she noticed Margaret and her sitting in the corner of the class and gleefully engaged in conversations. On a special day, when Margaret ate from Sujata's lunchbox, the news spread like wildfire in the school and the narration brought some middle-school students to their classroom so that they could have a look at Margaret.

Sujata was finally well adjusted and doing very well academically when a family friend advised her father to move her to a high-performing school so that her academic standards could improve. She told her father that she would join the new school only if Margaret went along with her. But Margaret had four siblings and she was the eldest of the lot. Her parents could not afford the high fees of the new private school. Sujata's father refused to submit to her incessant sobbing and like a tyrant asked her to follow his orders to join the new school. Out of fear, she appeared for a few interviews and against her hopes, she was selected to one of the schools in London.

The toughest journey of her life started at the age of fifteen, when she had to envision her school life without Margaret. This school was patronised by prosperous, elite and entitled local white families. There was a vast difference between her and their economic standard of living. She had no expectation of finding another Margaret and this thought made her come back home crestfallen, almost every day.

As Sujata began to reconcile with her new reality, she started to participate in extra-curricular activities to find her mojo back. In one event, a boy named Charles was assigned to be her partner in a school quiz competition. They had never spoken before. He and his brother, Ronald, were twins and studied in the same school. Sujata was a slightly introverted girl and consumed by the new environment, she had not made efforts to engage with many students. She could sense that Charles looked disappointed with her being his teammate, given their lack of familiarity with each other. He even tried to persuade the quiz teacher for a change before the qualifying round.

Charles was academically a good student and so was Sujata, but in her case the evidence was more in her test marks and not in her classroom participation. In the qualifying round, Charles was surprised to find her all energised with all the correct answers on sports and music. They did well in the qualifying round and beat all the other teams. Charles finally found her worthy of association and tried to make up for his earlier coldness by giving her a chocolate and introduced his brother, Ronald, to her too. The chemistry that commenced was beyond colour. It dawned on her that Charles and Ronald were going to be the new 'Margarets' of her life in the new school.

Ronald and Charles were sons of diplomats and exposed to different people across countries. They were colour-blind and attached value to friendship and capability. They respected Sujata for her abilities, integrity, diligence and her earnest endeavour to perform well in school.

Sujata's mother was not very comfortable with Charles coming over to their house every other day to study mathematics or science with her daughter, but she never made any outright objection either. Charles was from a prosperous and well-educated family and he introduced Sujata to his friends, thereby expanding her social network. Soon they became closer friends, much against the wishes of her mother. Neither the colour of the skin nor the difference in the economic standard stood as a barrier between their friendship anymore. Charles's family was very open-minded. Their unbiased attitude filtered down to their children.

Charles is Sujata's husband today and Margaret was the bridesmaid at their wedding. She is also Sujata's son's godmother. Some relationships have strong foundations and skin colour evaporates once the magic of love, friendship and respect spread its glitter. Such associations are to be cherished for the strong foundations they create for the future evolution of human bonding.

Sujata's relationship with Margaret was born out of their innocent love and compassion for each other. Sujata found refuge in her endearing care and concern for her; it engulfed her and she reciprocated positively. Margaret made Sujata feel included at a time when she was confused and alienated. She gave her a sense of inclusion and positivity. This relationship fulfilled an emotional need for Sujata. Life is all about forming memories and being enriched with the learnings from each other's experiences.

Sujata's relationship with Charles commenced as a friendship. She had never thought that this would become a lifetime commitment. As both of them evolved, discovered solace in their compatibility beyond their differences, the relationship became stronger. His admiration for Sujata's adaptability reinforced her confidence. His willingness to share the darkest and the deepest secrets of his life brought them closer. Her comfort of sharing her insecurities in a mixed-race environment, with him, brought her peace. Charles's presence in her life from a stranger to an undesirable team member to a friend and then to a lover and now husband demonstrates how love and mutual respect has the ability to transform a relationship.

In order to have a life well-lived, we need to form honest relationships with people without dwelling too much on their origins and skin colour. Today, Charles and Sujata laugh together and weep together, well not always, but most of the time. They are very much a part of the fabric of each other's worlds. Her companionship with Margaret and Charles taught Sujata that the greatest joy is in sharing and caring and in loving and being loved!

The Dalai Lama has propagated that love and compassion are necessities in their own right.

SECURITY AND FAMILIARITY—NECESSITIES OF MERE MORTALS

The American writer, Alan Wolfe, has rightly said, 'Behind every citizen lies a graveyard.'

In the US, most current citizens originally belong to a different country. Hillary Clinton put it well when she said that the US is a country made by talented immigrants. All of us are born in a certain race somewhere without a privilege to choose. However, we do have a choice to decide where and how we wish to lead our lives.

When we refer to a community of people who have the same race, we may be stating a certain way of how people 'look' or 'behave'. As per a few not so open-minded people, greater diversity is presupposed to generate conflicts of values and interests across races. Isaac Marks at the Institute of Psychiatry, Psychology and Neuroscience (IoPPN), London, warns that feelings of hostility and suspicion towards outsiders are latent in almost all of us and there is a small xenophobe hiding within us. Economic impact contributes to its external manifestation. This is the reason why conservatives always resist racial mixing.

A research paper written in 2001 at the Harvard Institute of Economic Research titled, 'Why doesn't the US Have a European-style Welfare State?' by Bruce Sacerdote, Edward Glaeser and Alberto Alesina, dwells on the thought that in the US a large amount of tax income goes to the minorities. This is an economic reason due to which some local citizens are insecure about immigrants occupying national space because they are afraid of a larger amount of tax revenue paid by them to the government going to blacks or Hispanics, even though many of them contribute hugely to the economy as well. Hence, there are benefits that accrue from the contribution of the minorities. However, the psychological insecurity coupled with economic insecurity results in welfare states being averse to asylum seekers or immigrants. Robert D Putnam, an American political scientist at the Harvard University and a renowned analyst of social capital, has studied around 30,000 people across forty cities within the US in recent years. His studies have revealed that all other things being equal, more diversity in a community today is being associated with less trust and this is true for both among and within ethnic groups. Colour is being seen only through a narrow lens.

The incidence of less trust is born out of the fact that anything new or ambiguous makes us so fearful and insecure that we fail to see through the benefits of it. Humankind has been struggling for ages to understand just how much diversity is optimum and beneficial. But, at the end of it all, relationships are a matter of emotion rather than rational calculation, or at least that is how it should be. Relationships based on benefit do not last long because as soon as the derived benefit ceases to exist, the relationship also vanishes.

Denmark has a more 'nativist' and restrictive approach to immigration as only 6% of the population is foreign born. Local Danes enjoy superior welfare benefits as compared to any 'outsider' or non-white people. Denmark has a two-tier welfare state, which offers higher benefits to 'insiders'. Multiculturalists have come to the conclusion that hostility to diversity can be perceived as a form of 'false consciousness' in people. Multiculturalists further argue that a single national story or narrative is not a strong base on which a common culture can be developed if a society is also fragmented by race and religion. It may work in small countries and cohorts that are stable with little need or ambition to grow, but in the new world, across the globe, there will be groups of the rich and the poor.

A study undertaken at the New York University and the Harvard University, which was published in the *Science* journal, an academic journal from the American Association of the Advancement of Science, in 2005, had revealed that racism originates from the ease with which people learn to fear other people from different ethnic groups. The research found that when people have an unexpected encounter with someone of a different race, the impact lasts longer and fosters fear and prejudice whereas an equally disturbing experience with someone from the same race is forgotten and forgiven. Are we programmed to fear differences?

In our professional and personal space, mutual love and respect build relationships that are based on solid fundamentals and are not hollow. It generates compassion and affection, which are active emotional stimulants. Even when it comes to the relationship between a leader and his team, a poignant question asked of most leaders is: 'Do you like to be feared or respected?' Fear creates hatred; it destroys the idea of love and squashes it. Hatred, in turn, does nothing to boost the performance of an individual on a sustainable basis. Also, the quality of work is hampered in the process. But respect makes the team feel an innate sense of love and admiration for their leader, which helps the team positively to perform better. The love for your leader or your colleague or friend brings a whole new dimension to the relationship. Our task is not to control the other person or change them in any way, but about mutual respect that acts as a catalyst to motivate people to do their best or perform a particular task for optimum outcomes.

Human beings need to find love for themselves first, before making an attempt to find love for others. Martin Luther King believed that infinite love has the boundless power to unite all, never mind the colour of their skin or their origins. Love always wins whenever it's unselfish and unconditional. Love brings a sense of tolerance in a human being, which prevents people from resenting other cultures or ethnicities.

Hate cannot drive out hate, but love can do that.

SUMMARY

1. Love knows no colour or ethnicity. Love is the most veritable binding force, which is the strongest opponent to the forces that foster racism. Love forges relationships, which are sustainable and erases barriers and boundaries.
2. Differences between communities create fear, which further leads to hate. Authentic engagement helps us, peek into each other's thoughts, smoothening such differences. It helps find common purpose and a shared vision.
3. Friendships are a manifestation of our love to extend ourselves. Forge relationships with those who understand you, respect you and are willing to walk with you in life. You will find them. You just need to open your mind and extend your hand to find a friend.
4. Mutual appreciation helps to eradicate malevolence and fosters tolerance and acceptance.

Objectivity

Avni is completing her project paper as Sid and I Skype her (at late US time) at her college.

Mom: 'Hi Avni, How have you been? You haven't called for a week. All okay?'

Avni (in a frustrated tone): 'Hi mom, sorry, I have been a bit caught up with studies and projects.'

Mom: 'You don't sound yourself. All okay?'

Avni: 'Mom, the project has been tough and to top it, among our new project group of three, I have this person from Romania, who is so restrained and unsocial. I am not sure if he really understands how it works here.'

Sid: 'Whoa you are really upset Avni di! Is he that bad?'

Avni: 'Honestly! Only if I can make this person understand how to communicate!'

Mom: 'Why do you say this Avni? You are not from the US either, but you have figured it out!'

Avni: 'C'mon mom, I have lived all over and most of my friends tell me that people like these are always behaving in a strange way!'

Sid (rolling his eyes): 'Really? They behave like you.'

Avni: 'Sid! I would appreciate your being quiet.'

Mom: 'Avni, I wonder if it's his communication issue or yours. For a minute, put yourself in that individual's place and feel what he is feeling. Can you try and respect the person as someone who is different, but not wrong? Confines of our mind sometimes show us what it wants us to see, but not always what you should see.

'It could be about seeing this situation more objectively, thoughtfully, understanding the other side without prejudices and developing an inference that is real. Don't fret about knowing the new people that come into your life. Good people come for a reason and a season. Try a fresh start with no pre-coloured lens please.'

Avni: 'Okay, I will mom, thanks as always. However, it takes some effort to sense what it is like to be him. I will speak to him objectively and try and make him understand us as much as we try and understand him!'

Mom: 'Yes Avni, someone did it for you when you were new in the US. Pay forward, my child!'

In a few weeks, the project was completed. Avni and her team members presented it together to the dean. They came out with flying colours.

Breathe, pause, hold your judgement and your ego. Real truth lies in data and knowledge. Let's discover what's real!

Awareness brings out the hidden truth in our life, one which sometimes we fail to realise when blinded by too much social chaos in our mind. Therefore, the separation of information from manufactured truths is essential to remove the bias, which could be unconsciously deep-seated in our minds. Earnest attempts have to be made to seek reality by shutting out the external noise at times, so that our minds are not mired in shadows. The quest for reasoning can help us to comprehend the indisputable facts so that we can sieve out the fiction from the non-fiction.

Objectivity demands that we seek knowledge, data and reason to eliminate unfounded perceptions and biases. That is the only way in which we can develop a logical and non-partisan mindset. In this world where people develop prejudices that hamper our awareness, deep understanding and thinking can prove to be a saviour.

FIGHT THE CLOUD OF BIAS, TRUE SELF WILL SHINE OUT!

'Rahul, we think you have the capability for this international assignment our company has for you. After observing your performance during the training period, we think that your contribution has added value. So pack your bags and head to California. Congratulations!'

This was Rahul's manager, the one he was reporting to in India, in one of the world's most reputed hardware companies. He soon received an email regarding his international assignment. Swarup, his Indian manager, had closed all the transfer formalities with Rahul's prospective white manager in California. Rahul was super excited and was really looking forward to this assignment as well as the move. The popular public perception (PPP) theory of racism that he had had limited exposure was yet to unfold before him.

Reflecting back, Rahul reminisced that during his graduation from IIM Kolkata in the 1990s, he was exposed to a large number of racist stories from Indian corporate honchos with experiences in foreign countries, who were ready to spill the beans in secret conversations of what to do or not to do. The IT industry was booming then and every second software engineer he spoke to was 'running away' to the US. *Amrika* was the place to be for every IT professional and the US had opened its arms to welcome all the Indian software skills and imports.

Management schools and engineering schools in India too provided their students with lucrative packages and glamorous international placement opportunities and the Indian students were lured into it. A reputed hardware company had already made an international offer to Rahul even before he had completed his management education. He was perplexed initially because he had struggled to get good grades in his management education and had no such expectation of getting to go to *Amrika* on his first job. But he was thrilled to show off to his peers. Further, all his relatives were duly informed by his mother and he had rapidly become a role model for his nieces and nephews.

When Rahul set foot in California, he was pleasantly welcomed by the warm sun and warm people who were so 'cool'. With so many white people around him, Rahul became aware of his own dusky colour for the first time. He now realised why his mother had felt it was all her fault that he was this colour, whereas he had been unapologetic about it. She had taken an oath that she would get him married to a fair girl so that at least his children would inherit a better complexion. He chuckled at the thought of marrying a white girl from California!

Rahul had been trained in India for six months before he was sent to California. His team here had only white people and no black people or Hispanics. Rahul was the youngest member of the team and perhaps the most inexperienced. He felt a bit unsure about how to navigate his way in the team as they all seemed so different in their styles and preferences—be it food, clothes or time out. He kept himself calm and objective so that he could understand the new culture better. Rahul joined their informal evenings over beer even though he did not drink; even went to a few shows that did not interest him, just to get to know his colleagues better.

Discrimination laws in California are the toughest and the strictest in the country. The state authorities, in the last decade, had formulated laws that prescribed severe civil damages and penalties for employers who engaged in unlawful discrimination at the workplace. Workplace discrimination and harassment practices in most organisations in California are neatly formulated to reduce and eliminate racism or discrimination of any kind at the workplace. This was one of the many reasons why California was a popular place for coloured people like Rahul to work in the US.

Rahul was assigned on a project, which required him to work for close to twelve hours each day. He had been sensitised that a few managers on the floor were from the mid-west of US, not familiar with emerging markets as they had not travelled much. Their orientation to diverse workforce was not as inclusive as they had been brought up in a very conservative environment. Hence, Rahul was sensitive and cautious so as to not attract any unwanted attention from these seniors. This was his first job and he sought a lot of support and guidance from his managers. However, as foretold by his colleagues, his team lead, who had some reservations towards coloured people, was beginning to make things tough for him. Rahul was being put on not-so-important tasks of the project and subtly excluded from key meetings. He had to learn a lot of new things and expected to comply with some tough targets too that did not make things easier.

Before Rahul came to the US, he had not really explored how it may be to work with different ethnicities. He believed that good talent will always find its way and will definitely be supported and recognised. His education and upbringing had taught him to segregate the truth from perceptions, to embrace enlightenment and discard ignorance. However, he now realised that he needed more awareness and learnings to settle into this new environment and people.

Rahul tried hard to adapt, connect and communicate, but his manager was not overly comfortable with him. The manager once shared with Rahul that his house was broken in by a brown person a few years back. His other exposure to brown people was the movie, *Slumdog Millionaire*. It really does not help when a certain country or race is shown in a certain way, which may not be their entire reality. However, media and movies do have an overbearing influence on people's perceptions. Rahul's behaviour (communication, way of dressing, food habits) was different, yet not disruptive, and that's what kept the manager going along with him, but in a distanced way. The condescending tone and rolling eyes gradually started to impact Rahul's morale. He began to sense some office banter around him.

Things became tougher. Rahul was not sure at that point whether he could term the management's behaviour as racism. He was not allowed to take leave even if he was sick, he was often blamed for any error in the product design and he was reprimanded for underperformance after working for close to twelve hours every day. But, when some doors shut on you, others open up.

Some of Rahul's white team members had developed an affinity for him, thanks to the pints of beer that they consumed every day. They were not just his colleagues, but had become his friends and family in this busy city. One of them, Lawson, born and brought up in California, helped him to find and move into an apartment with one of his university batchmates closer to the office. Rahul would spend his weekends with them and their shared interests were spread across a broad range of gadgets, tennis, soccer and technology. He did feel lonely at times as he missed Indian food and his family, but Lawson and his group of friends ensured that Rahul recovered from his temporary bouts of homesickness. Peter, another friend, found a good Indian takeaway outlet and treated Rahul to it every weekend.

One day at work, Rahul was accused of not meeting a deadline for submitting a revised version of a particular product design. The truth was that the entire team had not been able to deliver on time because the client had come up with last minute specifications, which could not be incorporated in haste. But Rahul was the only one to be summoned into the manager's cabin (the product division head), and was given a sarcastic mouthful without an opportunity to explain anything. He was enraged and his face turned red with humiliation.

Lawson and Peter along with many others on the floor witnessed Rahul being berated from a cabin that had glass walls. They felt upset for their friend. They could see that this was less to do with Rahul, and perhaps more to do with his colour. They knew that the manager had a closed mindset and was not inclined to focus beyond life in the Midwest or the West Coast, leave alone the entire country and the world. At their risk, they decided to have a conversation with the HR department and requested them to intervene. HR reached out to Rahul, who was terrified to raise anything formally, but conceded to share if he was protected. This intervention helped. The manager was counselled (reprimanded I think) and Rahul was shifted under another team manager, who was more diverse in his thinking and exposure.

Both Peter and Lawson were children of immigrant parents and in some ways, they shared Rahul's pain, even though they were born in the US. Somewhere they empathised with Rahul and could gauge adverse reactions from others more objectively from a shared perspective. Since Rahul was an introvert and could not express himself very well, Lawson supported him in the trial through a different environment. Peter drew him into team discussions and debates to share his viewpoints, which always helped the team.

Peter and Lawson supported Rahul emotionally throughout this period and were his pillars of support in his new workplace. He went on to work with them for over eight years after which Lawson left for his PhD at Princeton University.

Lawson was a perfect example of an individual focussed on building a human connection with an objective way of looking at situations and then applying an empathetic approach to resolution. He had the ability to suspend his judgements, withhold his emotions and map the right objective to the right action. When Rahul asked him the secret to his connect, Lawson had said, 'When I talk to you, I only see you objectively, no colour, no race. I see your thoughts, your motivations and how you relate to me. That's it!' Rahul kept in touch with Lawson over the years and they forged a brotherly bond. Rahul stayed on in the US, his children are biracial and their bicultural identity as Indian-American is indeed unique.

Human barriers of segregating people on the basis of their skin colour, religion or caste can be overcome by an objective and open mindset. Our mind is the strongest driver of different thoughts, perceptions, notions and ideas. It is the engine that drives our thinking and we must teach it how to think and not just how to react. The ability to conceptualise, comprehend with data and to do so within the social paradigms depends on the power of our mind. Colour exists, but only in our mind. The rest is information, which can be constructive or destructive depending on the lens applied.

'Chinki': Confront the Countenance of Racism

India is extremely diverse and well known for its community identification. I have explained this to many of my friends, colleagues and acquaintances from other countries that some parts of India could be as alien for me (in spite of being born here) as they are for them. I may not know the language, food or customs of a few regions in the country. However, it is this diversity that makes it so unique. We derive our strength from our coexistence. This integrated state can help us find collective solutions towards living together in communities.

In our quest to be objective, we must understand that we need to focus towards the relevant aspects of a community or an individual that underlines their existence. We need to gauge what has been the history in the making of certain values and drivers. It requires us to go beyond the obvious physicality to keep the mind balanced and realistic. Intelligence without wisdom is dangerous; and similarly, objectivity without sensibility is useless.

We are under social pressure to believe whatever has been passed down to us from generations, which sometimes distorts the locus of our original thought process. The disability to sieve the right opinion from the volley of information, which is bombarded at us at every point in our lives, thanks to the digital revolution, further spurs us to live in falsehood and untruths. Objectivity suspends the judgement, pending evidence, and resolves the conflicts that help us dwell peacefully with ourselves and others.

> *'Dispassionate objectivity is itself a passion, for the real and for the truth.'*
> *—Abraham Maslow*

In late January 2014, Nido Taniam died because of a street brawl in New Delhi. Nido was at Lajpat Nagar market with some friends. They stopped at a shop where the shopkeeper passed a rude comment about Nido's clothes and the colour of his hair, called him *chinki* (a slang used to describe a person of Chinese origin), and laughed at him along with some other people at the shop.

This allegedly provoked Nido to raise his objection at this treatment. He banged his hand on the shop counter, which shattered the glass and triggered a scuffle between him and the shopkeeper. According to Nightham Apam, one of Nido's friends, the shopkeeper and six other men threw chilli powder in Nido's eyes and beat him. Nido was beaten with a wooden stick. They also slapped him several times across his face. The shopkeeper called the Police Control Unit, and the local police too reached the spot.

Both parties were taken to the police station, where police brokered a settlement and made Nido and his friends shell out ₹10,000 to pay for the damages at the shop. Nightham said the matter, however, did not end there. According to him, a few hours later, men from the shop cornered Nido at the end of a narrow road and beat him again. The police said Nido complained to them after the second incident, and both the parties were again taken to the police station. They were made to submit written apologies before being let off.

Friends of twenty-year-old Nido Taniam last saw him alive at 6:00 AM after he had spent a sleepless night, agitated about the previous evening's incident, and complaining of uneasiness and pain in the chest. The friends assumed he had drifted off to sleep after that, but got worried around noon, when he still hadn't woken up. They took him to the hospital where he was declared dead. He died after suffering internal injuries from the brawl. The wounds were not just internal, they were perhaps on his departed soul.

There were three people accused. A charge sheet was filed by the Central Bureau of Investigation on May 2014. Delhi police had registered a case of murder and nabbed two accused.

It is no secret that India is a land of multiple ethnicities and indigenous people. There are visible differences in the physical appearance of Indians across the land. This diversity extends to lifestyles and value systems as well. Many North Indians may feel alienated in South India and vice versa. At its worst, this may lead to an unfounded view that similar looking people should live in the same region and those who look different do not belong to the country.

Racial barriers form the crux of various debates and demands actions, from time to time, for separate specific privileges including 'reservations' citing a disadvantage of being a minority. In the Nido case, when you delve deeper, the inhabitants from the North East of India have always been given a collective isolated identity due to their facial features, and the individual identities of the different states (eight states) have always been ignored. Reservations haven't been able to build the integrative mindset that is the need of the hour. So this needs more focus if we truly believe in inclusion.

The various ethnic groups in this region have their own stories of origin and migration. Each state in India's north-eastern region has its own culture, religion, festivals and language. Kamei Samson, an Indian scholar at the Indian Council of Social Science Research, claims that the idea of Bharat or Hindustan identifies with the Dravidians or the Aryans and not the Mongoloid groups. The inhabitants of the North East do not evoke a sense of identification with India. Since their physique and facial construction is similar to those from South East Asia or China, they are quite often associated with the South East Asian populace.

Many north-eastern students who reside in other parts of the country are not always welcome beyond unskilled jobs. They confess that people outside their communities do not embrace them and continue to treat them as 'outsiders', while local people refuse to mingle with them. Most of them are docile, soft-spoken, hard-working and extremely efficient in their work. A well-known recruitment agency shared that in spite of racial hardships, they remain calm, mature and demure, and their attitude remains professional.

A survey conducted by Reachout Foundation with the help of Policy Research made some startling revelations. Almost 1,000 respondents participated in the survey. Around 54% felt that discrimination was a reality in the national capital, whereas 74% felt that Delhi was the 'most unsafe' place in terms of racial and ethnic discrimination. According to the report, which was released by the National Human Rights Commission of India (NHRC), 67% of the respondents felt that they had been victims of ethnic or racial discrimination. The worrying factor in the report is that 63% of the respondents felt that the main reason for discrimination was their ethnic origin.

In fact, there were also several complaints about facing discrimination by minorities like north-eastern communities, Muslims and black people in India. They faced issues while looking for a house to rent, wherein they were charged more than the market rate. An article on the website of Al Jazeera[3] contains an honest rendition of a North East Indian journalist (who is an employee of the news service) about the names by which he is referred to on the streets of Delhi. He has been forced to hear racist slurs like 'King-Kong', 'Chow-Chow' and 'Momo' being hurled at him. When he confronted the young men who called him by such 'names', they misbehaved with him and his sister. Initially, the law enforcement was not always available. For a force already hard-pressed on other issues of law and order, a complaint about a 'racial slur' seemed a 'non-issue' until things actually got out of hand.

It is evident that the people of the Indian mainland have a psychological disconnect with the north-eastern region of the country. Biased views and discounting of real facts have led to their exclusion in the mainstream population. They are legitimately Indian citizens and it is shameful that even after decades of independence, some minds are still enslaved in the shackles of ignorance. The critical factor while dealing with issues of discrimination is the acceptance of the fact that severe racial attitudes exist in the country and then resolve it. Most of the time, people are in denial of race issues. It does little to solve this disturbing problem, which has the capacity to threaten the peaceful coexistence of human beings from diverse cultures in this secular country. An independent, data-based view will foster a mindset that is objective, inclusive and positive. We need to hold our judgements to understand motivations, characters and abilities of others who may be different looking than us, to foster a peaceful existence of our communities.

> *'Racism is a refuge for the ignorant. It seeks to divide and to destroy. It is the enemy of freedom, and deserves to be met head-on and stamped out.'*
> *—Pierre Berton*

3   Bijoyeeta Das. 'India's northeast speaks out against racism'. *Al Jazeera*. 16 February 2014. https://www.aljazeera.com/indepth/features/2014/02/voices-from-india-northeast-2014218113146008558.html

The story is not very different in other parts of India either. Prejudices exist and persist in India and skin colour seems to be a major factor even today. Globally, the scenarios playing out in other parts of the world are not any different. We remain oblivious to the objective rationale of how the human race itself was nomadic at one time and convenience and comfort led to each person settling in a region within circumstances of their choice. This led to an evolution of race and ethnicity. Over time, this regional groupism has manifested itself into more rigid and concrete enforced barriers—in our minds and souls.

South India v. North India: Match between Colours

Carl Zimmer, the famous *New York Times* journalist, had made an interesting statement, 'For centuries, skin colour has held a powerful social meaning—a defining characteristic of race, and a starting point of racism.'

The subject of racism in India spoils its national 'unity in diversity' rhetoric and is a thorn in the articles and the speeches that applaud the ability of Indians to indulge in peaceful coexistence in a multicultural and multilingual land. For decades, we have ignored or lightly acknowledged the biases that people in the North and the South have against each other. We tend to normalise embedded prejudices that the North Indians and the South Indians have for/against each other. In the Indian context, racism is intertwined with a variety of subjects such as history, caste, religion, politics and most importantly colour.

The colour black or *kaala* is associated with a sense of 'not so good'. At its extreme, it symbolises destitution and grime. White effectively is reminiscent of our colonisers, the tea-drinkers, the powerful, sophisticated and prosperous beings who are superior to the rest of the world. The *gora-chitta* (fair skin) populace of the North takes pride in their 'tribe' because of their skin colour.

In fact, some individuals in North India think that *gora* or fair is the standard complexion in India and those who are not, belong to the 'other' part of the country, which is the southern part. There are a large number of South Indians who are also fixated with lighter coloured skin and deem it to be lovelier than dark skin. Colour prejudices vary according to different shades—the darkest shade (popularly known as the *Mallukallu* colour, which means the skin colour of the Malayalees in Kerala) deserves ridicule, the 'wheatish' complexion (the colour of Bengalis and Oriyas in eastern India) merits sympathy and the *gora-chitta* (fair and white) complexion deserves praise. It is not very uncommon to witness reports of discrimination due to colour-related oppression in India. In fact, the practice of dowry sometimes follows on from the 'unpopularity' and 'inadequacy' of dark women as prospective brides. More dowry is paid for darker brides to compensate for the lack of fair skin.

The difficulty in being objective comes from the difficulty to let go of existing mindsets and ideologies. We need to consciously work hard on changing our belief structures irrespective of whether the thought or opinion is handed over to us by our parents, grandparents, professors, office seniors, religious leaders, politicians or the society at large.

As an individual, one needs to be strong enough to accept an alternate way of looking at the world of colour. Constant enquiry is the best way to indulge the mind to search and assimilate with fresh, different and appropriate paradigms of how people can be. Sometimes to be a part of the crowd, to fit into a contextual sitting, we compromise with our thinking and follow the crowd mentality. There are various paradigms of reason, which are positioned as reasonable to us, but we must revisit the relevant paradigm with facts when faced with a dilemma. The world around is ever-changing. The beliefs of the past cannot define the path of the future. Some of them need to be challenged to be 'fit for the purpose'.

Dr Tishkoff, a geneticist in the University of Pennsylvania, US, shared that it is an error to identify skin colour as a symbol of race. She further explained that there are eight genetic variants in four narrow regions of the human genome that starkly influence pigmentation, which makes some people darker and some lighter.

These eight gene variants were discovered by Dr Tishkoff and her colleagues in Africa and in various other continents. The DNA of our distant forbearers about 900,000 years ago contained the strains of these variants. For example, Neanderthals split off from their ancestors approximately 600,000 years ago and spread across eastern Asia and Europe. Some of their DNA has still survived.

According to Dr Tishkoff, these hominines inherited the same combination of skin colour. These gene variants are present across the globe and were present in our ancestors millions of years ago. European nations have lower variations in skin colour whereas African and Asian nations have higher variations. The genes that produce lighter skin and the ones that produce darker skin were both found to have originated in Africa and were carried from the continent by migrants. The Africans interbred with the Neanderthals on several occasions as they moved into Europe and Asia and that is how the genes were distributed across the world.

If looked at objectively, the colour of our skin we inherit has come through evolution and it is ever-evolving for a revelation.

AFFECTION OVER AFFLICTION

The process of adoption is indeed quite trying and difficult. It is an emotional process by which you make an unknown your very own. In fact, all parents who have adopted children would know that the most difficult part of it all is the moment at which you decide to reveal that you are a foster parent and not a real parent. At this point, the deep understanding of the environment and that of each other foster a relationship that surmounts all the differences.

Steve Markle and his wife, Linda, had been grappling with the decision to adopt for the longest time. Linda had been dealing with the problem of infertility for years. Steve felt that adoption essentially starts with an urge to extend your love. Linda and Steve were both African Americans. Linda was Kenyan and Steve was from Botswana. Their parents had migrated to the US for education and settled there permanently. Steve had also lived for a few years in Indonesia when his father was working there. He was well conversant with the world, its shade of colours and how that had manifested for him.

Steve and Linda wanted a family and colour was irrelevant to them, perhaps not even a matter of consideration. However, their experience did show them that the small number of those willing to provide loving homes was quite disproportionate to the large number of those who were in need of affection and safety of a loving family. The implication was that the number of parents willing to adopt children was much smaller than homeless children in need of foster care. Steve and Linda were provided with a few choices by the agencies; however, they wanted a baby girl from a humble background, they wanted to help someone who was in real need. On their lucky day, they were called with the news that their bundle of joy was here. She was a bit sick, she was white and pale. The concerned Central European orphanage was unsure if a white baby should be handed to prospective black parents, but could not prevent that under the law.

'Why a white child from Eastern Europe?'

This was a question they were asked often. During his stay in Hungary and Bulgaria, Steve had received a lot of information about the difficult financial conditions there, in spite of them being European countries. Steve had witnessed many young children addicted to drugs as they were made to work relentlessly for twenty-four hours. He wanted to help in a real way and decided even if he could change one life, his mission would be fulfilled.

When the call from the orphanage came, he was briefed that this girl child was born to an unwed mother in Slovakia who was unwilling to bear the consequences of conception. Her mother had kept her for some time, but one day left her at her cousin's doorstep and ran away. Her cousin did as was expected and compelled the child's grandparents to take care of her. The mother's parents themselves were living in destitution and could barely afford meals. Then, the grandfather passed away only to make the life of the child and the grandmother quite arduous. The struggle was real and the parentless child and the grandmother were starving for days together with no respite in sight. Every adopted child is a victim of surrendered love and likewise in this case the child was taken to an orphanage as there was nobody left to take care of her. Then, an NGO came to the rescue.

Racial mapping is a tricky process as there are no real studies supporting what works or does not. Hence most adoption homes are driven by past experiences and their own views about multi-racial relationships. There is a subtle preference to give children to similar coloured families on the assumption that they may adapt better. That may have some relevance, however, key drivers in family relationships are mutual trust and bonding. Only if people could place all races at the same level and then apply the human lesson of love, care and compatibility will we get desired outcomes for families. However, this level of objective assessment is largely missing. Biases often drive the predicament.

In spite of this harsh reality, Linda and Steve believed that the best way to nurture humanity and altruism was to take care of those who have been left with nothing and no one. They were guided by the Bible, which mentions that Jesus never discriminated among his followers and he considered each and every person's life to be precious and eternal. Hence, Linda and Steve decided to adopt this child from Slovakia. They were keen to adopt this child to not only fulfil their parenting wish, but to also help a longing soul find a home. But, the implications of their resolution had not dawned upon them till they started living with their adopted daughter back in the US. Steve felt that people around him had not warmed up to the idea of such multiracial families and found it quite tedious and frustrating to lead a normal life in his predominantly white neighbourhood.

Transracial adoption has had its own difficult history. In 1972, the National Association of Black Social Workers had famously declared that white parents adopting black children was almost akin to cultural genocide. The case here was a step further, a black couple adopting a white child!

Steve knew that cynicism associated with the adoption of white children by blacks was quite real, yet he was determined to do this. When Baby Angela was brought home, the visible difference in their skin colour did not bother them, but it bothered the neighbours, society and essentially the world at large. They were confronted with the misperception of black affection harming a white child that was prevalent in some minds. Some nearby social workers wished to get into details. A few went to the extreme of accusing them of child abuse and trafficking in cross-racial adoption. However, the parents persisted with their strong convictions and tided over these perceptions. Their strong bond with Angela kept them going. They kept calm and objective while dealing with baseless comments hurled at them, attributing it to ignorance

Steve and Linda had mustered the courage to face all kinds of issues as they were able to differentiate fact from fiction, and focus on their priorities. The rest was not relevant. As Angela grew up, she did have a lot of questions about why she was different from her parents, why others stared at them. Steve and Linda ensured that the affection they had for her made up for all the dissimilarities that existed physically and in their origins.

One pertinent incident that Steve recalled was when all three of them went out to have a meal and noticed many of those present at the restaurant staring at them. Angela was around ten years old and she became increasingly uncomfortable with other people's gaze. Linda, sensing her daughter's discomfort, suggested that they should leave the place, but Steve was adamant that they would not be driven away by strangers. The waiter served them with a glass of water, but nothing was offered to Angela. In fact, the waiter went to ask them, 'Sir is she with you? Is she related to you?' Steve answered in the affirmative and shared that she was their daughter. A lady at the nearby table found that amiss, 'How is that possible? Have you kidnapped her? Hey call the police! These kind of people I tell you. Taking all of 'em, the kids, our white kids!'

Linda felt shattered at this statement and broke down in front of everyone in the restaurant and Angela screamed, 'Mama, please don't cry, I am sorry I am white, people say bad things to you because of me.' Angela started crying too. Then, she turned to the lady who was speaking earlier and said, 'My Dada is not a kidnapper! He is a good dada! He loves me and tells me bedtime stories!' Crowds from other tables started to surround Angela. They still looked at the parents suspiciously. One of them called the manager to ensure valid checks were in place so that the child was indeed safe. This tore Linda and Steve's heart. However, Steve remained calm and objective as always. He knew the ignorance of others had to be reciprocated with his wisdom gathered over the years. The manager came by and asked Steve some questions. It reminded Steve of the time when he had adopted Angela from Slovakia, the gruelling scrutiny they had been subjected to, due to mistrust. It felt that Steve and Linda had to be scrutinised again and again to prove their noble intent of helping a child. At this tumultuous intersection of identity and ethnicity, Steve felt even more determined to make things work

He showed his ID card to the manager and a copy of the residence permit where Angela was listed as his daughter. The manager profusely apologised to the family. He tried to offer free meals and desserts to compensate for the incident. However, the deed had been done. The family left the restaurant. Angela was old enough to understand what had transpired that day—her parents were ridiculed and she felt hurt. She demanded to know why people behaved the way they did with her family. On that cold Sunday evening, Steve had to walk his adopted daughter through the trauma of her past, because he had no choice in the social reality they lived in. He had to explain to her that though she was not born to them, God made sure that they found her. She howled and cried and then all three of them cried. They consoled and comforted each other, to heal the wounds of biases hurled at them.

Steve and Linda also found it difficult to get Angela admission into schools because she was white and her parents were black. So, the parents were interrogated, their credentials and motivation rechecked. Sometimes the questions were humiliating because the school administrators would cast subtle aspersions on their character. Some even thought that perhaps this was the second marriage for either Linda or Steve and perhaps the first spouse was white. It was painful to make Angela understand why she was not securing the admission when she had answered all the questions correctly in her assessment. Finally, with the blessings from the good deeds of Steve and Linda, she made it to a private school. Gradually Angela learnt to deal with the colour differences that bothered all others around her more than it bothered her. In school, she would often be asked by her classmates, 'Are they your parents? No, that's just not possible!' She would reply, 'They are Godsend and more than my parents.' Children are innocent, but they can be quite harsh. They can ask straightforward and direct questions, which might hurt one's sensitivities, but how was Steve's little girl supposed to deal with all of it at this tender age? It is ironical how generations of wealthy white American children had been brought up by the servitude of black and brown African-American women. Unknowingly, that fact guided some naïve tender minds.

It was a battle that Steve and Linda fought every day, like soldiers. They became accustomed to people prying about their family background and heritage. Their only regret was what their daughter was subjected to because of their colour. Steve and Linda blamed themselves for the harassment that Angela went through. To make up for it, they simply loved her more.

Sometimes, something does not leave you, no matter how hard you try. Steve and Linda were barraged with questions for the greatest part of their early years with Angela, right from the cashier at the supermarket to a curious neighbour at a neighbourhood ceremony. But they moved forward with a smile on their faces, patiently and objectively alleviating the curiosity of the people around them. As time went by, with every passing incident, Steve hoped that the treatment meted out to Linda and him for being black would not be meted out to Angela. It sometimes bothered him that she was indeed bearing the brunt of having black parents, when she was essentially born white. She deserved better.

Even though Steve and Linda lived through the ups and downs of multiracial parenting and its associated challenges, they never gave up. A sense of holding off their judgements of the ignorant helped them keep on course. Faced with racial challenges, they navigated through the issues through open dialogue and driving awareness of multiracial parenting. Their clear thought process helped them. They learnt how not to let hurtful comments touch their core. Slowly, but surely, their anger became their force to provide for Angela. Steve learnt to deconstruct his ideas and reconstruct them so that it could accommodate the dynamism in black and white relationships. He believed that all three of them were one family and were destined to be together. They felt the need to educate people around them about parenting being fluid and transparent. There was no space to colour it in any other way. Angela grew up learning what humanity is really about and is now successful in her own way.

The colour really is in the mind. The binary thought process that accommodates one type of thinking and abandons the other kind needs to be discarded. Let's not abandon each other and instead, make an endeavour to coexist irrespective of the colour or the nationality. Our thoughts and our ideas have a social and an institutional dimension, which successfully supersedes darkness of biases. We are lured by socially imposed values to believe in that which is untrue, baseless and falsified. Hence, our quest for truth and facts should continue to motivate us to adopt a more authentic thought architecture so that the populace is not divided into segments by our own minds.

Looking at things or situations factually without judgement helps us to see them with a clear lens. It perhaps helps us understand things much better. It teaches us how to be thoughtful. Our unproven hypothesis about people and places can be soiled by our imagination, bias or perceptions. Hence when overwhelmed with an emotion—pause, reflect, inquire for facts and then decide. Find the objective truth, without any distortion. Objectivity removes the clouds in the minds and the dust in the haze of muddled thoughts. It is only then we can truly understand how people were really meant to be. They may be different, yet they an extension of ourselves.

Altruism, Affinity and Affection: Benevolence without Bias

Jhumpa was sent to South Africa on an international assignment by her software services company and she narrates how she lived and witnessed the unexpected.

'*Hallo! Goeie more! Hoe gaan dit met jou? Waar kom jy vandaan* [Hello! Good Morning! How are you? Where are you from]?'

Jhumpa's prospective neighbour greeted her in her own language when she was just about to enter the house, which was going to be her home for the next few years. She was sent to South Africa on a large-scale IT project by Fifo Technologies. It was an interesting phase of her life as she had not contemplated working overseas earlier. Jhumpa was a happy young woman, five feet in height, with a dusky colour. Her parents were originally from Bangladesh who had settled there after the partition. She had heard of a large number of racist and safety issues in South Africa and if she was honest, she was quite apprehensive to work and stay there.

However, in retrospect, she realised that her beautiful experience in South Africa taught her real affection and concern for one another that goes far beyond racial boundaries. She reflected how life becomes richer if you can objectively embrace the diversity around you. Her client in South Africa was one of the largest retail chains in the country and had a mix of Afrikaan-speaking blacks and whites as employees. This gave her ample opportunity to learn and engage with local communities.

However, the senior leadership in the company consisted largely of white people; black employees were generally at the lower and middle level of the hierarchy. Jhumpa was heading the delivery project and had to oversee the delivery of the end product. Because of her short stature, she had always struggled to make her presence felt in the office, and now she had her brown colour to deal with among black and white Afrikaans. Who wondered which 'camp' she actually belonged to?

Given the evolving racial landscape in the country, she was advised by her black colleagues to be careful with regard to her interactions with white people in senior management. Her white seniors shared with her that she must be diligent in ensuring all her black colleagues were not 'lazing' around. All this left her a bit perplexed in this mixed-race work environment. It was her first project outside her country and she was determined to make it work. She carefully got to know the relevant information about most people around her before letting the varying shades of colours taint her lens. Her work environment was a bit factitious which made her pause and study them to see the reality in the way it really was with regards to the history, present dynamics and everyone striving for a better future. There were white Afrikaans in the team who had a predisposed, not-so-positive view of her capabilities as they equated her with black cliques. This was likely driven by the social attitudes in that country during the time Jhumpa was there. A white operations manager in the company displayed continued dissatisfaction towards her with reasons that were not apparent. Jhumpa could not fully understand what drove it. She tried to do her best at work and attempted to bridge gaps with him. She tried to engage with him, and diligently incorporated his inputs while working on the project with fellow team members. But the dry and condescending attitude of the operations manager refused to change as far as she was concerned. Jhumpa attributed this to his apparent discomfort of working with coloured people.

As time passed by, Jhumpa felt slightly frustrated with this dynamic at the workplace. Her manager became a wall in the engagement that she sought from the seniors. In spite of her incessant efforts to engage with the black team members, they remained suspicious of her. She struggled, but kept her calm and did not generalise. She could see from her newly acquired knowledge and exposure to the country that divisions in her workplace were a reflection of the local community. She started to feel that she needed to really get into the cultural fabric by doing some volunteering work to help the local community and perhaps that would help her integrate better. She was determined to find friends and remained hopeful.

Just then something happened!

One early morning, Jhumpa got up feeling quite unwell. She had cramps in her stomach and knew something was amiss. She had been working long hours everyday and her staple dinner was a takeaway sandwich. Her body had had enough of it and was retaliating quite venomously with pain. Tears rolled down her cheeks and she screamed in pain, but no one heard. There was no one around. More tears rolled down, this time of loneliness. The oral medicines were not helping and her electrolytic balance was dangerously low. Jhumpa's neighbours called her, but she was not in a condition to answer their persistent calls.

Then Steven and Stacy, her worried black neighbours (after many ignored phone calls), broke open the door of her house only to discover Jhumpa in an ill and horrifying condition. Little did she know then that Steven and Stacy were going to be her saviours. Jhumpa was losing consciousness and could barely stand. Steven and Stacy carried her, made her sit in the backseat of their car and drove her to the nearest hospital. Jhumpa was immediately given intravenous antibiotics and electrolytes. Jhumpa had also contracted pneumonia and was suffering from lung infection, unable to breathe.

Steven and Stacy were joined by a few white colleagues from her office. They stayed in the hospital through the entire night. Stacy and Steven were there for Jhumpa, along with her white colleagues, to provide all the support she needed. Their intent was genuine and their concern was human. When Jhumpa's client discovered her condition, one of the white representatives of the company with whom she shared a good camaraderie, visited the hospital to see her. Jove, the white Afrikaan in her team, along with his wife, prepared Indian meals for her and brought it to her house everyday once she was discharged from the hospital. Jhumpa had never imagined that she would be so lovingly looked after by people in a foreign country who were now like her compatriots. She found a compassionate friend in some and a caring family in others. Her patience, hope, faith and this illness had brought some members of the black and white communities together.

Jhumpa, who a few weeks back was struggling at work and was unsure if she was coping well in this country, had been suddenly exposed to the compassionate face of the same people. This changed her outlook and restored her faith in her path of understanding colour. 'Don't generalise and don't judge till you have evidence' became her mantra. Her office experience initially drove her to misbelieve that the people in the country were fragmented and biased. Whereas the support she received during her illness made her realise how caring and supportive people of different communities/races could be in times of need. Every individual had their mindsets, but that may not speak for the entire race. She was pleasantly surprised at the kind of difference in behaviour displayed by individuals with the same skin colour and same birth place and the same culture. What really explains the difference? It is the lens through which different people conceive and perceive diverse people and diverse situations.

It was an experience that Jhumpa treasures till date.

Jhumpa did face apathy in office, which was induced by racial prejudices, but on the other hand, she also received the care she was yearning for. She did not have the slightest forethought when she set foot in this country that she would form relationships, which would last for a lifetime. She coexisted with multiple cultures and this diversity led to more harmony in her life. After her illness, the relationships with a few people in South Africa became so warm and pleasant that it never occurred to her that she was living a multicultural life. Jove, Steven, Stacy and Jhumpa did not let their origins interfere with their relationships with each other. They had a human connect because they had the desire and the willingness to learn about and learn with each other.

At the end of it, we are all made of the same emotions and we all have a heart, which responds to love and care. All we need do to help ourselves is to find the real truth in people by keeping ourselves focused on experiences and information that is authentic, and not handed down from elsewhere. Jhumpa's tenure in South Africa made her realise that a large heart and an even larger mind with real insights have no place for prejudices. The onus is on us, human beings, who inhabit the earth to ensure that we do not look at people through a narrow mind.

Objectivity is driven by the realism of life. It complements compassion, which arises when we can see things clearly. That gives rise to real human connect. Sometimes there is no common measure of assessing everyone as each individual is different. Behaviours are not usually ethnicity driven, they are mindset driven, which are different for each one. Generalisations can be dangerous and can lead to wrong judgements, thereby impacting our interaction with the world in a skewed way. Keeping ourselves free from judgement helps us to choose the right path.

Coexistence and Co-Creation

'Diversity: the art of thinking independently together.'
—Malcolm Forbes

Why is coexisting so difficult? Rather why is coexisting with people from different cultures so difficult? The reason is that we tend to be guided by the past where similarity fosters belongingness. This may be a fallacy, however this false wisdom tends to influence our thoughts and reasoning, curtailing objectivity. It is easier to go along with what is being said rather than testing it as that takes efforts. Also, beliefs become a part of our identity and challenging them implies we are challenging our being, which may create uncomfortable dissonance unless one is quite self-aware.

Coexistence with similar or dissimilar people in the long-term is driven by compatibility of thoughts and purpose. However, most times, we eliminate people from our circle of acquaintances basis what we perceive of their physicality to start with. Colour is an obvious driver and there could be others. This is a lost opportunity indeed. Respecting differences is the first step in the process of acceptance and consequently coexistence. God made us slightly different on the same planet. He could have put different colours on different planets if we were not meant to be together! Perhaps we need to dwell on the idea that being different is as normal as being similar. However, this requires one to make a mind shift, which is easier said than done. A first step towards this is asking ourselves 'why' whenever the feeling of not engaging with someone we don't know well surfaces. Objectively gauging the reasons that our mind throws up may give us clues about what's holding us back. Often I have heard people say, 'Oh! That person did not look too friendly or approachable.' How would you know what that person thinks if there has been no engagement? Looks can be deceptive and subjective interpretations may not be the reality. Open and objective minds throw up new thoughts for us. You can be objective if you have the courage to think in an unconventional manner. Your own thoughts might shatter perceptions and open your thinking chambers to face the truth. In this exploration, you should not be fearful of any dissonance as it is simply an indication of a new way of looking at life. Just keep going on to discover this new world.

In the age of global and multinational organisations, which operate across multiple geographies, cultures and time zones, companies do want to ensure the smooth operation of diverse teams across their branches in various countries. They do want to successfully navigate cross-cultural strategies and market differentiators to increase efficiencies and achieve their targets through productive performance. Successful companies do it on the foundation of optimising the potential of local talent with a deep global connect and understanding. This is usually done through open-ended processes and feedback where both sides are willing to engage with mutual respect and accept ethnic diversity as a competitive advantage. This anchor acts as a strong propeller for innovative ideas and diverse action plans.

The business case for coexistence and co-creation in the corporate world is of paramount importance because it is influential in building a purposeful value proposition for employees. The relationship between diversity and financial performance provides a strong economic and business argument for the adoption of policies, which promote diversity with regards to gender, race and ethnicity in the organisation. It is a strong nudge for the decision makers in various forms to approve and implement such policies. We find companies tracking ethnicity targets, but multiple research extend to find less ethnic diversity at leadership tables. Even today if you review the top Fortune 500 or FTSE companies, their boards and management team are not as 'colourful' as desired. One wonders why? This is top of the house leadership, has the data, understands the rationale, but still the momentum to drive ethnicity needs to be strengthened. This situation exists because there is no one to raise their voice, as a minority, on those leadership tables in many companies.

A research study conducted by McKinsey & Company spanned a range of industries in the UK, Canada, the US and Latin America, for the years 2010 to 2013. The study effectively demonstrated that companies with more diverse employees enjoy increasing returns because of improved customer satisfaction, decision-making, employee satisfaction and the ability to win high-quality talent. This implies that companies with a more diverse set of employees have a higher level of competitive advantage because the diversity in terms of gender, ethnicity and experience enhances the ability of such firms to retain talent.

The analysis revealed much more than just a statistically significant relationship between a highly diverse leadership team and better financial performance. It proved that diversity acts as a competitive differentiator due to which market share logically shifts towards companies which are more diverse than the others. In the US, companies with 10% higher gender and ethnic diversity on management teams and boards had an EBIT (earnings before interest and taxes) that was 1.1% higher, whereas in the UK, companies with same diversity levels had an EBIT almost 5.8% higher. There was a 35% higher likelihood for companies in the top quartile of racial or ethnic diversity to enjoy financial returns above their national industry median.

It is worth noting that the level of racial or ethnic diversity of a company provides higher likelihood, by several percentage points, as compared to gender diversity, for the company to see higher financial returns than their national industry median. Among all the countries, the US particularly showed ethnic diversity to have a much stronger impact on financial performance than gender diversity.

The following figures show how diversity and the component of diversity correlate with poor or better financial performance.

Figure 4.1 How diversity correlates with better financial performance

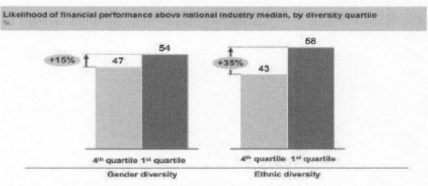

Source: McKinsey Diversity Database. 'Diversity Matters' Report. 2015

There were a few insightful takeaways from the research:

1. In the UK, whites form 90% of the labour force and the rest 10% are composed of coloured people. If the data for labour force diversity in the UK is taken into cognisance, out of the 107 companies, there are 13 companies that enjoy diversity levels in the range of 1–10%, 11 companies fall in the diversity level range of 11–20%, 8 companies fall in the range of 21–30% and 3 companies fall in the range of 31–40%.

2. In the US and Brazil, the number of companies in the higher levels of diversity range is lower when compared with their labour force diversity figures. The total number of companies taken for the US is 186 and that for Brazil is 67.

3. In the UK, the percentage of companies not representative of ethnic diversity is 78% as compared to their labour force diversity, which is lower when compared to the US and Brazil. UK overall scores better.

Figure 4.2 Compared with other countries, the UK is doing a better job in racial diversity, though it still faces challenges

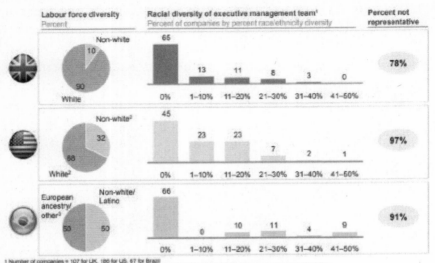

1 Number of companies = 107 for UK, 186 for US, 67 for Brazil
2 Undocumented labour force, largely Latino, estimated at 6 to 8 million (Bloomberg, Pew), has not been included in the breakdown
3 Other includes mixed race, African ancestry, native

Source: McKinsey Diversity Database. 'Diversity Matters' Report. 2015

Coexistence and co-creation are only possible when the mind breaks through conventional fetters to embrace neutrality at the start of any relationship, including that of employer and employee. We need to make an effort to be detached from the opinions about certain nationalities or skin colours so that we can involve ourselves in the process of being more inclusive. So long as we continue our quest to hunt for facts to corroborate our beliefs and ideas, we will reinvent our view of the world. Organisations become a larger social mirror of group think and need to focus on evidence-based thinking to ensure different ethnicities coexist today, to co-create innovative solutions for tomorrow. Living in a plural world can be tricky because we have to keep shifting the spheres of our sensibilities and our consciousness to adapt to a new place, a new idea and a new culture.

Peaceful Coexistence: A Challenge Indeed?

The thought of moving into our rented house in London had a calming effect on the entire family. Most people who have moved cities or countries can share the unsettling feeling associated with such moves that can only be assuaged when you find another home, your bed, your cupboard and, of course, your loo!

The house we chose was on Fitzjohns' Avenue in Hampstead, London, a distinguished area known for its serene surroundings, the Hampstead Heath, poets, literature, art, Camden, etc. It was a conversion house, with our apartment on the second floor. We had carefully evaluated the size, elevator, gardens, distance from school, neighbourhood and we were pleased with our final choice.

Our boxes arrived and over the next few days, we hurriedly opened each box to set things in order. The smell of your own possessions brings back comforting memories that help you settle quickly in a particular place. Happily, days passed by, weeks passed by and months passed by. We had come to realise that unlike our home country, culturally here, you don't simply knock on the neighbours' door or ring their bell unless you must. People coexist, but do not always connect as liberally. Conscious of our new environs, we simply followed the code. Only on Diwali, I did take the liberty of sharing some homemade sweets with three other families who resided in the property in other apartments.

One day the managing agent of the property called me to tell me that our immediate next door neighbour had complained of some smoke coming out of the chimney of our kitchen. I panicked and called my nanny at home to check in and she confirmed that there was no issue, however, smoke may have been driven by the boiling lentils that she was preparing for my son. I reconfirmed to the agent and informed him about the same. All good, all safe! However, next week I got another call from him that again a similar smoke and smell was emanating from the chimney. I called the nanny again and this time she was preparing cottage cheese curry for the children. I informed the agent, again. The week after that I got a call from the agent who apologetically stated that the neighbours had complained again of the smoke that comes through the chimney. He was actually subtly advising me to go slow on cooking, especially Indian food, as it is smoky and 'smelly'!

I was quite perplexed by the incident. It made me feel that I was being indirectly told that my cuisine and my lifestyle were interfering with the existence of other communities in the neighbourhood. I did not wish to do that. Hence in the spirit of camaraderie, I had refrained from complaining about the summer barbeque smell and smoke from the neighbouring apartment, which was a mid-week and weekend ritual for them. I was a vegetarian so the meat smell was not a pleasing one for me to bear with either. I was tolerant, but that was not to be reciprocated. This constant complaining made me feel as though I was purposely being targeted, because I was different, our ways of being were different and we were brown. I would have preferred if they had spoken to me and we had worked this through more amicably. I thought about it again and was unsure if we were really causing inconvenience or were we being singled out as the only brown family around. I was paying full rent, cooking basic stuff, was collaborative, but once or twice a week, a curry smoke was bothering our neighbours more than his barbeque smoke bothered anyone else. Being a vegetarian, I was expected to live with the smoky meat smell irrespective.

At this stage, I had had enough and told him that we ate all kinds of cuisine as hopefully they did too. My housing contract did not specify what I can cook or not. The agent could discuss the issue of the chimney facing the neighbour's balcony, with my Greek landlord (in Santorini)! They could choose to reconstruct and change the direction of the chimney, but, completely eliminating the ingredients of the cuisine that was a staple diet for us was not possible. More so, when we had been tolerant and never complained about the smoke from the barbeque emanating from their chimneys. The agent quietly slinked away realising that this may potentially become a bigger issue. We were mindful of not creating inconvenience in the community we lived in, however, we expected some amount of tolerance or mutual solution exploration to help each other. Time passed by and the noise ebbed a bit. I thought the issue had settled, but clearly we were in for another surprise!

My daughter used to park her little bicycle near the entrance where most cars were parked. The agent had advised us to do this after due checks. However, to my horror, I found one day that her cycle had disappeared. I was convinced that someone had broken the lock and stolen it, hence requested the agent to file a police complaint as per the local norms. The agent seemed reluctant, which felt quite strange.

After much back and forth, my neighbour sheepishly told me that it was he who had removed the cycle. I was aghast and asked him why he would do that. He replied that he felt it could fall on his brand new convertible Porsche, parked next to it and might scratch it. It was the most foolish explanation in my view. If there was a concern, it needed to be discussed and the place of parking the cycle could have been changed, but why have it removed and thrown away without our permission. This felt like a real breach of the line in community living.

The neighbour had tried his best to ensure that our stay in the locality would be so troublesome that out of sheer frustration we would voluntarily leave the place. It was obvious to me that he had not dealt with people of colour or race, instead his unfavourable views about them drove his reactions. Another family on the ground level confirmed this, when they saw us agonising over the cycle. It was apparent that he was conniving to harass us as we made him uncomfortable by just being 'us'. Why he behaved in this manner was not relevant to us, what was important was that we had not given him the permission to do this to us.

At this point, I was completely peeved off, so along with the agent I went to the neighbour's door, rang the bell and requested him to come out for a chat. For a change, he graciously obliged. I was calm and firm about what had just happened and firmly advised him how unacceptable it was. It needed to be compensated with an apology and in damages. He was not happy with the agent sharing the details of the 'bicycle disappearance' with us. He looked visibly frustrated and embarrassed (as if he had been caught out) as I continued to puff out the words. In a firm tone, I did share that I will need to take it up with the agency and my lawyers given these incidents were targeted and amounted to harassment. The agent tried his best to pacify me, but I refused to give in. His act had felt demeaning enough to me. I was confused that inspite of adhering to the agreements, we were being treated differently. I did file a complaint with the property services and received an official apology with a full reimbursement on damages, however, that did not heal the damage done to our dignity. I had come from a different country, but I was not flouting any rules. I had the capability to work in this country and was hired to contribute to my host country through my professional services. No one was doing anyone any favours here. I paid my taxes and contributed towards the economy of the country. Anyone thinking rationally would appreciate that I was adding more and subtracting less by staying in that country. This unwelcome behaviour was partly born out of the confusion in a mixed-race community where biases were imposed without any objective thought about their background, education and profession. It was a learning that equality is more than the sum of its parts. The message between the lines is subtle but that is where the biases rest.

Our company liberally moved us to another house close by which was more comfortable and in a more inclusive surrounding. After this incident, my husband and I remained cautious in the times to come. We had been rudely awakened by the fact that fair and objective rules don't guide people's behaviour; their irrational emotions do.

While we were staying in London, we wanted to do what was appropriate in that environment. Surely when we were performing all our duties, then we could live our life the way we wished to without hurting anyone else. However, sometimes the wilful suspension of consciousness of a few people leads to a situation wherein they are not accepting of alternative ways of being and blindly propagate their beliefs. Keeping ourselves objective and open is a key to a happy community living.

TRUTH OF THE WIDENING RACIAL WEALTH GAP

Human beings of different hues may be subjected to varying levels of exposure to racism depending on which part of the world they may be residing. The complex nature of the conditioned human mind to discriminate basis these factors limits connect and relationship development opportunities. Consequently, this results in the inequity of wealth and well-being. The data on the wealth gap between blacks and whites in the US denotes that it has widened over the years and even today, a large number of black people are at the bottom of the income pyramid.

Homogeneous communities breed on their good and bad attributes. The absence of mixed communities leads to a repetitive pattern of achievements or lack of it as in the past. Reason being people are programmed to believe and do what their ancestors have done. They derive their identity from them. Unless a colourful mix of diverse individuals breaks that cycle and awakens people to look at life differently, rise for their well-being and enable each other, the vicious perpetuity will continue. People who are uneducated believe that is how it was meant to be and people who are wealthy believe that it is rightfully theirs. Entitlement can be changed through different ways of doing things collectively.

> *'Everyone can enjoy a life of luxurious leisure if the machine-produced wealth is shared, or most people can end up miserably poor if the machine-owners successfully lobby against wealth redistribution.'*
> *—Stephen Hawking*

In 2016, African Americans owned one-tenth of the wealth of white Americans. The median wealth for non-retired black households (twenty-five years or older) was less than one-tenth of white households. Lately, the wealth of the black people increased at a faster rate than the wealth of the white people but starting point for black people has been so low, that there is still a long way to catch up. At the median, however, black people still owned less than 10% of white people's wealth. African Americans have a lower likelihood to have access to savings for emergency and a higher likelihood to experience negative income shocks due to a variety of factors like lack of access, past practices, biases, self-belief and resistance in the ecosystem. Hence, black households are in a greater need for personal savings than the white households. In fact, African Americans are less likely to be homeowners than other Americans and have fewer assets than the white people. In 2016, black people under debt owed $35,560, which is less than 40% of the amount of debt owed by white people ($93,000). Black people have historically owned high amounts of high-interest debt making them a high-risk community.

The phenomenon of 'systematic inequality' is widening the wealth gap between the black people and the white people in the US. It is creating a vicious cycle of economic struggle for the blacks. The disparity between the two groups of people has existed for generations because the policies across the ecosystem have implicitly or explicitly favoured the white people or discriminated against the black people.

African Americans lag behind their white counterparts as far as the rate of wealth creation is concerned even if they purchase a house, pursue higher education or secure a good job. Education drives wealth. Wealth is a crucial determinant of economic mobility and is more concentrated than income among the richest households. The study on 'Systematic Inequality' by Centre for American Progress also indicates that African Americans with little wealth are far more economically insecure than a small number of vulnerable white people who own less wealth as well.

A study of wealth and income shares of the top 20% of income earners by race and year in the US reveals:

1. In the 1990s, the richest 20% of the black people owned 51.5% of the total amount of wealth owned by all the black people in the US and that number has increased to 64.9% in 2016.

Figure 4.3 Wealth is substantially more concentrated than income

Wealth and income shares of top 20 percent of income earners, by race and year

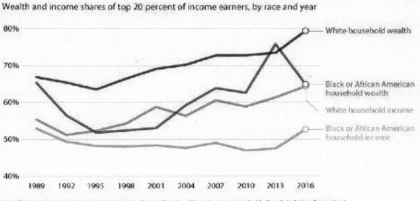

Note: Shares are based on separate distributions for white and black or African American households. Sample includes all nonretired households 25 years and older.

Source: Authors' calculations based on data in survey years from 1989 to 2016 from Board of Governors of the Federal Reserve System, "Survey of Consumer Finances (SCF)," available at https://www.federalreserve.gov/econres/scfindex.htm (last accessed October 2017).

CAP

Source: Centre for American Progress. 'Systematic Inequality' Report. February 2018

2. In 2016, the median wealth for black people amounted to $13,460. The median wealth of the white people was $142,180 and this implied that the median wealth of the black people was less than 10% of the whites. The Recession (2007–2009) caused far greater damage to black wealth than to white wealth due to which the wealth gap widened in the past decade. From 2013 to 2016, the racial wealth gap, which is the ratio of the median black wealth to median white wealth has narrowed slightly.

3. Even with regard to retirement savings, the amount of savings owned by the black people is approximately one-third of the savings owned by the white people; black people had $23,000 in savings, while white people had $67,000.

The changing dynamics of wealth distribution has to objectively start at the grassroots community and race level. Education and awareness help mitigate this and take the efforts beyond colour and race. Among minorities, exposing people earlier in life to possibilities, options and guidance available helps them break free from the identity formed in the past. Concurrently, taking support from well-to-do communities and engaging them to be a part of this journey helps. However, this is easier said than done! We do find that most races and communities do not open up to mingling so easily. Old age factors of comfort and familiarity create strong resistance. Also, the concept of wealth is always relative to poverty.

Cosmopolitan cities like London, New York City, Singapore and Hong Kong are great examples of what magic diversity can create. These cities have a good mix of races and communities that has led to an uplift of thoughts across mixed generations of children, evolving culture and overall prosperity.

The Life of a Multiculturalist

'My dada is Japanese and mother is European and I am Japanean!' This is something, which Carolene used to sing around as a child while growing up in Japan. It was quite amusing for Carolene to find people confused when she said that. Generally in Japan the answer to the question, 'Where do you belong?' was quite simple. It was just one word—'Japan'. But, Carolene was told later on in her childhood that this question had an even longer answer. She was told that her mother was an American, but of European descent and her father was Japanese but for the large part of his life had lived outside his own country. Carolene could not identify herself as Japanese in Japan. Somehow she felt she was quite different from the natives of that country. Even her name, Carolene Deseko, was a different one—half Japanese and half English or American.

Her parents consciously put her in an American school as opposed to a Japanese school. She did not entirely look like a Japanese. Japan was, and still is, a fairly homogeneous country with similar sounding and similar looking people with hardly any inter-racial marriages between different communities. Those who looked different were treated differently and that is why the diverse crowd in the American school was better suited to Carolene, especially in the context of her origins. The white children were quite the minority in her school, and then there were Filipinos, African Americans and various other ethnicities. A lot of US military personnel married local women. Hence, the

American school was full of biracial children. Reflecting back on her experience with a multi-ethnicity schooling, Carolene realised that attending a purely Japanese school would have given her a feeling of loneliness, a feeling of being left out, which definitely did not seem desirable at that young age.

In school, Carolene had a few European and Filipino friends and she got along pretty well with the African Americans. Her dad's Japanese family were regular visitors at home, so Carolene was quite familiar, amiable and friendly with her Japanese cousins and relatives. It was expected that she should engage with her blood relations frequently and her dad was very keen on ensuring that she got along well with her aunts and uncles. Carolene did wonder as to why most of her dad's family looked almost the same when her mom's family did not. Given that her facial features indicated a mixed-race, as a child, she did feel like the odd one out, leading her to behave in a coy demeanour, which was a natural consequence. She often felt, as and when she was oscillating between multiple identities, she was trying to wear different masks. She found the Japanese language quite difficult to pick up and was much more comfortable with English, especially because she went to a school where most children were bilingual or spoke only English.

She got a rude shock when she went to the US at the age of eighteen to pursue further education. It was quite arduous and exasperating for her in the first year to deal with the 'disorganised' American culture in contrast to the orderliness, tranquillity and discipline of Japan. She was used to a culture that was contemplative and thoughtful. In the US, she felt everyone was loud and large. She was astonished at the huge portions of food that were served in the restaurants relative to bento boxes in Japan. She realised that in her host country, it was a perquisite to win and winning was important. The 'aggression', relative to Japan, was quite starkly visible to her, among the men and women in the US. She found it quite difficult to reduce the sombre Japanese part of her to get attuned to the American way of being! She struggled with who she was and who she wanted to be in the US.

She looked different, behaved differently and that made people distance themselves from her. Not many would talk to her and it was even tougher to find friends. She gradually navigated her way with Asian friends, joined study groups, clubs and expanded her circle. Her evolution commenced with the baptism in cultural and racial fire pans. She tried, failed and then adapted, and then started liking the creative orientation of that country. After spending sometime understanding the US, her mind started to open up objectively to the immense possibilities that the place may have had for her.

People have a mind of their own and they tend to do what works in the best possible way for each of them rather than for the collective. Carolene was exposed to acultural and racial tension in the US, which initially left her a bit confused. The American population in the cities was diverse, but there was a certain amount of indulgence given to racial profiling. This is something, which never bothered Carolene in Japan probably because Japan was way more homogeneous than the US. She often wondered whether too much diversity was harmful for people to coexist? She studied American history quite extensively, which taught her quite objectively that the greatness of the country was founded on its diversity.

She understood that it is difficult for the human mind to remain objective all the time but it can be practised in moments that matter. On a positive note, when Carolene started working in the US, she realised that it is indeed a land of opportunities. If one was a fighter, sincere and industrious, then opportunities were galore. One had a high likelihood to be recognised and rewarded if one had the talent and tenacity. One had to be aspirational and then have the courage to go after their dreams. At work, she felt included and no one was unfair to her.

She understood from her experience that people succeed if they identify their strengths and then place themselves in the right opportunities. In Japan, there were not enough opportunities for outsiders/other races. There were some barriers to entry, even in the professional space. The US had been more accepting of talented and intelligent migrants like her. Japan had a higher respect for its own people and its own culture. Carolene did feel that there was one major difference between the two countries and that was the view on colour. She had never even heard of any crimes based on skin colour in Japan, but such incidents happened in the US and left her quite stunned! She was quite bewildered with this reality.

Once, her work took her for an opportunity in India. She was keen to do this assignment because she had not really worked in an emerging market economy. She loved the chaos, the excitement, the colour, the vibrancy, the diversity and the warmth. It was quite an eye-opener for her when she realised that the people, food, attire and their languages were so different in different parts of the country. There were not only state level differences, but also difference in religious sentiments and the diversity at such a magnanimous scale just blew Carolene away!

She stayed in Mumbai for three years and witnessed many hard-working people there. Their life struggles, as she could see, were real. The density of population was high, there were people everywhere. She was received very well, and she was subtly explained by her local colleagues that it was because she was curiously white! She did not know whether it was the colonial hangover, but she did find it difficult to fathom the fascination for white skin in India. It felt a bit subservient behaviour to her and sometimes embarrassing too, even though she tried to be as normal as she could be.

Carolene's engineering team was diverse in colour, religion, thoughts and jokes. Initially, she felt it would be quite a challenge to manage them. There were inter-regional and intercountry differences. She did not deny that she did witness that people from the southern part of India kept to themselves and those from the northern part kept within their groups. But, what was also evident was the conflict in terms of dark versus light, North versus South and the meek versus the powerful.

During her visit to a big fat Indian wedding in Delhi, she came across a hilarious banter between two women. They were discussing the skin colour of the bride with that of the prevailing daughters-in-law of the particular family. She could fathom from their conversation that they preferred light colour women as brides over dark colour ones. In fact, they went to the extent of discussing the various shades of light and dark skin, which baffled her. The glittery wedding was full of women who were looking three shades lighter than they generally do. Carolene definitely sensed the obsession with colour in this country.

Her husband is American and her children are biracial. Both Carolene and her husband have worked and stayed in different continents and hence they decided that their children should go to an international school, whichever country they worked in, including the US. It was a conscious decision because they wanted their children to be broad-minded and remain objective when they thought about different races. Also, it was very important for Carolene and her husband to help their children understand clearly, the nuances and the fine ideological differences between multiple cultures. From experience, one has seen that children who are put in a cultural environment very early in life acquire the innate tendency to become more adept in dealing with race and colour. They develop the appropriate emotional intelligence and acumen to interact with different cultures more empathetically. The way we react and respond to a person from a particular culture becomes a reference point for our being.

From her experience, Caroline feels, 'Everyone needs to keep judgements in control. Experience life and evolve your learning based on every bit of information that you stumble upon. Connect with people for who they are. Keep your eyes and ears open to understand people, their behaviours, their minds and then peek into their soul.' She feels that everyone needs to unravel the mysterious energy that keeps them together and merry in the midst of forces, which trigger hate. Her multicountry experience gave her deep insights into beliefs/practices of various races, their likes and dislikes, rituals and customs. It took away her judgement of people and situations. All that was left was pure curiosity to uncover facts and find a new way of living one's life. Her appreciation for different ethnic minorities emanated from her own struggles of being a minority in different countries. This in turn heightened her sensitivity to a level where differences became invisible to her.

Objectivity propagates that we focus on truth through data, without being marred by emotions. The mind attempts to distort the reality in line with our past experiences. At times when I am faced with conflicting views and emotions, I try to step out of the bubble literally. I imagine I am outside a bubble, and I can see myself dealing with a conflict. I try and see the situation in its entirety. This helps get a big picture view of the variables, which may have been missed when one was right in the middle of the action. It brings a sense of peace and calm. In situations of ethnic conflicts, this stepping out of a situation helps me get a balanced perspective of diverse views, thereby enabling better quality decision-making.

THE WIRING IN HIRING

An opportunity presented itself and he just could not believe it. It made him nervous, some others envious. He was shortlisted for an interview by one of the country's best technology companies. He did not tell his parents because his plan was to break the news once he had got the job. He was Konbe from Ethiopia. Konbe was the only black person to be shortlisted for the interview among all the applicants. Unsure why, but this made him feel proud of himself.

Konbe was aware that he was going to be facing a panel comprising some experienced and renowned names in the industry. He did have butterflies in his stomach, but he kept his confidence intact, given his strong technical background. It was just the kind of professional opportunity that he had been waiting for. The myriad thoughts in his mind convoluted to form a knot as he sat in front of the panel of four people. The panel was totally white—there was no colour in the panel and it felt a little intimidating to him. Konbe was unsure whether his mind was playing up or was he sensing a real discomfort in the environment.

One interviewer ruffled through Konbe's resume, another made some notes. Even though the process went on, Konbe felt as though they were done with the process in a few minutes. He was quite bewildered to see their countenance. It spoke to him. He felt as if it was telling Konbe, 'Why are you here? Are you supposed to be here at all? You think you can pull this through?' There was no verbal interaction between the panel and him for the first few minutes. There was a stony silence. Konbe had begun to lose his patience, but he thought of his purpose and knew that many of his countrymen dream of such aspirational opportunities. Therefore, he held himself from being intimidated by the panellists and pacified his emotions to respond and not react. He rationalised that the panellists must have seen some merit in his qualifications and professional experience for him to be shortlisted. He felt he may be over thinking about their body language.

The interview commenced and what an experience it was! He was asked his name and its meaning. He was then asked about his origin, and how/why had he come to the country. After he shared the details, they started to ask him about his experience of living in a developed market that was so different from where he came from. Till this point, it was all quite peaceful and comfortable. But the question of how equipped Konbe was to deal with a developed market, what he found challenging and what was easier felt a bit misplaced. He rationalised that they are curious even though it was not entirely relevant for the role at hand. The fact that he had been working here for the last eight years should have been comforting, but it seemed not. One of the white men, a seasoned professional in the industry and known to be quite hard on the interviewees, took over. He flooded Konbe with questions around general knowledge, and his views on relationships that had almost no connection to the job profile, the one he had applied for and the one for which Konbe had sufficient experience and knowledge. The interviewer did not allow Konbe to complete his sentences and interrupted him every time he made an attempt to explain the answer. No questions of relevance on skills, scenario and ambitions were posed to him.

Konbe's throat went dry and at one point he struggled to find his voice. He could see the twisted and ignorant expressions of some of the panellists. He continued to feel humiliated as more unrelated and difficult questions were thrown at him. He wanted to drink some water and breathe some fresh air. He was quite exhausted with the continuous repartee in the interview. His mind had shut down and he just wanted to leave. Konbe had been to many interviews (including with similar white men), but this one seemed quite different from all the earlier ones. The underlying tone was extremely racist.

Konbe had prepared well for this interview, but this was not an interview, it was something else. He felt misunderstood, cornered and ignored. He attributed this to lack of a diverse panel. Konbe was not the most street-smart individual amongst his peers. He could speak well, but English was an acquired language for him. He felt if someone similar to his ethnicity was on the panel, they would have interviewed and understood him better for who he was. He may have or may not have got the role, but atleast the process would have been more objective and fair. This process felt like the panellist were trying to understand his ethnic fit for the role instead of focussing on his capability and skills, which were stellar.

Konbe kept himself calm throughout the whole process, but his attempts to navigate the conversation in a constructive direction failed! Finally, at the end of an hour, it was evident to him that irrespective of the outcome this was not the kind of team he would like to work with. He did not wish to be a part of a working environment where he was judged for being different, he was judged to be a misfit. He pulled out of the process and went ahead with another offer from a company where ethnic diversity was not spoken but embedded in their cultural fabric. Today, he is the CEO of that company and has just acquired this other company, where he had been interviewed years ago.

Sometimes, the contours of our mind tend to get blocked when age-old thinking acts as a layer of rust that prevents new thoughts and new ideas to enter. People lack objective data and tend to be influenced by their ignorance. They tend to be guided by incorrect perceptions that lead to judgements and unproductive outcomes. Our false sense of good judgement can mislead us into believing that we are fairly impartial and indifferent towards various races when we are not. Objectivity requires holding off judgements and living with real facts and what matters.

Truth and objectivity are intrinsically connected. Our emotional views of others influenced by social norms around us, make it distorted. Truth defines the actuality of states of people, places and perceptions. It is a set of assertions based on evidence, fact and faculty, which gives us the real picture and not the falsified one. Therefore, truth tells us 'what is' as opposed to 'what is not'. Natural tendency of human beings is to run away from a discomforting truth or frame it in a way that removes the reality. It is born out of the fact that sometimes truth itself can be quite harsh and may cause social or personal loss. Objective truth should be the real driver for responding to others. It is not subject to interpretations. We do need to redefine the race narratives that distort our vision of the world.

Summary

1. We need to make careful observations to collect facts and process them with reason in a multicolour environment. The correct method of reasoning will help us to find the right story from the right piece of data or observation.
2. There is no common system of measuring everything and everyone. We need to practise objectivity with sensibility so that we are able to conceptualise and define each action and reaction according to the available context and circumstances for people around us.
3. We should make dispassionate and realistic assertions on people. Embracing realism and seeing the truth as it is will help us to identify the girth and see through the misrepresentation of facts.
4. Learn to embrace realities that you have experienced. We should learn to pause on contradictions and make our own well-informed judgements.
5. When we coexist to co-create, we collectively value add. This however is driven by connecting with other diverse people in an authentic way.

Understanding

Avni: 'Mom, I have joined a project team that is working on the mental well-being of students. Because of my previous experience in the area, my professor wants me to anchor the project and lead the team. As much as I find it quite exciting, I have all kinds of students from different countries. I'm not sure if all of them are happy to have me lead them. How do I go about this?'

Mom: 'How much time have you spent getting to know them Avni?'

Avni: 'Well…some of them are easy to talk to, but others are not! I also get a sense that sometimes they do not understand me!'

Mom: 'Okay, let's start with how you communicate.'

Avni: 'Huh! Like I normally do mom!'

Sid(rolling his eyes): 'Duh, she is so confusing mom, I never get her. When she says yes she means a no, when she says no she means yes!'

Mom (ignoring Sid): 'Avni, have you realised that your accent is different, you speak a little faster and the English you use may be different from the English they use, some words may mean different things.'

Avni(sounding confused): 'I don't understand.'

Mom: 'Exactly! Look, the country you are in, people speak differently than you do. So they will take time to understand what you say, so speak slowly to start with. It is sometimes too rude in their culture to stop you short or ask you to repeat. And words may have a different meaning. For example, in India a word like "interesting" has a positive connotation whereas in the UK or the US, it may sometimes have a dubious connotation.'

Avni (a bit bewildered): 'Really! I hadn't realised that!'

Mom: 'Yes, from my experience, once people can understand what you say, they can understand what your intent is. That may not mean they agree, but at least you are now on the same page.'

Avni (smiling): 'That's interesting—in an Indian way!'

Sid (winking): 'Avni di, you are interesting in a British way!'

Mom: 'Once you are able to communicate verbally or non-verbally, you are able to understand people irrespective of who they are or where they come from. However, before communicating, you need to know about what your purpose is and what are you trying to achieve from this engagement.'

Avni: 'That's never a problem.'

Mom: 'Well! You may be surprised, but more often than not, what plays below our consciousness has the biggest influence on how we behave. So be aware of yourself too. Life happens when we are busy doing much else.'

Avni: 'Hmm! Now you got me thinking. How do I do that?'

Mom: 'Explore, think, feel. Keep an open and compassionate mind for yourself and for others. It is all about creating a sense of acceptance for everyone, which opens the doors of their hearts and yours.'

Avni: 'Who am I? Who are you? Who are we? Are we understood?'

Start by understanding yourself fully before understanding others. The buds of empathy bloom when it is nurtured by the elixir of understanding.

'London, here we come!' my daughter exclaimed just as we were to board our flight to London. We were raring to go and start a new journey in a new country, together.

As the aircraft wheels touched Heathrow, our weary family opened their eyes to the bright, sunny London morning. It had been a nine-hour flight from Mumbai to London, with two young children. The soft sunlight welcomed us as the new residents to the beautiful city of London. The excitement overtook the fatigue and we woke up, ready to take on our London sojourn.

We were put up in a serviced apartment in Marylebone that was conveniently located between the high street and a park. We started to get ourselves acquainted with the surroundings and began to get acclimatised with the weather and food over the week. The daunting school search and house-hunt commenced immediately. I had taken two weeks off from work for our relocation and wanted to get all this sorted before my leave ran out. We narrowed down to a school in Hampstead and consequently a house close by, so that the children could walk to school. Happily sorted, we moved into the house over the last weekend before I joined office. Weeks went by and we started feeling more at home and my daughter started settling down in her new school.

Few weeks later, one day, she came back from school and started crying. She was all of seven years and a very happy child. I sat down with her and asked her what had happened. She said that she did not wish to go to 'this' school anymore and wanted to go back to her Mumbai school. She kept sobbing inconsolably and it was evident that something had hurt her deeply. It had really affected her young mind. We agreed to go buy her favourite cupcake from the nearby café. As we sat in the garden by the café, I gently nudged her to tell me what had really happened. She did not cry again with the cupcake stuffed into her little mouth, but her eyes grew moist. She started talking (thankfully) about how she was a bad person! I was really troubled by that statement and asked her what had made her feel that way! She went on to share how, over the last few weeks, most children in her class would not talk to her for some reason and that she was suffering from isolation.

That particular day, two girls had hidden her game kit. Subsequently, she had been pulled up by the teacher for not having a kit, made to sit in the classroom and not go for the PE session in the sports field. It was her favourite class. However, she was too afraid to tell the teacher what the two classmates had done. She let herself be subjected to the ordeal of further isolation and teasing about being a 'funny brown cow'. She was unsure why she was being treated like this, but it really bothered her. She then opened up and told me how some children played pranks on her by hiding her things, speaking rudely and pouring water on her shoes. A British Indian child told her that this happens when you are a brown person. Avni's accent was quite different from the other children in her school and she believed that most of them did not wish to speak to her. Further, she also struggled to understand the British accent in the first few weeks of school.

After having let off steam, I could see her much calmer, munching away her cupcake in pure delight.

As a mother, I was responsible for my daughter's well-being in every which way. I felt really guilty for not doing enough and realised that as parents, we both should have taken the necessary steps to ensure that our daughter transitioned well and not go through this suffering. It seemed to me that my daughter was harshly enduring this agonising time because of our relocation to an entirely new country. Neither we nor the school had made adequate preparations to ensure that she was inducted and enabled to adapt well, to live in a new culture with new people. Her pain hurt me deeply too. This little child, her mind, her feelings created a sense of anger and guilt, which overwhelmed me momentarily. That night I expressed my anguish to my husband who shared my woes and we agreed to take the necessary actions. I couldn't see how happiness is different for any child, brown, black or white. This emotion does not differ with colour.

Next day, I decided to visit the school and meet the head teacher and the class teacher. I was fairly candid about how my child was being treated, and that it was simply not acceptable. The teachers were concerned and a bit anxious. I was unsure if they were anxious because of the issue or the fact that an issue like this could have potential reputational damage for the school. They pacified me that this will be sorted out, but I insisted on a clear plan and accountability given that small children are not always straightforward when it comes to these issues. Their world view is driven by what they see and experience at home, an ecosystem which is not something a school will have control over. So, this matter had to be dealt with delicately. One option given to me was to change Avni's section, which I refused to do as it was not her fault. This could happen elsewhere unless the core issue was resolved.

Finally, it was agreed that the teacher would have class stories around coloured children and biracial families, and the teachers would talk to children about Asian mythology and cultures. In fact the two children, who were playing the pranks and were isolating a few children, would be spoken to through counselling sessions. All of this was worked through, over six weeks. It reaped some great results with the children. The entire class loved stories on Indian mythology and soon started to insist that their parents take them there for a holiday. Avni, my daughter, started to feel more included and she too developed a better appreciation of local culture with her new-found white friends. Colour started to disappear with this understanding and love started to blossom.

Avni went on for a long innings at that school. Recently, she met one of those two girls on her visit to Oxford, grown-up, beautiful and mature! They laughed about that incident and she confessed to her that it was quite a lesson in terms of changing her perspective on colour.

Reflecting back, it was obvious that there was a lack of understanding and exposure of coloured children and cultures for some of the white children in that school. In fact, children are usually very curious to learn about life and people, all they need is the right inputs and knowledge to develop a broader understanding of life. Most of the children in the school came from local households and perhaps inherited their family's world view, which may not always be well-founded. This generational legacy is usually not challenged by young children as they know nothing better. Therefore, as parents we need to help with spreading this awareness. Distance can be reduced between children and adults from different races by having conversations and providing them diverse experiences. Distinctive patterns of behaviour and the verbal or non-verbal mannerisms of people from certain races can be explained. Understanding the differences in such patterns will help enhance the appreciation of the various ethnicities and diverse ways of being.

Understanding emanates from the state of being unbiased and open. It involves making an endeavour to know a person so well that we get much closer to a person's soul. Understanding and empathising involve living in someone else's shoes and wearing their lens to see the world. The human brain is neurologically endowed to feel and have a sense of the other person's state of mind, but often it is blocked by the noise and clutter that we gather about different races along the way. For minorities, the feeling of being judged and observed apprehends a person and prevents him or her from being his or her natural self to understand others as well. Further, the need to understand ourselves is critical because it is through this self-awareness that we understand others better. We can observe tangible truths, and then tie it all together with a string of empathy to develop a sense of understanding of a certain race.

As children, we tend to learn what is taught to us because our sense of comprehension and discernment is in a nascent stage at that point in time. Over time, people can develop a conscious process of empathy, which clears illusions. The elders in a community need to guide the children and not be beguiled by their perceptions and half-truths. It is perhaps our collective responsibility to teach children how to think and not what to think. This may reshape how the future becomes more colour-blind.

SIMILARITY WITHIN DIFFERENCES

Our understanding of people is often smeared by the stereotypes formed in our minds. The human brain has an affinity for making generalisations. It constructs images of a group on the basis of witnessing one individual's behaviour, who belongs to the group. Most of us know this fallacy intellectually, however our unconscious mind prods us to behave otherwise! That's the power of unconscious which can be managed through understanding people with an open mind.

As I started my new assignment in London, my initial focus was to build a team that was capable of delivering the business agenda that I was tasked with. Over the course of the next few months, I interviewed many candidates and then selected a few. As the few came onboard, they built their teams and helped me get even better talent that we could collectively learn from.

Once we had most of the team onboard, I realised that we were such a beautiful motley crowd. Amongst my direct reports, I had a group of French, Indian, Jamaican and British.

Most people on the floor in other teams were curious about how our team dynamics worked given the diverse ethnicities. Our team had come together through merit and strengthened the bonds through a collective empathy and understanding of each other—be it the ways of thinking, approach to work and, most importantly, to friendships.

As time passed by, our diverse team became closely knit. There were common goals that bound us at work. We were not similar, but we complemented each other. Cec was always my third child, Toral remains the best friend that I always wanted, Raz was the rebel friend, John the polite one who reminded us to speak slowly as not everyone understood our varying accents, Jitesh was the calm guy, Leena was the forever young one and Fina kept us on time. There was so much we learnt from each other apart from work that has stayed with us till date. Some of my takeaways were:

1. If Cec is giggling too much in a discussion, then it means she is not happy! She would not express it any more than this.
2. If Toral was upset, you simply knew it as she would be ready to throw things at you!
3. If John was happy, you just get a smile in his eyes, read them carefully without embarrassing him.
4. When upset, Jitesh would be quiet for hours.
5. Leena always wanted to help (even when she did not want to) as she could not say no; in her culture that was simply rude!
6. Fina was open-minded and it was rare for her to keep a secret in our little community. It was indeed her family so everyone had to know everything.

The list goes on. We learnt that what may work in England certainly does not work in France or Jamaica. What worked in India could raise eyebrows or laughter in the UK. Initially, a lot of confusion prevailed on working styles, giving way to bonds as the team persisted to make things work. The key factor that helped us to keep moving on was that we trusted each other, never attributed any personal agenda and supported each other through the journey. We had our moments, but a candid process of discussion, debate and no retaliation was subtly followed. Also, we were conscious about our cabinet responsibility for our collective actions. It mattered to our clients and our team brand.

As I reflect back to the few years that we spent together working, growling and growing with each other, I wonder what made this work.

1. **An understanding of each other as friends before colleagues:** There were differing views on certain situations, but understanding the divergent perspectives helped. Personal and professional boundaries were navigated with trust. We had blurred lines without being too intrusive. I would invite the team for a meal at home as Asian hospitality is about a good meal with friends. If we like them, we feed them, if we love them, we feed them; basically Asians can feed you till you die! John would often schedule beer catch-ups to chat, Cec would ensure we get to the right French bars and Fina would carry home-cooked food to office. Although we were friends, the professional boundaries on accountability were never compromised. Some tough messaging would take place if things went wrong between people; however, the relationship would bounce back to normal as it was built on a solid foundation of understanding and respect.

2. **Breaking the biases:** Knowing each other helped kept biases at bay. We saw each other as people and not as people of colour. We realised that we all had the same ambitions to grow and even though our drivers were different, our values were similar. We felt the same hurt and pain even though sources were different. We felt the same compassion, and the triggers for annoyance were never different.

3. **Trust in our little community:** This was a significant glue that kept us together. We did not second-guess each other. It was an unsaid code that no one breached. Trust begets trust. Knowing

each other helped with trust-building. This trust built a strong relationship so much so that we are in touch with each other even after ten years of moving on. Our little WhatsApp group keeps us virtually together. I know they are there if I ever need them and vice versa!

Understanding each other's thoughts and beliefs infused authenticity in our relationships. We systematically and gently processed what each of us was doing in the professional and personal domain separately. The ability to do this further strengthened our bonds and our connections. Our thinking was open, we allowed ourselves to be porous enough to make corrections and supported each other. We must remember that we are all a product of our experiences and the way in which we borrow from the experiences essentially makes us who we are.

The feeling of reliability punctuated with a sense of understanding assists us in building trust. An openness to reasoning helps us to decode the mannerisms and interpret them in the right way. The wrong interpretation can lead to lifelong misunderstandings. The crucial ingredient in a relationship, just before trust, is understanding and this ingredient can go a long way in making the coloured relationships complete and beautiful, across multiple borders.

Published in 2005, one of the most elaborate and extensive studies on personalities was done by Robert McCrae with the assistance of seventy-nine collaborators around the world. His personality theory has been studied in different cultures and individuals.

The five factor model developed by Robert McCrae and Paul Costa basically enlists the following personality traits:

1. **Openness:** an individual's openness to new experiences.
2. **Conscientiousness:** an individual's thoughtfulness.
3. **Extraversion:** an individual's assertiveness and outgoingness.
4. **Agreeableness:** an individual's concern for other people and the ability to mingle with others.
5. **Neuroticism:** an individual's likeliness of feeling disturbed, depressed or sad.

Further to this, Scientists William Revelle, Luis Amaral and Martin Gerlach from Northwestern University in the US have identified four new distinct personality types—the average, the reserved, the self-centred and the role model. The average personality is someone who scores slightly above average on neuroticism and extraversion, but lower on openness. The reserved are not open or neurotic, but are emotionally stable. The role models score highly on all the traits except neuroticism. The self-centred people score below average in openness, conscientiousness and agreeableness and quite high on extraversion.

The study presented an aggregate trait score for each of the cultures by analysing the personality profiles of 12,000 college students from 51 cultures or races. Most of the personality tests, when given to people from different communities, revealed that the 'average personality' in one country is quite different from the average personality in another country even within the same ethnicity/race. We do tend to associate a typical personality type to a particular country, for example, the British are elite and high-nosed, the Japanese are polite and industrious and so on, but the research suggests that the assumptions may sometimes be widely off the mark for individuals who may be residing in that country or not.

Germans and Danes received the highest scores for 'Openness to Experience', whereas Kuwaitis, Hong Kong Chinese and the people from Northern Ireland got the lowest scores with regard to this trait. Nigerians, Moroccans and Asians got the lowest scores on 'Extraversion' and Brazilians, the French living in Switzerland and the Maltese scored the highest. It is worthy to note that there is quite some overlap between countries and races because these are average scores. However, there might be some people in Indonesia who are much more extraverted than some people in Brazil and, hence, there have also been complications with regard to the interpretation of the results. The personality questionnaire may or may not accurately capture the typical personality trait of a particular race or culture but it does definitely give us an idea of how perceptions may need to be evolved and not hard-coded for every individual as an outcome of averages of a certain community.

The studies, conducted internationally, also show that the basic structure of personality which is organised into five main traits remain the same throughout, but the average trait levels tend to vary between cultures and communities. It is possible that these personality traits may result in different reactions to similar situation from various races.

There is another study conducted by David Schmitt at Bradley University in 2007, which involved surveying 17,000 people from 56 nations/communities. The study revealed that Japan and Argentina scored very high on the trait known as 'Neuroticism' and the lowest scores were received by Slovenia and Democratic Republic of Congo. Interestingly, Japan and Lithuania scored the lowest on 'Agreeableness' on average, but Democratic Republic of Congo and Jordan scored the highest. In fact, with regard to the trait 'Conscientiousness', people in Africa scored the highest as compared to people in any other part of the world. People in East Asia scored the lowest on 'Conscientiousness'. However, it is important to note that one needs to be cautious as interactions on a one-on-one basis change the predictable dynamics between human beings.

The differences in personality traits do exist, and sometimes they are not similar to the popular perceptions or stereotypes of national character. For example, the average British person is considered to be reserved and very polite as compared to the average American, but this generalisation does not apply to everyone. Similarly, Sikhs with a turban or Muslims with a turban are perceived to behave in a certain way or engage in certain activities by the populace at large; and herein comes the importance of understanding. We need to delve deep into a person, through interactions and repeated conversations to get an idea of how that person thinks, feels and functions cognitively.

Sometimes, due to a lack of understanding, we tend to conform to the personality type in a particular community, even if it is our own, on the basis of what we see from childhood and what we are expected to be. There are various reasons which explain the differences in the personality profile, such as the pattern of historic migration in a particular country. People who score high on traits such as openness and are risk-lovers are more likely to migrate.

Differences in personality arise from the way we are brought up in different communities and cultures. Conforming to a popular norm sometimes can rob us of the opportunity of knowing facts that may have changed. Differences in expression might lead to difference in reactions or emotions. The feeling of pain, fear, love and compassion remains the same across all the countries and cultures.

CONVERGENCE OVER A CUP OF COFFEE

It was early morning and Rohan was just rushing into the office for a meeting at 8:00 AM. As he walked towards the elevators in the towering London office, the smell of freshly-brewed coffee wafting from the corner of the reception was irresistible. He was drawn to the Costa Coffee shop like a magnet!

He stood impatiently in the queue, waiting for his turn to pay and to get his shot of awakening prior to the meeting. As he reached the counter, he quickly shelled out £3 for his steaming cup of cappuccino and then waited on the next counter for his cuppa. He presented his bill, but felt he was not seen or heard. A few minutes passed by and his cup did not arrive whilst others who had paid after him had walked away with their cups of coffee.

Rohan looked at his watch and realised he was getting late so he called out for the person across the counter to inquire for his coffee. The server looked at him confused and rudely asked him, 'What do you want?' Rohan said, 'I want my coffee order!' Promptly the server said, 'You need to pay, there is nothing free here for you!' Rohan was stumped, he wasn't sure why this person was talking to him so rudely and assuming he had not paid. He restated that he had paid. Rohan insisted that he had presented the bill, which the person on the counter had not taken from him. The server asked Rohan for the bill again. Fortunately, he was holding the same and gave it to the server right away. The server just shrugged and said 'whatever'. Rohan had kept his calm all this while. He had kind of understood the dynamic. It was apparent to him that the server was unconsciously biased and this was perhaps his usual behaviour with certain people of colour. There was no difference between other people in the coffee shop and Rohan apart from the colour. Yet he was meted out a belittling treatment. He chose not to confront the server wanting to avoid an unpleasant situation in the morning. Rohan was a peace-loving person, but was hurt by the behaviour of the server. His coffee was still delayed and he was unsure what was going on.

Meanwhile, Sonia, a young Spanish management trainee, who was standing at the back and watching the scene, came to the counter and asked the server to apologise not only for the delay, but for the way he had spoken to Rohan who by now was upset, demeaned and annoyed. The server refused citing that he has had instances with a 'few people like this' not paying up. The server did not think there was anything inappropriate in what he did. It was surprising that apart from Sonia, all the others had turned a blind eye to this.

Sonia was quite infuriated to see Rohan being treated like this. She was from Madrid and was bold and courageous. She derived a lot of strength from her beliefs of self-respect having migrated to another country with her family decades back. She had seen her family work their way through bravely to the top. Hence, it was very unlikely for her to be tolerant of this kind of behaviour. She reacted because she had a value system, which compelled her to call out the racist and prejudiced treatment that Rohan was subjected to. Rohan was much more tolerant by nature as he was less conversant with cross-cultural dynamics.

Sonia was brought up in a zero-tolerance environment. She believed in fair play, which urged her to take a step and speak up to the server on his objectionable ways of dealing with a brown customer. She insisted that he apologise for the behaviour and also give a free coffee to Rohan, because of the delay, else she will complain to the management about the discriminatory treatment meted out to him. The server was taken aback as no one had really challenged his beliefs like this amongst the crowd there, leave alone his behaviour in the past. He just thought that this was the normal way of dealing with people. He never really understood the nuances of dealing with different people and was simply driven by ill-conceived stereotypes. Finally, the server conceded, but Rohan was not in any mood to accept this apology; instead he graciously thanked Sonia for stepping in as he fumbled with what just happened. Finally, he dashed out for his meeting.

What really happened here?

The server operated with an unconscious bias. It may have been driven by an experience of the past wherein he erroneously believed that a person with brown skin must be looking for a bargain or a freebie. It may have been based on a one-off experience the server had with someone else, had read in a book or seen in a movie; but, he had needlessly generalised it! His body language, his tone was unnecessarily negative and had left Rohan feeling belittled. Rohan's dignity had been hurt. The server who bred the preconceived idea about brown individuals had refused to open his mind and understand much more than what he already knew. One of the most important steps in trying to understand a person is to let go of the stereotypes in your mind and have the humility to accept the fact that you know close to nothing about that person. That's when the real discovery happens.

Sonia was brave in reacting to the incident in the way she did. Sometimes it is important to make one understand that he or she might have hit a wrong spot unintentionally, or intentionally, and should mend one's ways as appropriate for all. It helps them self-correct.

Understanding in itself is a simple process, but as human beings we tend to complicate it. 'I don't know' is a good place to start with when you move to a new place or meet different ethnicities that you may have had a limited interaction with. It helps you start on neutral grounds. Having assumptions about the behaviour of a particular ethnicity pushes us in a particular direction without fully being conscious of its propriety. We tend to submit ourselves to what we have learnt from others and to what is perhaps perceived as the truth. The lack of understanding between the server and Rohan was evident but the reason behind that possibly was quite pithy and petty. Rohan tried his best to be calm and composed, but the server overlooked his good nature and behaviour. The mind needs to be free from incessant droppings of popular public perception to be able to receive a human being for what s/he is and not what s/he represents.

> *'The improvement of understanding is for two ends: first, our own increase of knowledge; secondly, to enable us to deliver that knowledge to others.'*
> —*John Locke*

THE GOOD, THE BAD AND THE UGLY

Anjana Murthy had been staying in the US for almost two decades and gave a powerful rendition of the paradox, which exists for some Asians abroad.

When her husband and she first moved to the US from India, they had to live on one salary because Anjana was on a dependant visa and could not work. Her husband was a fresh graduate from an engineering college. They felt life was not as good as it was made out to be in the US until and unless one had better financial capital than they had then. Her husband and she were well-educated individuals who shifted to the US for better opportunities and a better life which was yet to shape up.

Anjana's husband, Shouvik's colleagues were very understanding of their circumstances. They were mostly white people and were very kind to them. Shouvik was great at building relationships and his hard work won a lot of hearts at office. His colleagues helped them find a new house and school for Ishaan, their son. Anjana was pleasantly surprised at the respect they had for her husband. Many of them had worked outside their countries and had a good understanding/empathy for people who leave their homes. They appreciated Anjana and Shouvik's willingness to stretch their boundaries (literally and figuratively).

After Anjana's home was set up, they needed a television set. She found a store in the mall close by that was offering good deals. So, the two of them set out, dressed in their not-so-posh Walmart clothes with just enough money to buy a TV. They got into their second-hand car and went to the mall. Usually in these stores, the sales people approach the customers and offer help. They walked around the store waiting for one of the sales personnel to come to them. The sales personnel were mostly Caucasians and were not very busy as there were hardly any customers in the store. Anjana felt a bit strange about this.

All the salesmen and saleswomen nonchalantly ignored them and they both were too timid to ask for help. So after an excruciating period of searching with lack of guidance, they left without a TV. Anjana and Shouvik were a bit perturbed by the behaviour of the sales personnel in the mall. They struggled to reconcile the two different kinds of behaviour—one of Shouvik's colleagues in his company and that of the salesmen in the mall. On one hand, they had white people helping them to survive in Chicago, and on the other, they had local sales personnel who ignored them. They understood that these were perils of ethnicity reality that they needed to deal with. Anjana braced herself again and went on to buy the TV from another small shop that did not have the deal but treated them like any other customer.

Since then, they have had many TV sets, the best that money can buy. But Anjana did not forget that brief trust with humiliation, which was her first brush with biased mindsets in a new country. She was hurt and irate with this incident, but after gauging the environment, she realised that the salespeople in the mall did not bother to take them seriously because that is what they had learnt to do. The city was dominated by white people and there had been a general perception that people from developing countries do not have deep pockets. Anjana and Shouvik did not have deep pockets, but had enough money for what they needed. The sales persons' reluctance to attend to them indicated a lack of empathy for people of different ethnicity. Their idea of 'people from developing markets' would have improved, had they spoken to them as shoppers. Instead, they chose to completely ignore them and in the process disrespected their presence altogether. Understanding requires a positive intent and disposition to respect the other person and engage with them as equal partners. That is the starting point of understanding another individual in any situation across any race.

A year later, Anjana's parents were visiting them. Her son, Ishaan, and she took 'Ma' (mother) and 'Baba' (father) to another city close by. They had a wonderful time, shopped in the mall and had a picnic lunch. They used the metro to go around the city because parking in the city was very painful to find. Ma did not like using the escalators because she was apprehensive of her sari getting stuck in them. She usually took a few seconds to gather herself and then got onto the escalator. People around her in public places usually waited for her to get on the escalator. They were usually polite and patient as Ma fumbled her way through. On the return leg, as Ma had to get on to an escalator again, she went through the usual ritual of holding her saree and waded her way slowly on the escalator. There was a man, waiting behind Ma, who became increasingly irate at her slow pace. He said to her in a demeaning, aggressive voice, 'Why don't you people just go back to where you came from.' These words were eloquently espoused by a white, middle-aged man who himself was helping his old mother get onto the escalator. His wife glared too and Ma was quite startled and embarrassed. Ma stepped aside and allowed the white gentleman to go with his family first. Anjana was red with fury and tried her best to gain control over her tongue when another old white gentlemen retorted back to the statement made by the middle-aged man, saying, 'And who gave you the power to decide and command whether they should live here or go back?'

It was quite intriguing to note that one white person was not empathetic towards Anjana's mother and chose to belittle her whilst the other challenged him. It played out beautifully where it reaffirmed her faith that all kinds of people exist in the world, but one should never lose faith in humanity. Some people understand and some don't, and that should not be generalised to one race or community. She felt affirmed that good people exist, irrespective of colour, who will step in to support people for the right cause when needed. She could have indulged in a debate with the not-so-pleasant white person, but her value system would not allow her to do that and that too on foreign land. Anjana attributed that his insensitivity to another race arose from the fact that some people have distorted thoughts and tend to generalise. A few warm words and respectful gestures from a person opens up avenues for further interactions so that all can avail the opportunity to know another person.

We do not need to conform to social biases or norms, we can always exercise our own choice, even though it is not always easy as the behaviour is so programmed. It requires effort to understand the other person, their struggles and their hardships. Making blindfolded comments and coming to unreasonable conclusions might harm other's sentiments. Understanding is important to give ourselves and the others a better experience in the moments we spend together, to give us a sense of fulfilment and that feeling of completeness which we all look for. Life is too short and no one gets out alive so let us be kinder to each other.

The Multi-Ethnic Factor

As per multiple research studies, multi-ethnic individuals are believed to have a deeper sense of understanding of human dynamics across races and therefore may sometimes find it easier to navigate in a global environment. The ability to observe and comprehend the behaviour, attitude and the non-verbal communication of diverse individuals is heightened in multi-ethnic individuals due to their early exposure to different cultures in their families. They are obviously more familiar with different kinds of cultures and are relatively more appreciative of them. The reason being that they themselves have grown up and lived with multiple racial identities and have struck a balance between knowing and attempting to understand the emotional landscape of both or more identities.

There are certain families where the father and mother are individually biracial, then their offspring obviously are multi-racial enabling an easier understanding of different cultures than the rest. For example, it is indeed an opportunity for a child born to an African-American mother and a Mongolian-Japanese father to understand Asian, African and American cultures altogether simultaneously while growing up. Since the child is exposed to a variety of cultures at home right from a very early age, it is but natural that the child will be more accepting of all the three cultures!

A survey conducted by Pew Research Center among multi-racial adults in the US tells us that they are disposed to have better understanding and a more open approach to people of other races and cultures. Around 59% of multi-ethnic Americans feel that their multi-ethnic or mixed-racial background has made them more accepting of other races and cultures other than that of their own. Around 55% feel, as compared to others, they have a deeper understanding of other races and backgrounds. Additionally, 69% of multi-ethnic graduates say that they have felt, when compared to other college graduates, that they have a better understanding of other cultures. In comparison to these, 52% of the multi-ethnic population, which is less educated, say that they are more open to other cultures.

The survey further reveals that three quarters of Asian and white biracial adults are more likely, as compared to other multi-ethnic groups, to acknowledge that their multi-ethnic background has made them more open to other racial groups. Fewer American Indians or American blacks have said that they are more open to other cultures due to their multi-ethnic background. Around 63% of multi-ethnic adults who are white and black and 62% who are white, black and American Indian say that they are more understanding of people from other backgrounds.

But the most interesting piece of data to ponder over is that very few, as low as 19% of multi-ethnic adults say that they can act as ambassadors who can bridge the gap between people of different races or bring them together by reducing the differences between them. That means only three in ten feel that they can bring people from different races closer to each other.

Therefore, the last piece of data essentially tells us that the process of connecting to another individual from a different race by using a multi-ethnic adult is a huge opportunity to explore. We need to understand the cultural and the ethnic nuances of the other culture and focus on insightful observations in order to understand the person's thoughts and ideas. Understanding each other forms an important part of steady cross-cultural connections and associations.

Further, we do need to understand ourselves better to understand others. It can be quite challenging for multi-ethnic adults to gauge who they are and where do they belong. In fact, most of them struggle to live with and identify with their own multicultural identity. Most often than not, they are in a dilemma with regards to which culture they belong to. The physical dissimilarities with their national counterparts also contribute to this confusion. Some of them spend a lot of mind space to understand why they are so different than the rest of the population of a particular region.

Such assimilation and education make a difference to an individual's sensibilities towards other cultures. It increases the bandwidth of the mind to comprehend the reason behind a particular attitude or behaviour type that a different person possesses. If one has not been exposed to multi-ethnic environment, then a self-imposed quest for research can help gather constructive information, equipping one to arrive at thoughtful and logical conclusions. It could help us to learn, unlearn and relearn in these changing times.

We have a term called racial identities. Sometimes people overtly like to find the name, the country of birth, residence and various other things to initiate a conversation. These parameters are used to judge a person and put them in a box even before really getting to know them. We think it helps us prepare with who we are dealing with whereas in reality it is reconfirming our stereotypes unconsciously. A peek into their character, their language, their interests may be a better way to connect. The lack of real understanding propels us to digress from the connect and from forming lasting relationships. We could be more appreciative and respectful towards each other's histories because until and unless we understand someone's past and present, we cannot be a part of their future.

C FOR CHINESE, C FOR CONFUSION AND C FOR COLLABORATION: THE SINO-INDIAN FRIENDSHIP

Prashant was sent on an international assignment to China. He was working with a Korean company when he got a good offer from a reputed Chinese electronics company. He thought that the new offer was exciting and challenging in a good way. His brother had studied in China and had also worked there for a considerable period of time and his experience had not been as smooth. When Prashant shared his decision with him, he did express some apprehensions related to language and key cultural differences between the two ethnicities, which Prashant would have to work through. Erroneously, Prashant assumed culturally Korean and Chinese companies work in a similar way, hence assimilation should not be an issue! Hence he did not really do much to prepare himself for the transition. Prashant joined their office in Bengaluru without much ado. Initially, he worked with locals and enjoyed the experience. He got along with his manager who was quite impressed with his performance and he shared a good camaraderie with most colleagues. Prashant was affirmed in his beliefs that if one has talent, creativity, and one performs well, one will be recognised, rewarded and appreciated.

In a few months' time, he was delighted to find that he was being sent for an assignment to the company office in Beijing. It was going to be his first international experience and he was going to work with the Chinese people for the first time. His brother endeavoured to educate him about two important subjects—how Indians perceive the Chinese at work, and how the Chinese perceive Indians at work. But, Prashant chose to ignore it and went to China with an open mind.

As he started working with the Chinese, he was faced with a very cold welcome. Nobody talked much, it was monosyllabic, and hence, he found it difficult to understand what they thought or felt about him at work. The culture was quite different. The Chinese preferred to speak in their own language when they did talk and were not very expressive in ways he could comprehend, so it was hard for him to read them. Prashant was largely engaged with product design; however, he noticed that in most instances, he was ignored and his inputs were not taken into consideration. Whenever he walked into a room with Chinese officials, they would stare at him as though he was not one of them. He was, indeed, an outsider. His extroverted nature struggled to deal with the coldness at the workplace. Prashant failed to decipher the reason behind it and decided to have the recommended 'one-to-one chat', as is popularly known in the corporate world, to resolve the mysterious conundrum.

One of his team members, Wang Lei, with whom he interacted more often than anyone else, was quite uncomfortable with the subject of this conversation. His reaction was one full of disbelief and shock. He believed and behaved as though he was oblivious to the phenomenon. Lei's wife worked in the same company but in a different department. Prashant decided to seek her assistance in formulating a solution. He had met Lei's wife earlier at a conference and in one of the busy shopping malls in Beijing, and they had struck a cordial relationship. Prashant met her again and indulged in an explicit and candid description of the ordeal that he had gone through in the organisation in China. Being invisible to many at work was consuming him.

Lei's wife gave him a patient hearing and very simply revealed to him that the fundamental reason behind the existence and the manifestation of the beliefs was the inward-focussed social character of the local Chinese people. They perceive too much of loud chatter as rude and superficial, and prefer to remain elusive. There are a large number of Chinese who do work and study in other countries and are quite cosmopolitan in nature. But the continuous exposure to the same kind of people in terms of physicality, culture and mindset cultivates the desire in us to prefer one of our 'own' and propels the formation of the unconscious bias against other cultures or ethnicities.

Lei's wife told him that he should have a conversation with all his team members, one-on-one or together, over a meal (a friendlier environment where they may lower their guards) to make them aware of what he was going through. He could reassure them that he was genuinely interested in forging professional and personal relationships with the Chinese. She also told him to make an attempt to learn a few words in the Chinese language so that he could connect with his colleagues at a personal level, reinforcing his commitment. Lei's wife was just the magic wand that Prashant needed. She had an astute understanding of Prashant through her interactions with him and being a local herself, she also understood his Chinese teammates' outlook to life. She seemed in a good position to bridge the gap here.

Prashant organised that 'special' lunch on his birthday after a few weeks. In the fun and frolic, he brought up his struggles with his teammates. He shared with them that he liked being with them and wanted to make lifelong friendships apart from his professional contributions. He requested for support and help for the time he was with them away from his family. Prashant could feel the empathy surfacing on the faces of a few people. A few of his Chinese team members inquired what they could do to help. He simply requested for some time and engagement to get to know each other better. They reassured Prashant that they will try their best to provide a conducive environment for him to work for his psychological, emotional and professional well-being.

Prashant was elated to discover that both his teammates and he together were a part of the solution to this problem. The next few days, weeks, months and years were most satisfying for him in this organisation. He started to get the needed appreciation and emotional support from his colleagues. He also had the good fortune of attending a Chinese wedding as one of his colleagues had invited him to be a part of the occasion. Prashant felt at home finally.

Loneliness away from home can be confusing and can make one feel alienated and insecure. When others make an attempt to understand you, it is reassuring and inclusive. Prashant did not want to sit on fractured relationships and also wanted to abstain from any fall outs due to a lack of understanding with his fellow team members. Initially, he was not frustrated with anyone else apart from himself for not getting it right. The feeling of isolation had created a roadblock for him socially. But Lei's wife stepped in and changed it all for him.

That sense of belonging, which is generated out of an individual's willingness to understand, created the magic for the human soul.

There are some cultures that are quieter, softer, contemplate more than they express. The manifestation of warmth and love might vary across cultures, however, the feeling is consistent. The way we understand others also helps us to explain ourselves to others. Sometimes we need to take a few steps back to decode the mystery and uncover the hidden truths which escape the common eye. The mystical part of us needs to sit down and process the physical and the non-physical factors, which affect behaviour and thoughts that reflect in our external and internal manifestations. We need to find the isolated spot of compassion in a relatively cold atmosphere in one culture to create the warmth in another.

We may be under an illusion that we know everything around us. This confusion can engulf us when we come into contact with different people and can't read them. Understanding a person is an ongoing process, a work-in-progress, that can never be complete. The process of understanding people and their stories should invigorate us to find out more about them. It will help us to learn some intangible truths about different ethnicities.

THE ROOMMATE CONUNDRUM

Three Indian students—Raghu, Mahesh and Ashish—headed for a master's programme at the Manchester Business School and its in-campus accommodation facility. It was their first time in an educational institution abroad and the year was 2003. Culture immersion was sought after and these students thought it was a great opportunity to try living with someone from a different country. The college noted their special request and agreed that they would try and do what best they can. A month later, three of them were told that there were no Americans or Europeans available to share a room with, but they could possibly share rooms with a few Chinese students who are keen.

The Chinese? The college got them to meet up but Indian students were hesitant to take it forward. They felt unsure about how they will all communicate with each other, how they will discuss social issues and 'their Chinese food-eating habits' would not sit well everyday!

Perhaps the issue was not about the Chinese, but of the known versus the unknown, an unwillingness to understand someone different. The Indian students realised in a few weeks that the three of them too were a bit different in many ways. Two were non-vegetarian and one was a vegetarian. There was one person from southern India and the other two from northern India. They had different political ideologies too. However, having agreed to stay together as 'Indians' they went on with their life.

One cold evening, Raghu was heading back from college to his apartment. The freezing cold fuelled him to walk faster. Being from southern India where the temperature is never below twenty degrees Celsius, this weather was killing him! He loved the warmth near the fireplace in his shared apartment. It was Diwali time and he had just received some extra money from *Amma* (mother) and *Appa* (father) to buy gifts for himself. He was really looking forward to the weekend shopping as he had already narrowed it down to his favourite phone. He had also taken out some money to buy sweets.

Suddenly, two people appeared from nowhere. They were masked, bigger and taller than Raghu and had knives on them. One of them punched Raghu and asked him for his wallet, watch and any other valuables he was carrying! Raghu was stunned and froze. He had never been mugged before. A lack of response from Raghu led to stabbing in his arm, gagging and more beating. They snatched away everything, including his money, watch, ID cards, and left him with a few books in his rucksack. He lay bleeding on the icy cold road. He could see his life slipping away and an unconscious dark night taking over his mind, eyes and everything around him.

Just then, he felt someone pick him up, shake him and slap him awake. This person was shouting for help and calling a few people in a language Raghu was not able to understand. He tried hard to open his eyes, but he collapsed.

When he awoke, he was unsure whether he was alive or dead. He found himself surrounded by his teacher, a few Chinese people and a nurse in the college hospital. He soon realised that one of the Chinese students was the same person he had refused to share the apartment with!

He looked for his roommates and realised that they were away for the Diwali holidays that week. As he tried to raise his head, he squealed in pain as his collarbone was fractured. He looked at his teacher, questioning what had happened and how he had got there.

The teacher told him that he was left bleeding on the road after the two goons fled. These Chinese students had found him and had carried him to the hospital. They had ensured that doctors and nurses arrived timely for the much needed surgery and medication. Then they called the professors and the matron too to ensure Raghu was in good care.

A sense of gratitude swelled in Raghu's heart with tears in his eyes as his thoughts went back to the time where he led the discussions on not sharing his apartment with the Chinese. What was he thinking? He had disregarded the basic understanding of human bonds whereas the Chinese individual had not. A person in need is a person indeed and he had stepped up to the duty of care for Raghu when his own roommates were not around. Raghu had learnt an important lesson about humanity that day.

More importantly, as he turned his head to the side table to get a glass of water, he found some *sambar* and rice on a plate for him, which was his favourite South Indian food and was arranged by his new-found Chinese friend!

Appreciation and understanding of basic human bonds enrich us! It does not take anything from us. In school, when we learn a new topic or a new subject, it is tough in the beginning and then it gets easier and then it becomes a part of our thought process. This is no different than learning from different cultures. There has to be a willingness to learn, and not be afraid of it.

Apart from social engagement, some common drivers, motivators and areas of interest can help us to understand each other much better. It further enables us to peek into each other's mindsets and perspectives. Understanding others is also another way of exploring ourselves, what we are capable of in our personal and professional capacity, and how we can leverage it to make the world a better place to live in. The Chinese friend surprised Raghu and changed him for ever. Raghu had closed his doors on him, he had believed in the stereotype and was swayed by his unfounded beliefs about the Chinese people. The mishap in his life in college gave him the opportunity to respect the humane and the caring nature of the Chinese friend who left no stone unturned to make him feel special and at home after the gruesome incident.

The Chinese boy felt for a fellow student away from home. They were both Asians who had come there to study for better academic and professional opportunities. Therefore, the commonly felt sense of loneliness, a feeling of homesickness especially when you are ill, was well understood by the Chinese friend. That is the perfect example of what the magic of human affection and sensitivity can do. The Chinese friend had managed to break the stereotype and had it not been for this mishap, perhaps Raghu would have never realised the real person beneath the skin of the hard-working Chinese boy whom he had refused to have as a roommate.

The lack of understanding provokes us to stay away from cultures and people that look discomforting to us on the face of it. We often do not make an effort to see what lies in the heart of these individuals, we get blinded by our misunderstandings. Difficult or tough situations tend to bring out our natural humane self at the forefront.

Understanding and knowing each other better every day will help us practise tolerance for people from different cultures. This tolerance will help us pause, reflect and give time for clouds of confusion to disappear to allow the acceptance of the truth. We are then well equipped to transform our beliefs in the long-term.

THE TOLERANCE OF RACISM

Sometimes, racism is normalised and tolerated as a way of being and working. The selective conscious and unconscious bias prevails against the various races because of lack of compliance of anti-discrimination laws across the world.

Alem Dechasa's death lifted the lid on the plight of migrant workers in Lebanon. Alem was a 33-year-old migrant worker in Lebanon and she had made the heart-rending decision of leaving Ethiopia to work as a maid in Lebanon for a better life for her children, Yabesira and Tesfaye. Alem committed suicide after she was allegedly beaten up on a street in Beirut. The dehumanising incident only depicted the plight of Ethiopian maids in Lebanon and the entrenched form of slavery which still exists in Ethiopia. Human Rights Watch, an international non-governmental organisation in New York that conducts research and advocacy on human rights, says that atleast one migrant worker dies in Lebanon each week. This incident is perhaps indirectly evident of the fact that anti-black racism still exists in the Arab countries.

Anti-black racism in some countries originates from their desire and aspiration to be rich and powerful like in the colonial era. Their image of prosperity and strength is of people who are tall, sturdy with light skin, ruddy cheeks and straight hair. This is far removed from a physique that boasts of a short stature, coiled hair, broad hips, big legs and melanin-rich skin or dark skin from some continents. The latter image is a symbol of penury, subordination and indolence. This phenomenon has continued in a subtle way even though decades have passed by. The oppressor feels it is normal to believe and behave in this way and the oppressed feel that this is how life has been and this is how it was always meant to be. No one challenges!

The fact that racism is a normal phenomenon on some platforms is best described by the dating apps. RajnishVahera, an Indian man who works as a marketing manager in Vietnam, uses various dating apps and feels that racism is quite rampant on these platforms. He says he struck a conversation with a white girl on one of these apps and to his surprise, he got an alarming response which said, 'Asians are weird'. A sufficient number of ethnic and black singletons have had to face racial abuse on these dating apps. There are various profiles that one can run through on the apps that say 'I'm not attracted to Asians' or 'no Asians'; for coloured individuals to glance through such 'signboards' can be quite denigrating and rasping.

Monifa Olayinka, a Nigerian colleague says people have incorrect perceptions about other people who have a particular colour or ethnicity. Monifa received messages with words that implied that black women are aggressive, abrasive and gross. In fact, a large number of plus-sized black women are recipients of such insults. It is quite intriguing to see how these apps give us a slice of how society is predisposed towards colour, even to this day. Physicality among human beings forms the first parameter of judgement. Social conventions play a huge role in our lives and decide who we want to engage with and how we want to approach others. However, often life goes on as these biases are not fully challenged!

Researchers in Australia published a paper in 2015, and shared that more than half of the users of a dating app believed that they had been victims of racism and almost 96% of the users believed that they had seen atleast one profile that included some form of racial discrimination. Also, another shocking revelation was that more than one in eight people accepted the fact that they themselves had displayed racial behaviour by including text on their profile which discriminated among people on the basis of colour. When online platforms encourage racial behaviours, then that basically amounts to naturalising the whole phenomenon of racial discrimination.

Some users suspect that these apps contain in-built algorithms, which recommend partners on the basis of preference for a certain ethnicity by recognising certain kind of images. These apps have been structured technically in such a manner. Although most deny, but it is possible that some of the apps do give suggestions for potential matches based on contacts, previous swipes, image preferences and current location. It is important to observe that if any app requires the users to define themselves in terms of ethnicity, then the app is getting to know who we are and our racial preference once they track our activities. Each click on an image will tell the matchmaking algorithm exactly what it needs to know.

Normalisation of racism is a phenomenon wherein people, influenced by their prejudiced mindset, believe that this is their reality. But we have to make an attempt to reduce this social and emotional distance between people from different cultures by being open to have a dialogue beyond our comfort zone. The process of human resonance that we have been endowed with tends to assist us to appreciate the other person's feelings. So let's get to know each other better as a human race.

WHEN HATE SURPASSES ITS OWN UNCONSCIOUS THRESHOLD

Daniel Jabolonswki was Polish and he came to Ireland about fifteen years ago. He had come with the optimism and hope of building his life in the country. He had heard many stories of how some of his fellow Poles had migrated to Ireland and had settled there well. The eastern part of Europe is yet developing relative to its western part. Contrary to perception, Poles do not always occupy unskilled jobs in Ireland. They are also well off in white collared and business jobs. Daniel came to Ireland in search of some livelihood and he happened to meet a gentleman, Fennel Bates, on the train who worked as a manager in a restaurant and was looking for a supervisor.

In the train, when Daniel was just about to give Fennel his full name, the manager happened to meet his friend Percy. Both of them spoke incessantly about a Polish business partner who had apparently duped them. They were quite upset with their decision to trust their Polish partner, and were upset that they could not trace him down anymore. Daniel's conjecture from overhearing this conversation made him think that he would never be able to get a job in Ireland, if he were to reveal his true identity. He was eavesdropping further when he heard, 'These Poles, hmm…never work with them, they are not the ones to work with. Why do they come here?'

Daniel shuddered. He was aghast to learn how one incident can do so much damage to the reputation of an entire populace.

After that brief conversation, Fennel turned around and asked for Daniel's full name. He fumbled. Then, he blurted out, 'Daniel Woodlands' indicating he was a local! There was a queer silence among all three of them. Daniel was an incompetent liar. Perhaps, it was showing on his face. Fennel patted him on the back. He could not think of anything else. If Daniel were to be questioned further, he could have done no justice to his manufactured stream of impromptu falsehoods. Fennel asked him some more questions about managing restaurants and let him off the interrogation. He then asked Daniel to assist him. Daniel was glad that he would be earning something if not anything. His tribulations had come to an end, at least for the day. Fennel asked him to give details of his identity to the administration staff of the restaurant to complete certain formalities. Daniel's throat became dry. He did not know what to say. He pondered on his Polish nationality and what he had disclosed.

He later realised what a complete fool he had been by hiding his identity. In any case, a relationship based on falsehood is no relationship at all, even if it is at work. He stared at his passport and other identity documents. It was going to be a tough task to undo what he had already done. However, he had to clear it all the following morning. The guilt inside him did not allow him to sleep. It was causing so much discomfort within him that he found it difficult to breathe as he played that conversation with Fennel in his mind. But, he realised that he would have to do a full disclosure. He would have to reveal his true identity and that might have consequences on his chances of getting the job.

The next morning when Daniel went to the restaurant (the address had been given to him), he showed Fennel all his documents. Fennel was quite alarmed at first when he realised Daniel was Polish and not British as he had understood earlier. There was a stunned silence. Daniel gathered all his courage to tell Fennel why he had concealed his surname from him as the conversation on Poles in the train had suddenly alarmed him.

Fennel appreciated his honesty and gave him the job! Daniel was delighted and his faith in honesty was restored. He learnt all he could about managing restaurants from Fennel. In fact, their relationship grew stronger on the foundation of honesty. Fennel started to treat him like a brother. Daniel had studied till high school in Poland after which he had to look for work because he was trapped in a financially compelling situation. Fennel helped Daniel complete his studies and promoted him as a restaurant manager.

Over the years, Daniel settled down in Ireland, got married and had a son. Daniel worked day and night to build a good life in Ireland with his wife, Elena. She too provided all the support she could so that their only son would not have to take up an unskilled job to make a living. Elena was Irish and Daniel had married her after they had met at a grocery store. Thanks to all their efforts, their grown-up son, James, started to work in the research laboratory of a famous pharmaceutical company. A few months ago, his son bought a car from his savings and he wanted his parents to take the first ride with him. Daniel's heart swelled with pride. Daniel and Elena had worked so hard all these years to ensure their son had a good life.

James decided to drive his parents through the city in his new car. On the way, he stopped by a café to get some hot chocolate and burgers for the family. His parents sat in the car while he went to get the food. They suddenly heard a few people screaming behind them. The verbal duet transformed into a fight within minutes. Elena opened the door of the car because she was concerned about the safety of her son who was somewhere out there. In the meantime, a few men started to throw stones and eggs at the car. Daniel was quite startled to see this. In so many years, he had never witnessed this kind of an incident. It filled him with pure anger and apprehension. A few men surrounded the car and threatened to break it down into pieces. That's when his wife shouted loudly, 'Daniel, Daniel please leave the car, let's run.' Daniel was shivering with fear inside the car. Suddenly, he heard a few people shouting out his son's name! He could see that his son was being beaten up, but the car doors were jammed and he could not get out.

About thirty minutes back, while James was buying the burgers and hot chocolate, he noticed the manager in the café speaking quite rudely to one of the waiters. He decided to intervene because he felt that the waiter was being humiliated for a petty mistake. James had no idea then that the waiter was Polish. The manager was quite furious at his intervention, since James was trying to defend the waiter. The manager realised that James was Polish, as he saw his company ID card on his shirt. He felt James was like those 'evil immigrants' and was trying to protect his own. He reacted and immediately called in a few people. They started to shout rudely and hurl comments at him about the Polish minority; they even threatened that if they do not leave the country, the worst will happen. Then, in a few minutes, out of nowhere, a few more men on bikes arrived outside the café and asked the warring factions in the restaurant to come out! They singled out foreigners and started to beat them. A huge crowd gathered from the surrounding areas to passively watch this mayhem unfold.

This episode spiralled into something much larger than expected. His son was engaged in an unnecessary scuffle with two more anti-socials because they had abused the waiter. Daniel could see his wife trying her best to calm down the people around her, but in vain. The new car was in a horrible shape, the windshields were broken and the body was scarred with stone marks. Finally, Daniel somehow got out of the car, with a wound on his head from stone pelting. He heard the men screaming, while they punched James incessantly. Elena lay on the ground with her face upside down, because someone had pushed her while she was trying to run away. Then, she tried to get up, but was pushed down again. Daniel was so scared that he could not move. His legs were frozen.

Daniel was in disbelief—was his son getting beaten up because he was Polish or because he was defending a Polish person. He quickly dialled the police. Then, he called the nearby hospital and got the ambulance arranged. He lifted his son into his arms like a baby. James was seriously injured and his head was bleeding profusely. The police finally arrived on the scene. What a day it had been for him and for humanity!

Daniel could not feel the pain, the emotion, the person he was. He could not feel anything. There was a strange silence all around him. He had stopped thinking. He was quite numb to the truth that had unfolded before him today. It was the lull after the storm. He collapsed on the seat of the ambulance. The entire day had just finished the life within him. He could see his wife holding onto their dear son and calling out his name again and again. James was declared to be in a coma upon reaching the hospital. It had happened all too soon and all too fast. Daniel felt responsible for whatever had happened that day. He regretted ever coming to this country to start his life, a country he had felt was his home. The myth had been shattered for him. It did not matter that he had lived his life in this country with honesty and integrity. The fact of the matter was that he was basically an outsider. He was taken back to the train conversation that he had overheard decades ago between Fennel and Percy. Had nothing changed?

His family had to suffer for no fault of their own. The incident had catapulted his wife into a state of permanent fear. She could not talk for days together. Daniel found it difficult to sleep at night. The grief had consumed him to the extent that he had started living a dead life. Hatred had won and humanity had lost.

The understanding between Daniel and his manager, Fennel, had ensured that they both worked comfortably for twenty years in Ireland. The manager knew that Daniel was Polish, but that never affected their relationship. Daniel was a sincere worker for Fennel and, therefore, it did not really matter where he came from. However, his Polish origin mattered to others.

The sheer lack of understanding of the manager at the café and his idea of Polish people had led to an unnecessary feud. James had stood up for someone because that individual did not have a voice and needed help, not because he was Polish. The waiter was driven to tears by the manager's rude demeanour as witnessed by James. He chose to protect an innocent man from being further humiliated. He also made an attempt to make the manager understand. The manager was antagonistic and lacked any understanding of human race, leave alone colour. He was devoid of empathy. He was so blinded by his own prejudices and biases that when James intervened, out of misplaced rage and fear of assault, he called a few other people to wage a war! Presumptions lead to anger that arises when we do not even make an endeavour to comprehend the other side of the story, when we stick onto what we think is the reality. This leads to some very harmful incidents that scar the lives of people forever, just as it did for Daniel's family.

Understanding is like a window, which needs to be kept open. The concocted beliefs sometimes need to be distilled to cull out the real truth. Folklore and distorted narratives need to be clarified with proper evidence to enable us to formulate a better connect between the pieces of information. Sometimes when we fail to understand the difference between objective truth and subjective opinions, we end up manufacturing a volley of narratives, which may be inauthentic and unreal. Let's try to lead a real life.

Summary

1. Grown-ups need to provide children an exposure to diverse environment so that they can get the opportunity to mingle and learn from different ethnicities. This will help build a richer legacy with more open mindsets and an appreciation of cross-cultural dynamics.
2. We need to reflect and reassess the stereotypes that each country or colour may be distinct and may have an assumed culture or mannerism or image. We need to deconstruct and reconstruct basis our own experience and understanding.
3. We all feel the same emotions—love, hate, anger, fear and sorrow. The essential need is to decipher why different cultures have different ways of expressing or responding to them.
4. We need to be more self-aware—we need to pause, sit and self-introspect to understand ourselves and our emotions better.
5. The process of understanding is a long one and will continue to be a work-in-progress. Therefore, we should not react in fear to ambiguities and always keep the window of understanding open.

Resilience

Sid: 'Mom, when I was on the exchange programme in Europe, there were some things that I felt were different and strange. I had mixed emotions about who I was! Avni di, have you ever been in this state?'

Avni (confused): 'Like what? I am not quite sure I understand!'

Sid: 'Well, first, when I reached the host family's home, some of them were quite surprised that I spoke good English. They were confused where I was from and when I said I am an Indian native from England, they seemed unsure about how to interact with me.

'And then one day over a meal, the hostess did not put cutlery for me and when I requested for a knife and fork, she laughed and said that she thought all Indians ate with their hands! I did not know how to react, but shrugged her statement and told her that we do eat Indian food with our hands, as touching the food in a certain way adds sensory pleasure. Remember mom told us?!'

Avni: 'Hmm, that is rude indeed. I am glad you handled it well.'

Sid: 'Yes, but in that moment I felt angry and hurt!'

Avni: 'It happens, Sid!'

Mom (who had been eavesdropping): 'No, it should not happen. We live in a zero-tolerance environment for such interactions. Do no do bad and take no bad!'

Sid and Avni turn around as they notice their mother in the room.

Avni: 'But mom, not everyone understands! Is it wise to pick up a conflict all the time? Though I am not like Sid, who knew how to handle it.'

Mom: 'This kind of behaviour emanates from a lack of awareness and sensitivity to different people. It does not have to be conflict always, you just have to speak up to try and change things in a respectful way. Mindsets are difficult to contend with but if you do not raise your voice, you may be implicitly agreeing with them thus legitimising hurtful behaviour consciously or unconsciously. Sometimes it is these simple conversations, other times it is awareness and education of others and self. Finally, there will be times where a statement of what is acceptable or not has to be explicitly made. Life is larger than your fears! Look beyond your doubts and you will find the new sun of conviction rising.'

Sid: 'But people can be mean and rude, if I raise my voice would that not hurt me?'

Mom: 'You are stronger than you think, the courage is within you, don't let anyone steal it from you! Self-belief and focus are the key to a smooth climb on the mountain of life. If you believe you are being unfairly treated in any way, then do something about it or don't moan about it. There is just no one solution for every such situation, but I can tell you that each such situations will change if you try and change it. There will be different responses to different situations, but start with speaking up.'

Avni: 'What if that isolates you further?'

Mom: 'Well, you can choose to isolate your real self, live a life that is not really yours or raise your voice in the right way and be authentic. Find communities, networks to support you. There are plenty of good people in the world and many who face similar challenges like you. Create an ecosystem that fosters and nurtures the best of you.'

Avni: 'I feel better hearing about this now, mom.'

Mom: 'It doesn't need to be how things have always been, they can be changed. Just because the world said so in the past may not be right for the future. You have a thought process of your own and your heart murmurs a different song to the soul—your ears listen and your mind gears in to follow this song. That song, I believe, is for the world to follow too. You deserve to be happy! Don't let anyone take it away from you.'

We don't see love, but we love, we don't see air but we breathe, we see colour and we assume what we don't see.

Colour Neutrality: Easy to Preach, Difficult to Practise?

In 2004, Divya had two options to choose from—one of marriage and the other of a dream job from a reputed hardware company in the US. It was an arranged marriage and the groom's family did not want her to go to the US for the job opportunity. However, given her penchant to explore the world, she took the bold decision of deferring the marriage proposal and packed her bags to head straight to North America. Divya's parents were concerned about her marriage since she was on the wrong side of thirty and a brown Asian. But, Divya had been waiting for this opportunity and she grabbed it as soon as it came her way.

She was alone when she arrived in Texas to work in the new company. At the airport itself, she felt she was different from others around her, a feeling she had never experienced back home. She found herself segregating the brown and the white people, unconsciously looking for someone from her community. Her penchant for the much needed comfort with familiarity pushed her to find someone who could make her feel at home.

At the new office, she struck an instant connection with the few Asians in the organisation. They helped her settle down in the city as well as in the organisation. She was assigned to a team which had one Asian and the rest were all white Americans. In the beginning, her interaction with the whites was limited because understanding each other's accent and language was a problem. She was from a vernacular medium school and her spoken English was far from being perfect.

Her past overseas experience was quite limited hence she made all conscious effort to adapt to the new culture as fast as possible. She read books, watched movies and documentaries and tried to learn from fellow Indians and Americans. Her team lead was a white American who had been working in the company for a fairly long period of time. He was from the Midwest and did not have much exposure to people beyond that. Divya made repeated attempts to strike a connection with the team lead. She knew that to be successful, she had to have a good professional relationship with him. In the beginning, her inputs for the project under consideration were duly acknowledged in the meetings she attended. Ignorantly, Divya assumed the early politeness to be an indication that she had got something right and was an equal partner.

Gradually, this engagement started to fizzle away with the team lead, followed by others. As she brought more of herself to work, some white team members started to withdraw from interactions with her. They found that beyond work, there were no common interests, her food habits were different and she was not as exposed to their world. Only one out of the ten core team members engaged with her beyond the professional domain. She gradually realised others would not even respond when spoken to in meetings. Some of them would give her a cold look, if she raised concerns on any project plans. She had a feeling that something was amiss, but was at a loss to define what it was! It made her feel dejected and miserable. Divya started to feel irrelevant.

Each passing day, humiliation was fuelling a fire within her, which if left unaddressed would incense her dignity. She was conscious that if she did not resolve these dynamics, her career and the project might be impacted! After living with this for a few months, she mustered up the courage to confront the few colleagues who were not inclusive.

Her first few attempts to have these conversations with them failed. She persisted, however, and involved Stephen, one of her teammates with whom she shared a better interpersonal relationship. He was empathetic and advised her that this would need some persistence as the team had very limited international exposure and could be quite unaware of their behaviour and its impact. Stephen acknowledged that she was at par with them in terms of knowledge and skill, but culturally she was quite different. This unconsciously may have been creating a gap in relationship-building.

Matters of the mind are complicated. Divya started on her mission, but struggled to get time with them.

After a few days, the team members got together in a project closure meeting. All had gone well and the team was happy. Celebratory drinks followed; Divya decided that it was time to precipitate the discussion, given the happy disposition of the team. She approached each of the four people individually and started to share that she wanted to contribute more, but was not feeing included. She requested for their advice and suggested that having some operating principles for the next project would be helpful. She shared how she respected all of them and needed support as she was on a journey to add more value to the team goals, than she had been able to do. A few changes in communication and engagement would help her do that. Some of them, reluctant to speak on this issue, deflected the conversation in another direction citing that Divya may be incorrectly interpreting their behaviour. It was not about what they said or did, what was important was them knowing how she felt about it and its impact on her. Any intended or unconscious behaviour that made one feel isolated was not desired in any culture. Divya persisted, she explained how the last few interactions had made her feel. She expressed her desire for more interaction with them as fellow colleagues as she felt there was so much she could learn from them, if they would only allow her to do so.

Finally, everyone shares a human core that manifests itself when one touches it. It was obvious to Divya that these four members had not fully realised how hurtful their behaviour had been towards her. The team lead finally shared that he had had some bad experiences of being in India where his luggage was stolen and he felt quite harassed by the way people talked to him there; it was too loud and uncouth for him! Somewhere he agreed that erroneously he had generalised it to each and every Indian and that was reflective in his behaviour. Another member was bullied by an Indian child in his US school and those memories still haunted him! Yet another shared that she could not connect with her emerging market world view on work–life balance. In some ways, others were also following the team lead and that realisation came about. The examples set by seniors makes a certain behaviour legitimate when it is not.

As Divya dug deeper, she found out that their one-off experiences had somewhere formed a generic opinion about all brown people and she was a victim of that. As soon as this rose to their conscious level and they realised that there was no real rational for this generalisation, she could see their body language change to a much friendlier disposition towards her.

She then scheduled a one-on-one catch-up with each of them every week to keep the engagement going.

They all knew the significance for more collaboration and knowledge-sharing among core team members. Divya used the one-on-one sessions to make them realise that she had made a brave attempt of disclosing herself in the team. Stephen joined her in team meetings to emphasise the fact that misunderstandings among the team would ultimately prove to be harmful for the final performance of the company.

Since he was a senior manager of the organisation, she knew his words would be taken seriously. Stephen also stressed the fact that the organisation needed to invest in innovative and effective unconscious bias trainings to ensure that people appreciate these dynamics better. Over the course of time, Divya's relations with the team lead and the four members improved. She was reminded of the song, 'We Shall Overcome', by Pete Seeger, as she dealt with her tryst with biases at the workplace.

When I feel left out
When I am not made to feel a part of the whole
When I am left to fend for myself
I do seek for help
I get some but not from everyone
Is it due to my colour?
The one I was born with?
Even though I cannot change it
Such irreversible facts have reversible consequences!
Please don't see colour,
Let your eyes see 'me'

When we are faced with tough situations as a lonely stranger with a new set of people, unless we face up to the challenges and push the limit, unless we persist on an unchartered and sometimes frightful path of conversations, we will never be able to fathom the extent of our resilience! The way we frame our response to an adversity, affects the way we deal with it. Divya had an internal locus of control that helped her navigate and keep up the optimism. She channelled her emotions as a force to build on her inner core. She was not just looking for any external affirmation or appreciation, what bothered her was lack of collaboration and empathy. Divya had given up a lot personally to be where she was professionally and her biggest learning from the incident was that if no one is applauding you for what you have done sincerely, you should learn to applaud yourself, internally and quietly. However, she kept working on building her relationships without giving up on her team.

We need to fight our own battles and sometimes a little assistance from a colleague or a network can make a difference. If you have self-belief, then the win is yours too.

As quoted by *Psychology Today*, 'Resilience is that ineffable quality that allows some people to be knocked down by life and come back at least as strong as before. Rather than letting difficulties or failure overcome them and drain their resolve, they find a way to rise from the ashes. Psychologists have identified some of the factors that make a person resilient, such as a positive attitude, optimism, the ability to regulate emotions, and the ability to see failure as a form of helpful feedback... But, even after misfortune, resilient people are [blessed with such an outlook that they] are able to change course and [soldier on].'[4]

In life, often our reaction to various situations is driven by our conditioning and our internal wiring. It is our positive intent and will to persist against odds that can help surmount hurdles. When I was growing up in a predominantly brown environment, I never felt or thought I was inferior to anyone as I was surrounded by similar people. It was only when in college and at work when I

---

4 'All About Resilience'. *Psychology Today*. https://www.psychologytoday.com/us/basics/resilience

stepped into a mixed colour environment that I was taken aback by how much difference this could make. I struggled with certain reactions—subtle or direct—of being subjected to not-so-affable non-verbal cues and somehow was suddenly conscious. However, I remained positive and comfortable in my skin. I learnt to believe that I liked what I saw in the mirror. One needs to observe or ignore the non-verbal cues, depending on their relevance, and not get disheartened by a rude reaction or comment that may be driven by a mindset outside our control.

Adversity is an opportunity to embolden ourselves to strive much more than we did in the past. We can leverage adversity to change the set practices and norms. Life will have its ups and downs and it is our courage to keep going that helps us bounce back. The emotional turbulence, which accompanies each hard-fought battle, should enrich us. We can assimilate our learnings for the future whilst increasing the intensity of persistence within us. The combination of courage and conviction should provide the necessary power at each point of inflexion in our lives to not accept defeat and change the curvature of life for the better.

ZERO TOLERANCE!

Last week in Dubai had been unexpectedly hectic to say the least. My flight was at 9:00 PM and given the stressful day at work meetings, I was carrying a headache back home with me to Mumbai. I reached the airport on time.

Finally, I boarded the flight that was ready to take off. By then my headache had gathered more intensity and was drumming up a world war inside my little head. Fortunately, I found a pill that could help alleviate some of this pain. I requested the steward in the cabin for some water. He heard me and went ahead to the tray areas. I waited and waited, but he did not come back with a glass of water for me. Given the flight was busy, I decided to be patient. As he passed by again, I signalled him again for water and he waved his hand and nodded his head, but there was no water in sight even after fifteen minutes.

My head was about to explode soon! I spotted the same steward again, talking to another guest ahead of me and I assumed something more urgent may have transpired there. As he passed me by again, my co-passenger waved and asked the steward for a blanket as I struggled again to voice aloud my request for water. In a minute, the blanket arrived for the co-passenger, but still no sight of a glass of water for me. It was really odd. I was suddenly overcome by an overwhelming wave of anger and humiliation that was beginning to surpass my patience now. So, I pressed the attendant button, the light came on and an air hostess arrived. I asked her to get the cabin manager or the captain as I wanted to raise a concern; in fact, I wanted to do this in writing. The anger was swelling up within me so much so that I could not feel my headache at all now. The air hostess tried to calm me down, but in vain, for that time had passed.

In a few minutes, the cabin manager arrived and very politely and patiently enquired what he could do to help me. I fought my anguish against his surprisingly appropriate demeanour, unlike the white steward. My simple complain was that I had requested for a glass of water three times over the last thirty minutes. I was not well and needed to have a medicine quickly. It was annoyingly evident to me that I was not being treated at par with other guests, given that a lady next to me was heard and serviced instantly, while I was being ignored. This was quite unacceptable, more so as I had bought a full fare business class ticket, which I assumed included a glass of water! Further, I shared with him that I felt the differential and not-so-good treatment (as possible reason for ignorance) relative to the other guests. The fact was that I was a brown person among many white people. Thankfully, the white lady next to me supported my case. I insisted I would like to log in a formal complaint for this treatment and would like a response to this incident. For me this was a racist treatment unless the cabin manager could explain to me otherwise.

The cabin manager heard me very patiently and cordially. Once I was done, he did seem perturbed and apologetic, but that did not take away my trouble. He did agree that I could raise a complaint, but at the same time, he was profusely apologetic about the behaviour of his colleague. He promised me that he will have a conversation with the concerned individual to check what may have triggered this behaviour. However, it was obvious to me that he had realised what I had been trying to tell him. Perhaps he knew what I knew about colour!

As the flight took off, I realised that the steward was removed from the cabin and I was showered with 'special' treatment all of a sudden. I simply detested that part. All I wished was for a 'normal' treatment. I felt the airline was concerned about the issue and was trying to pacify me, which did not help. However, my dreary state took over me and I finally settled in my comfortable seat and retired to the goddess of sleep.

I chose to raise my voice to display my dissatisfaction, frustration and disappointment so that the airline ensures that no such incident happens in the future. I made efforts to get the service that I had paid for! Sometimes negative events help us to have a reverse focus—they tend to expose our vulnerability and make us more aware and determined. I realised that had I been passive for the sake of public image and peace, I would not have been able to make the staff realise the extent of my indignation.

Expressions and emotions have to be channelled rightly at the right time to have the right impact to address an issue at hand. We must not be carried away by our feelings to the extent that we lose our focus from the main issue. Resilience may or may not be a learned behaviour but we must all muster the courage to deal with disrespectful behaviour.

Whether it is an airline issue or an office colleague issue, it is all about why and to what extent you are willing to tolerate this and what you are willing to do about it. Simply asking for being treated professionally, compassionately and empathetically is not asking for too much. It is a basic dignity we deserve and owe to each other. If violated, it is something we need to ensure is corrected and the appropriate mechanisms are put in place. Sometimes, it takes a soft dealing when it may have been an inadvertent miss, sometimes a confrontation and sometimes an escalation. Often some people avoid conflicts of this kind knowing well that they are in the right. Fear or hesitation, irrespective of whatever it may be, we need to rise to the occasion when appropriate or else not complain!

Is it really an issue if someone ignored you or 'forgot' to get you water inspite of incessant requests? The answer is yes, it is an issue, as the behaviour seemed like a manifestation of more deep-seated beliefs. If this went unchecked, then it would be repeated and would become a part of the legacy that we will hand over to our children. When we feel hurt, we feel vulnerable; we could make that vulnerability our strength and fuel it to raise our voice appropriately for the right reason.

The intention to correct the behaviour or misdemeanour should not arise just because it is a professional courtesy or a professional imperative, but rather a conscious need and requirement to address prejudice and discrimination wherever it occurs, in whichever part of the world. The need to raise such issues should arise from the fact that we allow such incidents or misdemeanours and discourtesies to prevail upon us because somewhere we are in this mode of acceptance that we deserve this kind of biased behaviour. Hence, it is our responsibility to respect ourselves before we expect others to respect us. We need to develop the emotional resilience to deal with such incidents so that whether it is anger or sorrow or frustration, it should be channelised in the right direction so that the perpetrator of such irresponsible behaviour can be made to realise and made conscious of his behaviour.

Confrontations are tough for most of us. They may come to a few naturally whereas scare other people. However, confrontations can also take the form of discussions.

BATTLING RACISM: BUT AT WHAT COST?

Jason Shen is an Asian American who went to the US from China at the age of three. He attended Stanford University later in life, and is also an example of the quintessential successful Asian American. Jason circulated a survey in 2015 on the experience of Asian men in the US—this entails their experience with dating, working and everyday life in the US. Jason circulated this survey because he felt that there was no emphasis given on the understanding of how Asians felt being in the US—which was and still is a predominantly white people's land. The survey received about 354 responses, all from Asian men in the US. Two-thirds of the respondents of the survey were between the ages of twenty-five and thirty-four who had Asian parents, but were themselves born in the US. Almost 55% of the respondents held four-year college degrees and 75% were East Asians, who filled the survey. The survey revealed some very interesting facts.

In the survey, almost ten different Asian stereotypes were listed which were 'being good with computers' or 'kung fu skills' or 'speaking with an accent'. The survey revealed that 65–69% of the Asian men were uncomfortable with the stereotype of being good at computers. Also, 69–71% of the Asian men had been uncomfortable with the stereotype that they were good at maths. More than one-third of the respondents felt that as compared to white people, they were treated in a far worse manner. About three-fourths of the respondents felt that they were treated much better than the non-Asian minorities. Around 20% of the respondents felt that they had been bullied at school and only 4% felt that they had been bullied at work.

Almost half of the Asian men have heard someone say that they 'did not wish to date Asian men' in their presence. A lot of Asian men are asked the question, 'Where are you from?' and such an instance where the interrogator wants information on the country of origin has occurred more than six times. Racial stereotypes like 'being good at math', and 'good with computers' are still prevalent even today. Inspite of this, Asians continue to survive well in the US because they come with the intention of building a life there. This intent is built on a foundation of resilience and determination to better their life. Resilience has been the key to their survival—they have deep beliefs, which are reinforced by strongly held values, the continuous effort to make life meaningful and the endeavour to improvise, both personally and professionally.

The unhappiness in certain parts of western countries has been rising slowly and steadily. The rising mortality rates among middle-aged uneducated whites, the reasons being suicides or poisoning, also points to the fact that uneducated and poor whites have also been discriminated against. A November 2015 report 'Rising Morbidity and Mortality in Midlife Among White Non-Hispanic Americans in the 21st Century' by Angus Deaton and Anne Case showed a considerable increase in all-cause mortality of high school (and below) educated white, middle-aged, non-Hispanic men and women between 1999 and 2013. Mental health and the ability to conduct daily activities also saw a marked decrease in this group, which also indicates that there is a growing amount of stress. Further efforts need to be made to measure the extent of the crisis based on certain measures such as stress, pain and anxiety in addition to well-being and life satisfaction.

The gap in life expectancy between white people and black people has narrowed over time—in 1990 this gap was seven years and in 2014, the gap narrowed down to three years.

These findings may reveal a gamut of information, which may help us draw some inferences. Minorities such as Hispanics and blacks have fought tough battles, which has led to the improvement of certain metrics. The resilience that they have shown in combating discrimination and prejudice has further helped them to ameliorate their condition. As far as the black people are concerned, there is a significant improvement with respect to certain parameters such as education and wages. As the competition for low-skilled jobs increases, the economic status of the whites has considerably fallen. Across income groups, gaps in education attainment and proficiency have widened, but they have narrowed between whites and blacks at the same time. Black males earned 69% of the median wage of white males in 1970 and 75% by 2013 and the proficiency gap today between poor and rich children is twice as large as that between white and black children.

Andrew Cherlin discovered that poor and middle-class blacks are more likely to compare themselves to parents who have been worse off in the past when they are in the process of assessing their status. An American economist, Paul Krugman had noted that the expectations of the present generation of white people had been higher driven by their past status and, therefore, this group has had a tougher experience with bad economic setbacks.

An open mind
A sincere heart
Candid confessions,
Filter-free expressions
Honest laughter
Genuine tears
Authentic anger
Leaves me to ponder
Does purity in all its forms exist?
I surely wonder!

THE HARLEM HELLFIGHTERS

Their enemies, the Germans, called them 'The Harlem Hellfighters' out of reverence and fear. The French, their allies, called them 'The Men of Bronze'. The Harlem Hellfighters were the first black regiment in action in World War I. In fact, they were officially known as the 369th infantry regiment and they were formed in New York City at a crucial point of time in American history. They went on to become the most decorated and the longest-serving units of the Great War. The unit suffered a large number of indignities at the hands of many white officers in the US but they stood up against all odds and were famous for their valour and prowess.

At that time, the black were not treated as equals and were not empowered in the US. The country was set to enter World War I. Racism was prevalent in the US and the period between World War I and World War II was replete with incidents of racial violence against the black in the US—and the Harlem Hellfighters were black too. It is intriguing to note that many individuals in the regiment who returned as conquering heroes were marginalised irrespective of their achievements. They were used as a means to an end in a mercenary way. The discrimination was rife as the regiment was assigned to fight along with the French army (on behalf of the US) as many white American soldiers refused to combat with them in the unit, which was well-equipped with helmets and rifles, whilst the Hellfighters were given none.

As they went into the battlefield, many American officers believed that African Americans lacked the intelligence and the strength to fight fiery armies in Europe. But the regiment achieved a fantastic combat record of fighting continuously for 191 days on the front. They disproved their sceptics by spending the longest duration in continuous combat and winning it. Self-belief was the key for them and external perceptions did not deter their courage. They did not only fight the enemies out there but also the thoughts and actions of being treated differently and unfairly. They persisted and they resisted this attack and did not let it impact their might and focus. Their resilience was unparalleled.

The Harlem Hellfighters are a great example of what resilience can do. The blacks in this regiment continued to fight with great fearlessness and fortitude inspite of being exposed to so much racial disparity. Their heroism and resolve to persist on the trenches for the longest time affirms what determination and focus can bring about. Some of them hailed from very humble backgrounds and gave up their lives while fighting the longest war with Germany. Yet they were undaunted and stubborn, leveraging their inner strength and power to deal with the difficult conditions at war, expecting nothing in return.

In the remote contours of history, the Harlem Hellfighters have passed the test of resilience in body and spirit. They fought to protect those who never recognised them for their valour and fortitude. Their heroism has been documented in history but unfortunately it was not appreciated at the right time during their existence. They were dedicated to their profession and were determined to not let spirits down. A special recognition in their history is the reverence and gratitude shown by the French towards them. The French government honoured them for their exquisite fearlessness and diligence which was on display at the battlefield. The regiment was awarded by the French government and close to 171 individual medals of valour were bestowed upon them. Croix de Guerre is an award bestowed upon soldiers from Allied countries for bravery in combat by the French government and the regiment got this award after spending close to 191 days in front-line trenches. Eventually, the US handed over this regiment to France.

In those days, discrimination against the blacks was much higher, and it was in fact difficult for them to get into military services. The Harlem Hellfighters are held in high esteem and regard for their boldness to get into the services among so much of resistance and obstruction. It is not always easy to pledge your allegiance for those who do not acknowledge your contribution. We should salute their resilience.

RESIST, RISE AND REMAIN—CALMNESS DOES NOT EQUAL PASSIVENESS!

Kay was working in an e-commerce firm in India when she was sent to the US on a particular project. Her husband stayed back due to his professional compulsions. It was a difficult decision but they both agreed to try and make it work. Kay had been working in her firm for over a year and enjoyed her work tremendously. She had worked in the US earlier as well, so there was some familiarity that she enjoyed with the culture of the country and its people. She was looking forward to her new role. When she reached her new office, she was quickly introduced to her colleagues, vertical heads, including Jennifer Woodlands.

Woodlands was one of the influential team members who was handling one of the most important projects in the IT department. Over the next few weeks, as Kay started working on the project, the working hours got longer and longer that started to impact her well-being. She continued, trying her best to overcome the fatigue. As a result of her ill health, she only focused on work and could not join the team engagements, lunches and dinners. She was so immersed in work that she could not find time to make friends. However, she always conducted herself in a collegiate way with peers and assisted younger colleagues in whatever way she could.

Kay's team had largely local Americans. She was yet figuring out how to navigate and connect. She admired the way Woodlands, took all the right steps to mingle and engage with her teammates, especially with the head of the IT department. Kay wanted to learn that skill from her but felt there was an invisible wall every time she tried to reach Woodlands and a few others. She knew she was different but it was obvious to her that this 'difference' was standing between 'her' and 'them'. After trying a few times, Kay decided to embrace serenity and continued to focus on her work to deliver her goals. She channelled her energy to constructive ways of engaging with people outside of work and joined a few non-profit groups to give more of herself to others. Strength of mind and character, both are required to tackle challenging situations such as these.

The project came to an end and the team successfully delivered. However, Woodlands and another gentleman from the team, Paul, took most of the credit for the timely and proper delivery of the project. Kay was the key driver for strategising and final implementation but it went unnoticed in the shadow of Woodlands and Paul. The lack of recognition was hurtful for her. As days went by, she felt miserable about it given the attention bestowed on the two, which she felt should have been co-shared with her as she had left her family behind to commit herself truly to this project.

Given the project launch was successful, the unit now needed to go to the board for a go-live, and big investment dollars were needed for it. The team was summoned in again to prepare the presentation. Woodlands and Paul were leading the team and were overconfident to deliver the pitch. The board was diverse and had members from different parts of the world. To ensure all goes right, Kay did put forward her views to the project team about placement of the product in different parts of the world, but was ignored. Yet she continued her research and diligence as she was confident about her insights and approach. She had a high ownership of the project and was not willing to have interpersonal dynamics mar it in anyway.

The crucial morning to present to the board arrived. The presentation commenced. Woodlands and Paul were in the flow. Suddenly a board member stopped them and asked how this would make sense in Asia or Africa. The two leads stumbled and tried to murmur something on customisation. The board member was not convinced. The conversation veered towards doing a US launch first and then the rest of the world. The board members were unsure about how a testing done in US would really work for emerging markets? And, since the product is catering to the needs of emerging markets, why launch it in the US? Also, a huge revenue potential lay outside the US too. Given the lack of convincing answers from the ill-prepared project leads, the team could sense the investment was beginning to slip away from the project. Uninvited, Kay stepped in with her views! She may have crossed a few boundaries here, but she felt it was the right thing to do.

On the basis of her extensive research and diligence, she took them through the launch plans in South America, Africa and certain parts of the US, which could provide lessons for the emerging markets. Being familiar with Asia was an advantage for her as she could share her insights and connect the product in the US to Asia more aptly. A barrage of questions followed from other board members and Kay was in full form, as this discussion infused more life back into the project. After an hour of the debate, the board signed off the money to go ahead with the implementation in line with what Kay had shared. As Kay walked out of the conference room, the project team stood up and a round of applause followed!

Her getting in front of the board to talk was not driven by her need to prove someone right, wrong, superior or inferior. It was simply to salvage the project. It felt like the right thing to do inspite of what Woodlands and Paul did. Today, Kay had nothing to tell anyone, but everyone knew.

Throughout the entire episode, Kay tried to gain strength from herself. Her self-belief kept her going, it spurred her to persist and keep a positive social disposition. Sometimes we worry and ruminate too much about issues beyond our control, which can make minds cloudy and impact confidence. Kay did not give into any indulgence to any such prophecy, rather concentrated on how she can do better. She had herself as her companion in her moment of distress. Kay derived strength from her self-awareness about what was important and then she focused on that irrespective of all odds. She held herself accountable for what happened to her and that gave her the power to change it as well. In tough situations, it helps to don a fearless yet collaborative attitude and let your faith be larger than your fears. She kept calm and carried on!

Resilience demands faith in self, life and our values. Awareness keeps us on the path when the going gets tough. It is natural to feel flustered in tough situations, however when one does not give up and keeps trying, there is always light at the end of the tunnel.

Tryst with Racism as We Step into the World!

Stepping into the world of college education can be exciting! One leaves the comforts of home, security of family, to find a new identity in the dynamic world. One seeks new friends, new alliances, relationships and perhaps a new way of being! Now superimpose this with a new country, a new culture and a shade of colour to deal with. This is what a student faces who decides to pursue education outside their home countries. Many a time their decision is driven in pursuit of high-quality education and better opportunities. Some acquire skills and learning to return to their homelands, whilst a few wish to persist with some overseas experience to gather a rounded perspective by working globally.

We often find that in many emerging markets like Asia, students gravitate towards the Ivy League or other top colleges in the US or UK, in search of greener pastures. The fees for international students in all countries are multiples of what the local students pay. There are families who can afford it, whilst others spend savings or take loans to propagate a high-quality education for their children. It is seen as an investment in the next generation's future.

When so much is at stake, these students have to toughen themselves to take on the challenge of any change. It is, however, not easy if they have never worked in a mixed-race environment. Adaptability is the key and resilience is crucial.

Mongkut was from Bangkok. His father worked in a consumer marketing company who had always aspired to study in the US but his parents could not afford it. Mongkut's father had worked hard throughout his life, was educated locally and took up a job in a good company. Over the years, he did well and was ecstatic when Mongkut received an acceptance from an Ivy League university. He felt his own life's mission had been fulfilled with his son going to study in a top US college. He felt really proud, and happily shared the news with friends and family. He took time off work to drop his son for this significant milestone in his life.

Mongkut loved the college and its surroundings. He was in the US for the first time. Like a little child, he was filled with wonderment. The size of the burgers, the wide roads and lovely green pastures, all this was new for Mongkut. He loved it all. His roommate was a local white American who had his own busy life with his friends. He was cordial with Mongkut and had brief conversations when he was back at midnights! Once the initial euphoria was over, Mongkut realised he was in an extremely competitive environment and it was not going to be easy to establish himself like it had been in school. Everyone in his college class was very good so he had to really rise to the new benchmarks. He studied hard to do well academically. However, that was not enough. In college, being a part of social groups is very critical to have access, a network and a status!

Mongkut discovered the social networks—fraternities (frats) of boys—that were essential to be a part of if he wanted to embed himself in college. To enter the frats, you have to 'rush' and meet the 'brothers'. If they 'liked' you, they may induct you into the group. Mongkut's social skills were not the best for this hyperactive college as he had never experienced this environment before. Somehow, he managed to get into one of the 'frats'. Every weekend, the frats would have chapters (meetings) and he would try and attend these. However, not being from the US, he did not have knowledge of the local games, sports icons or friends from local schools to lean on. He tried to learn, to be one of them in the meetings, but he felt lonely and lost in the crowd. The feeling of not fitting in socially started to gnaw at him gradually and he started to feel depressed!

As this feeling built up, his grades fell and he stopped engaging with the other students socially. He was afraid that they may think he is not good enough for them. This led to a vicious cycle of not feeling socially adept that led to more loneliness. Sometimes he wanted to rush back home to Bangkok, however, his father's dreams kept him grounded. He knew he had to make the most of this opportunity.

One day, Mongkut saw Arnold sitting outside the library. Arnold headed a fraternity group and was munching his sandwich alone. Mongkut mustered his courage and boldly (not his usual style) joined Arnold on the steps. He mentioned that he had seen Arnold in a frat session. They got talking about a project that Arnold was working on. The topic was familiar for Mongkut and he shared his invaluable insights. They discussed for a while and Arnold was very impressed withMongkut's thoughts. He invited him to the project team. Some people in the team were unsure why Mongkut was there as he was a freshman whereas the team was full of seniors. However, it was a matter of a few days and all of them realised that he had a lot to offer towards the project that would benefit all of them.

As Mongkut conducted research on the project, he approached a professor who had an opening for the teaching assistant's role. Impressed with Mongkut's intellect and perseverance, he offered that assignment to him. These two engagements helped Mongkut expand his network. The feeling of isolation started to metamorphose into optimism. He knew he was opening his wings and was beginning to fly in the direction his dad would have wanted him to.

Reinforced with his successful engagements, Mongkut decided to create more awareness about South East Asians and created a band to introduce music from that region. He identified a few music-friendly students in the university, approached them and motivated them to join in. The band started small, but became a big hit for its novelty on the campus. Mongkut's popularity soared.

In a new environment where one is dealing with different set of people, culturally or otherwise, keeping faith and optimism is critical. Often when one is navigating through a new and unfamiliar cultural jungle, the trick is to keep tuning yourself and experimenting to find a new path. Embracing a new culture without judging it is key whilst keeping your core self intact. Mongkut's courage in approaching the professor and commencing on a South East Asian band at a time when a lot of people did not believe in the idea was a symbol of his tenacity and his determination. He was an introvert and a bit reclusive, therefore, for him to connect with seniors in a new college to form a band was really stepping out of his comfort zone. Taking the first step towards a change is difficult. However, life starts at the edge of your comfort zone.

A national survey conducted in 2016 across 1,500 first-year college students in various two and four-year institutions by Steve Fund and JED Foundation revealed that 75% of the coloured students keep their feelings about facing difficulties in college to themselves whereas only 61% of the white people tend to open up more. In fact, about 47% of the white students felt that the college was not living up to its expectations as opposed to 57% of the coloured students. Additionally, 36% black students felt more academically prepared than their peers as opposed to 50% of the white students on campus. The power of endurance of the black students is a determinant of their ability to deal with micro-aggressions on the campus. In some places, black students attend non-elite schools, which are perceived to be less rigorous so that they could perform better there. This points to 'mismatch theory' which means that policies which are race conscious do more harm than good to minorities in the long run as the coloured students learn far lesser.

The concept of 'double consciousness' as coined by William Edward Burghardt Du Bois tells us that coloured minorities are pressurised to view themselves in the same way as the white majority perceives them and are compelled to live with two identities. It can be quite overwhelming to manage the stress that arises out of the continuous exposure to racism in academic and social domains on a regular basis. Therefore, a significant amount of emotional and psychological energy is required to navigate through all the anxiety and the trauma. That's the journey of resilience.

EXCELLENCE TRIUMPHS OVER COLOUR

Babu was an aspirational young man when he went to Australia to study for his master's degree. He did his MS in Radiology from the University of Sydney and consequently started working there in one of the hospitals as a radiologist.

His family lived in India and that made him a bit lonely, being away from his own. Over time, he learnt to adapt himself to the Australian culture and created a world of his own. He had not experienced much trouble finding his first job but he definitely found it difficult to keep it going amongst a very purist local Aussie working environment. He was conscious of his brown colour. While growing up in India, he had witnessed relative comparisons between fair and dark colour with not so great associations with brown or black. This unconsciously played up on his mind.

Babu was one of the students who passed his course with flying colours and was conferred with the Dean's Award in his college in Australia. He was even requested to come back to the college to teach new students. He was applauded for his uncanny aptitude to be able to see things from a different perspective. In the college, he had earned his laurels by going beyond what machines could show to a radiologist. His early diagnosis in some cases had even saved a few lives.

As he commenced his new assignment, he was welcomed by the medical faculty with open arms. However, when he started working with the patients, he noticed that a few of them were quite uncomfortable getting their ultrasounds done by him. He found some of them would ask for an alternative doctor or go to another hospital. Babu was unclear what was driving this behaviour but he did not feel good about this. He knew he was capable and more qualified than many other doctors around him, however, some patients were yet not comfortable with him. Not fully aware of the issues, he continued on his path unfazed. Ultrasound is a test where certain body parts of the patient that have to be examined are exposed, so that the doctor can capture the scan of the organs. Babu felt that perhaps he was not conducting something properly and hence the concerns were being shared by the patients to the administration. He became extra cautious, given that the Australian rules and regulations with regard to medical health are very rigid and one has to be careful while giving the diagnosis report to be compliant.

Then, his worst fear came true. In one of the ultrasound interactions, the Australian patient asked him the name of the country he belonged to. He then asked him how clean is the place and what were Babu's hygiene standards. He even pushed Babu to reconfirm that he had washed his hands! As Babu continued with the ultrasound, after a few minutes, the man said he was not comfortable. Babu was disappointed and requested him to share the issues, so he could do better with the next patient. Uncomfortably, the man shared that he had never seen brown doctors in his town. Most such people were cab drivers or unskilled workers. Hence, he was worried whether Babu really knew what he was doing and was fully conversant about the Australian medical system.

Babu felt shattered. He actually felt heartbroken, but now he understood that this perception may have manifested into some kind of discomfort for the other patients who refused to get treated by him. His horrific memories of fair and dark colour in India bubbled up. It was evident to him that his ethnicity created doubts in patients' minds, with regards to his capabilities. It did not matter what an ace doctor he may have been or how many degrees he might have to prove it, what mattered to them was his colour that was associated with their lack of confidence in his competence.

Babu then informed the officer in charge of the radiology department about these incidents that were driven by ethnic undertones. To salvage himself, he requested the officer to check on his procedures so that they could instil confidence in the patients on his work rather than moving them to alternative doctors. Consequently, whenever some patients shared their concerns that may have been triggered by a colour bias, the officers in the administrative department were asked to counsel the patients and educate them about Babu and his credentials. This enabled the patient to stay with this best radiologist rather than be guided by their biases.

Patients were made aware that Babu had received appreciation from senior doctors in the department for the way he carried out his diagnostics. These efforts paid up and over due course of time, he became one of the best-performing radiologists in the hospital and also received an award for outstanding performance.

The first thing to do to remove any bias is ensuring it does not touch one individually. One needs to immune themselves to manage their thinking and response towards it. The second thing to do is to persist and seek support as appropriate. For the individual, it is best to allow your work and your strength of character to become your spokesperson. Last of all, those who are biased need to be made aware that their thinking is unfounded, else they will not be in a position to get rid of it.

When I start doubting myself,
When my knowledge is questioned
When my education can't fight the colour bias
When I give indulgence to self-deprecation
Yet,
I am reminded of my tenacity
I am able to recollect the sleepless nights
I recount the days when I felt homesick
I had the courage to continue
Because I knew I was empowered
Because I knew I could prove myself whenever required
Because purity of heart can defeat prejudices of mind

Babu believed in his capabilities and persisted to the best of his abilities. His self-respect was of paramount importance to him. His penchant to thrive intellectually in his profession gave him the confidence to navigate through difficult and uncomfortable situations. Babu knew that he was dedicated and honest to his profession and that was enough to keep himself resilient.

Babu also shared that engaging with people and trying to make them see an alternate point of view really helped him tide over the situation. He strived to break the false glass ceiling of myths and biases and wished people focus on capability that knows no colour. Babu utilised support from other doctors/officers to educate himself on ways of working locally and also the patients about his pedigree and experience. He derived strength from his confidence, from his self-belief and from his well-wishers too. It was imperative for him to educate some of the local people that what matters in a doctor is his competence and not colour.

The German psychologist, Norman Garmezy, aptly explains how our ability to perceive a situation in a certain way helps us to be resilient. At times, we may find a situation to be confusing. We immerse ourselves in it in a way that it becomes an opportunity to learn and grow, so that we can become stronger in the long run.

Colour at the Top?

It takes a lot of grit and perseverance to reach to the top of a corporate pyramid. Leadership is a lonely journey and sometimes colour makes the climb up the ladder tougher. Success has no shortcuts. I have not heard any individual stating that s/he had it easy, but possibly a person of colour or one belonging to a minority had it harder. Being a leader is tough and everything becomes fair in love and war. During leadership battles, all variables including race, colour and gender will be thrown at you. It requires courage, conviction of choices and one needs to go against the tide, if needed. To rise and fall and rise again is an important ingredient of a leader. When a leader transcends the depths of the oceans, sharks cannot be avoided. One needs unwavering faith and clarity of purpose to overcome odds.

The data does show that ethnicity ratios at leadership level in global companies are not great. Research shows that a few have had the courage to persist and rise but more people need to persist to get the balance right. Since 2002, the number of coloured CEOs in Fortune 500 companies has touched the lowest figure across the world. According to research from UCLA, in the C-suite of the US' largest companies, the representation of African Americans has witnessed a downward trend. There have been only sixteen black CEOs since 1999, who have been at the helm of Fortune 500 companies.

The following figure shows the share of minority directors being appointed to the open board seats of the Fortune 500 companies. There had been a steep rise in the appointment of Asian-American directors to open board seats after 2010 and consequently there has been a sharp fall in 2012. At less than 4% of new board seats, Asian-American director appointments saw the sharpest fall in 2012. In 2013, the share of the appointment of African-Americans directors in new board seats was the highest, at over 10% and now has plateaued at a single data point for two years. Interestingly, there has been a sharp rise in the share of Hispanic director appointments to new board seats as the number has risen from 4% in 2015 to 6% in 2016.

Figure 6.1 Minority appointments to Fortune 500 boards

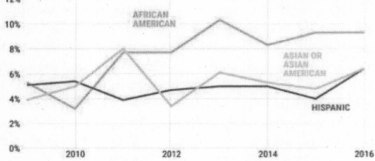

Source: Heidrick and Struggles' 2017 Board Monitor Report. Grace Donnelly. Fortune Magazine. February 2018.

The number of coloured people at the helm of companies are countable. It requires a systemic and focussed effort to change these stats. Ethnicity targets are legal in certain countries, however, compliance is sketchy. An ethnic diverse workforce brings ingenuity and innovative ideation for the future. Whether companies are global or local, diverse thinking gives birth to a new way of doing things which can become a competitive edge for many. Different ethnicities bring a different viewpoint to a global business that may actually be truly beneficial for companies, clients and shareholders.

POWER AND PERSEVERANCE

Ramen got placed in a French MNC as soon as he finished his undergraduate degree in engineering. He was elated to join the company. After working for the company in Asia for three years, he was sent to France on a long-term project, which he thought would provide a substantial boost to his career. He was placed in Paris, a city he had wished to explore for the longest period of time. It was indeed very exciting for a young man, in his 20s to have got the opportunity to participate and contribute on an overseas project for a reputed organisation in a city of his choice. The French experience was refreshingly new and unexpected. The language was definitely a problem outside the office and the work culture in Paris was quite different. There was consideration given to work-life balance and the French prefer not to overwork themselves relative to Asia. As Ramen started work on the project, he began to understand the importance of interpersonal dynamics that played a key role in collaborative alliances at the workplace. It was difficult for him to establish strong, tenuous relationships with the French team members because communication was a real barrier.

Although, his colleagues spoke some English, they were much more comfortable speaking in French. Especially, when there were informal conversations, they definitely did prefer to speak in their mother tongue. Ramen struggled to integrate at work. He found his local colleagues a bit more inward-focused and reclusive. Ramen was an extrovert and he felt most of the office people were too quiet. They even smiled a lot lesser than they should, he thought. He liked a few friends and acquaintances around him but they too had limited time for him. Hence in Paris, he had no one to really share his experiences with. He wanted to go out, explore the city, learn new things but it was odd for him to do this by himself. However, he kept his positive outlook, focused on his learning at work and exposure to greener pastures in Paris.

Ramen was fortunate enough to meet a young black fellow team member, Alex, who was from Kenya, but had been educated in the US. He had been working in the company for a year and this was also his first proper opportunity to work in a global project. He seemed as lost as Ramen did! However, given their similar circumstances, a friendship commenced.

After meeting Alex, Ramen had one pertinent question which was on his mind—'It is fascinating how minority/coloured individuals connect easily to each other on foreign land. Why does this happen?' Alex and Ramen were both alone and became good friends due to a different shade of colour they shared as foreigners in a new place. They started to explore Paris, its cuisine and its historical treasures. Alex was well-versed with the French language and helped Ramen learn a bit of workable French.

At work, with this new-found support system, Ramen found it easier to push his way around. The feeling that he had another colleague to fall back upon if something went wrong was powerful. He started to use his broken French to communicate which was much appreciated by his colleagues and they soon started to talk to him in their broken English too.

A few in the team who had never worked with Asians behaved strangely, as if Ramen was unskilled. Even though Ramen was a topper in his college, he did not take this personally and was polite with everybody. He was unsure if those few would ever respect him for his competence or will ever get over his colour. There were certain times, when Ramen took a back seat when he found his French colleagues not warming up to his thoughts and recommended action on the project.

However, Alex rubbed off on Ramen. He was quite a calm and charming individual who did not get perturbed by such attitudes with racist undertones. Instead, he asked Ramen to exercise patience in that environment and concentrate on the output of his work. He told him, nothing succeeds like success. Alex and Ramen worked very hard and persisted to perform well at work. As they did well, the attitude of those few teammates changed a little. The partnership and support that Alex and Ramen provided to each other helped them stay the course in a new and different environment. Ecosystem and support are key ingredients for us to progress and persist in the pursuit of our vision.

This experience taught Ramen that colour can connect people. His support system in the form of Alex provided him the much needed social support to keep going. They were from different cultures but they did identify with each other's life story and there was an instant empathy. They provided comfort to each other and knew they were there for each other. If one stumbled, the other was there to get him back on his feet to start again. Power of friendship fuels the power of resilience. It was evident that certain shades of colour came together and helped each other to become a stronger shade that can override any colour bias.

Harsh History, Hard Reality

In the aftermath of World War II, the Jews immigrated in large numbers from Eastern Europe since most of them were being executed in public places or were removed from government ranks. Some surviving Jews tried to return to their pre-war homes, but they were unwelcome. The National Council of Jewish Women in US set up the department for immigrant aid to protect female immigrants at the time of arrival. In fact, the council assisted immigrant Jews with regard to health, employment problems and housing. The US was one of the largest centres of Judaism in the world after World War II. The Jews in the US have invested in education and formed themselves into a rich community of educated individuals. They largely immigrated to the American sunbelt—Los Angeles and Miami.

Today the story is a little different. Although the American Jews have played a role in active economic development and local politics, and are welcomed in country clubs and universities, the march of the white supremacists in Charlottesville in the year 2017 carrying torches and chanting, 'the Jews will not replace us', is an evidence of the anti-semitism growing in the US. All of this coupled with anti-Semitic graffiti near synagogues and various other places such as Jewish homes certainly raises an alarm with regard to the position of Jews in the US. There has also been a rise of about 57% rise in anti-Semitic incidents in the US in 2017, according to the Anti-Defamation League in the US.

It was October 2018 when Joel woke up to a number of messages on his phone from his family and friends. There had been 'some kind of' shooting in Ohio by some senseless white supremacist who had declared all Jews must die and then took the sinful step of gunning himself in a place of worship.

At first Joel shook his head in disbelief. What had he just read? He read the messages again. He went to the washroom, washed his face and read the messages again, and again. His hands shook and he had almost turned into stone. He had numerous missed calls from friends and family that were made to him while he was asleep. He went numb and could not feel anything for a few moments. A lot had taken place during his slumber and he felt that perhaps he had woken up at the wrong time or he was still in a scary dream.

As he read the messages, he started crying. This shooting had changed everything for him as he had lost his parents and his two friends who were natives of that town and were believers of Judaism. His shock overtook his grief and then it transcended into anger. As much as he did not want to, he kept turning back to the face of the perpetrator asking the question, why? He recognised the hate in the shooter's eyes for his people. He knew that hate and resentment because he felt the echoes of it in himself. But, why harbour hate for another, for his non-white skin colour, for being Hebrew, for observing Sabbath and for going to a synagogue?

Whether it was hate or some other underlying reason, Joel was writhing with anger at one point and howling at some other time. The barrage of emotions consumed him. His ears could still hear his mother's voice and his father's footsteps, he stared at the last WhatsApp message, from one of his friends, whom he had lost in the incident. He read about the incident in detail, again, and was shivering with anger. His phone was ringing, but he refused to take the call. He was not in a position to speak to anyone, his mind was flooded with questions and most of all the strong desire to meet the perpetrator.

Joel ran outside his house, he ran for a good three kilometres before he fell to the ground and broke down. He had never imagined that his origin and his identity will cause him to lose his family, and, therefore, everything in totality. He never thought that hate for his community could have fatal consequences, never realised the fact that he and his family were so unwelcome in the country that they would be killed, wiped out in a few hours. He could not bear it. His entire body was in pain, and he could not explain it. He did not want to get up. Life perhaps had come to an end.

In fact, it was natural for Joel to be angry, but the anger was born out of irreversible loss, which made him think, why would anyone do this? Incidents such as these sometimes have such as a life-changing and lasting impact on our lives. We reach an inflexion point to rethink or redefine our outlook towards us and towards the other. Joel was deeply disturbed and yet bewildered. He could find no justification for this incident, of the kind of fate his parents met with. It was difficult for him to fathom the fact that hate can take such a form, that too hate for those who follow Judaism. He was perplexed when he thought about his own future, his own presence in this world. It is important to get inside the mind of such perpetrators and understand the reason for such hate which transcends into such consequences. But, we are all human beings and it's just one world, why not live happily together? Where do such unreasonable insecurities arise from? This world will not get peace by spreading hate but rather love and respect would do the needful for sustainable peace and harmony.

Quite a large number of young Jewish families had migrated here from Israel, only for a peaceful life.

As a child, Joel knew that he did not exactly look like his neighbours. He spent hours looking at his facial features in the mirror. Like his local friends, he wished to be more fashionable, bleach his hair golden and mesh with the crowd. He wanted to change his surname.

He wanted to lead a normal life and most of all, he wanted to be happy. He wanted to mix with his neighbours, forge sustainable and lifelong relationships. His family was quite open-minded and had encouraged him to believe that all humans are equal. In fact, he had also learnt that colour does not indicate a person's nature or character; instead, it is the way we are, the way we think and behave with others, it is our soul which perhaps is the important indicator of a person. The physicality that draped his body often filled him with questions—who are we and where do we belong? His family were God-fearing, good people. A common and widespread mistake is to confuse Jewish people with Muslims. Some people ensure that their ignorance manifests itself in various ways and it spreads like fire and distorts information. Living in constant threat of being evacuated from a country for no fault of yours can be quite a difficult task, especially in a country which has been your home for close to two decades.

Joel was left wondering, was it his fault that he was born a Jewish? It is at these points when a human being is left helpless because he cannot find the answers to his questions.

Joel has battled ever since that shooting to come to terms with his loss. His initial reaction that day was that of avenging death of his parents on his own. It has been difficult for Joel to deal with this kind of a mishap in his life. He spent most of his time asking questions and not being able to answer them. This incident shook him, but it also forced him to introspect and realise the malaise, which afflicts society and perhaps the whole world.

It is their will power and hope that has kept Joel and all other Jews in Berlin and any other parts of the world alive. The hope that one day they will be accepted and their histories will not affect their present or their future.

This is perhaps the best example of an instance when unchecked hate and illogical hatred for a certain community or culture takes a fatal turn and results in irreparable destruction. In a country like the US, which is a land of immigrants and has always welcomed Jews across the land in every sphere, such incidents point towards a certain seething ill-informed mindset, which is growing so fast among the white supremacists that it smells of danger and will ultimately lead to emotional damage.

The need of the hour is to have a dialogue and unravel such pent-up feelings, which can manifest externally in such harmful ways that it can cause an individual like Joel to lead a listless life. We perhaps are required to stand in solidarity to prevent such hate and prejudice from spreading. For those who come from another land and with much hardship make the new one their own, such incidents are symbolic of the fact that they are undesirable. But even then, I would say that these are the inflexion points sending out alarm bells for us to get out and act together, to locate the real problem and find the right solution.

SUMMARY

1. You are your largest source of strength. We as human beings tend to draw support and strength from others because we forget that it lies within us.
2. We need to realise that no matter where we go, there is an ecosystem that we can build to tide through tough times.
3. Persistence and unwavering courage is the key to resistance.
4. Believe in yourself and trust those who believe in you!
5. Living in fear is not a solution. Sometimes we need to stop and find solutions that do not exist for problems of today.

Looking Ahead

A journey of a thousand miles starts with a small step.
—Lao Tzu

…I think we have already taken a few steps in our tryst with colour, but there is more distance to cover…

CAN FUTURE BE 'COLOURLESS'?

Connect, Openness, Love, Objectivity, Understanding and Resilience are sewn together in a word for a reason. They represent what 'colour' actually implies. Any other meaning is a matter of interpretation when applied to the human race.

As I ponder over my childhood art book after thirty years, I look at all the colours again. I realise how much I have been in awe of the vibrancy of the interplay between colours that actually infuse life into the paintings. Each colour evokes love, optimism and energy that makes me hopeful. Over my life's journey, I continue to decode what's hidden behind these colours for us. Black has this beautiful mystery that wants me to get closer and discover it more. It evokes an emotion of power, authority and elegance. It is considered to be an absence of any colour, with insurmountable depths. White feels light and innocent. It is born when the goodness of all the other colours is reflected out to the world. It evokes an emotion of peace and security. Brown denotes earthiness, stability. It reminds us of that earth that is all embracing and honest. It provides a sense of warmth and reliability, which unfailingly becomes a foundation of feeling whole and in unison with others. I wonder if one could simply apply these feelings to people of these colours too. That would make our life so beautiful!

As I talk to my children, I often share experiences of my time in diverse locations in the Americas, Europe and Asia. Traversing the world to find livelihood as a brown person has been the best experience I have had. If I were to go back in time, I would do this all over again. This is not to say that it was smooth and easy, but it made me a different person and helped me shape a global outlook. I had my own cultural challenges of dealing with the different languages and mannerisms of different Asian countries. I adopted a very straight-on, outcome-focused and bias-for-action approach in the US and a subtle and consensus driven way of working in Europe. Every time I moved, multiple racial and cultural challenges surfaced, making me unsure of why I did this to myself! However, there was always that 'someone there' to hold my hand and navigate me through the forest of cultural alleys.

There is something inexplicable and beautiful about this human connect. It is beyond religion, colour and nationality. It is just a simple bond and a feeling of care and compassion. It is about giving. In my experience across countries, I have had to contend with many who held views about me just by reading my name or by taking a single look at me. A few ensured that I was discomforted and excluded to a point of giving up, but then there were also those who would step up to mitigate this negativity and help me navigate the maze. I was always the same person, but different people looked at me differently, depending on their own predisposition. When I was frustrated in Asia, my manger helped me understand the acceptability of words and mannerisms in the same continent with somewhat similar people. When I was burnt out in New York, a colleague taught me to pace myself in the marathon that was the corporate race; I had been sprinting too fast. When I almost gave up in a European office after being targeted by a few, when I thought the predominantly white work group would never accept the hybrid Asian and American working style of a *desi*—they were there to hold my hand. My support system was colour-blind and saw me as colourless. Those relationships were born out of a certain chemistry, connect and understanding. Most of them had worked outside their home country and empathised with me.

The cross-cultural experience also helped me change my perception of certain races. I did not realise that I too had biases until I became a minority myself. From far away, a country always looks beautiful in post cards, but when you live there with its people, it forces you to look at your lens of life. In my early days of working, I found it difficult to push back or challenge any unfairness. Our formal education teaches us many things, but not much about how to manage life. I was put into situations at work where I had no option but to fight back or perish. So, I fought back to survive. I got it right sometimes and not at other times, but I got better each time. I became aware of my inner strength and capabilities, which helped me keep moving in the right direction. As a minority person, it can be scary sometimes; not just because of the environment around oneself, but also because one lacks confidence and support when one is lonely. Through my early conflicts, I learnt that my self-belief, my self-confidence and unrelenting determination were my best companions. Being guided by them kept me on my journey as I travelled past thick and thin.

NATIONALISM OR RACISM: WHAT COMES FIRST?

We do have our similarities and differences with other people, but I don't think there is any homogeneity in any race. People vary within the same bands of nationality, colour or religion too. The need to belong to a group may be driven by power or security, but how is a group defined by country, nationality, religion or colour? Issues emerge when this debate is leveraged for a self-centred agenda. As a British Indian, do I have to choose my loyalties? I can't vote in India, but do I have to explain why my vote must matter in England even though I am brown?

The relationship between nationalism and racism in modem times is a really interesting one. As we know racism is an age-old ideology, with the human body as the focus. Nationalism, synonymous with patriotism, is a constructed faith in a geography leading to ideologies such as liberalism, conservatism and socialism. In the current geopolitical times, nationalism is often seen to drive racism across. Superimpose this with religion and the debate gets more complicated. Oft-heard comments in developed markets are, 'XYZ country or people took our jobs away', while not realising that more jobs are being lost to robots than to other nations; 'Migrants impact our economy', although there is no domestic workforce to take up unskilled jobs; 'Minorities live off our national system and burden our tax payers', when most minorities do pay their taxes too. I am not saying things are perfect across, but we are starting this debate with a positive intent to find a solution. Otherwise, we could always perpetuate the earlier debate of power and security, where people like me are good and people like you are bad.

Nationalists tend to give more importance to their own 'people'. Every country has nationalists, but if we were all strictly nationalists with allegiance to our nations alone, then colour or religion ideally should not matter in secular geographies, but they often do. When nationalist chants are drummed up, suddenly what is 'home' to an ethnic minority may become a place of fear fraught with vulnerabilities. 'Supremacist' sentiments tend to prevail in such climates. Supremacists believes they are superior to others, leading to dissonance at many ends. This belief is then combined with many other variables in geopolitical situations, rupturing human bonds. Even within the same race, there are different groups, hence, homogeneity is a myth.

There are many drivers of human minds. Inspite of the politics, it is difficult to explain why Hispanics and blacks will vote for a US leader who is perceived to be supporting 'white supremacists'. Why will Muslims support Hindu leaders and vice versa? Why? Perhaps people are voting in the hope for change. Perhaps this is the best choice available to them?

People have similar needs across the globe. Is it possible for all people to coexist with some common, shared thoughts without being coerced to act in a certain way? No two people are similar whether in a family or in a group, but colour and race somehow magnifies and distorts these differences, leading to hostility in its extreme forms.

As we peek back into history, some of these debates are cyclical. However, the fact that we can debate this openly today—that itself is huge progress. From a recent past of dark slavery to passive submission to awareness and debate are steps in the right direction. The world around us will keep evolving and changing, sometimes a few steps forward and sometimes a few steps back. However, it is you and I who have to continue to pursue the journey forward in the right direction. Our collective resolve with learnings from the past can help us build a better legacy for our children that is filled with natural colours, but devoid of any racist colours.

> *Won't you celebrate with me*
> *What I have shaped into*
> *A kind of life? I had no model.*
> *Born in Babylon*
> *Both non-white and woman*
> *What did I see to be except myself?*
> *I made it up*
> *Here on this bridge between*
> *Starshine and clay,*
> *My one hand holding tight*
> *My other hand; come celebrate*
> *With me that everyday*
> *Something has tried to kill me*
> *And has failed.*
> *—Lucille Clifton*

We have made progress, but we still have issues to deal with as the debate of race and racism impacts our daily life. These issues can be overcome as long as we keep an open mind to resolve them, as long as we don't shun them, we don't avoid them, we don't run away from discussing them, we don't treat as a problematic or taboo. If we are able to do this together, we can keep our future generations from suffering and living with conscious and unconscious bias.

RESOLVE TO RISE AND STAND TALL

Thought leaders around the world have been doing their bit to ensure that the definition of beauty is equated with character without any splashes of skin colour. Nandita Das was one of the first women in India to lend support to the 'Dark is Beautiful' campaign. The campaign was launched in 2009 by the NGO, Women of Worth, and Kavitha Emmanuel, the founder, had said that it was a campaign that aimed to foster inclusion. It was not necessarily an anti-white campaign, but rather ran advocacy programmes in schools to educate children about colour bias at a young age. The campaign was one of the first of its kind in India, which gave people an open platform to share any stories of skin colour related bias. There are many women and men who spend years denying their natural skin colour and use a number of products only to get a lighter skin tone. Nandita Das, in all the interviews and other media interactions for the campaign, had shared that she would often talk to a lot of young women and men who were not confident and had low self-esteem because of their dark skin.

Oprah Winfrey, who has been quite vocal about her experiences with racism, took a remarkable step in 2018 when she decided to address the colour bias at the Golden Globe awards. Ironically, in fact, she was also the first black woman to be honoured with the Cecil B. DeMille Lifetime Achievement award, an honourary Golden Globe award. She used her place under the arc lights to talk about Sidney Poitier, the first black man to win the Oscar for Best Actor and the Cecil B. DeMille honour at the Golden Globes. She was also one of the few black women to have started a series on racism in 1992. The series consisted of thirteen episodes dealing with racism, which according to Oprah was prevalent all over the country. The Oprah Winfrey Show conducted a series of experiments in the wake of the Los Angeles riots in 1992. The people who came to Oprah's show were divided on the basis of eye colour. The blue-eyed were given a green collar and made to wait outside whereas brown-eyed individuals were told to stand in front of the line. Jane Elliot, a diversity expert was invited by Oprah to explain how the blue-eyed individuals voiced their frustration when they saw the brown-eyed being treated in a better way. The idea was to separate people on the basis of a physical characteristic over which none of them had any control, and as a result create frustration among those who were not treated well. She explained that melanin was the reason why the pigmentation of the skin or the eye was different and it is an illogical basis on which discrimination and prejudices are harboured, manifesting in ways that impact our world view.

Courage, on and off the Field

LeBron James, one of the finest US NBA players was on the wrong side of the colour bias. He faced quite hurtful incidents, including racist slurs being pinned on his house gate in California. LeBron has spoken at length about the incident in public because such incidents psychologically demotivate a person over and above spreading hate in society. LeBron has consistently voiced his solidarity with all those who have been at the receiving end of such disrespectful treatment and has also openly denounced such activities. He has been instrumental in raising awareness about police brutalities and has also made significant contributions to uplift communities with his charitable foundation.

LeBron's speech[5] during the ESPY 2014 awards is indicative of the larger truth underlying racism and how we need development to reduce its incidence:

'What are we doing to create change? [...] Let's use this moment... [for] all professional athletes to educate [themselves], explore these issues, speak up, use our influence and renounce all violence and, most importantly, go back to our communities, invest our time, our resources, help rebuild them, help strengthen them, help change them. We all have to do better.'

---

5   Messer L, and D Caplan. 'LeBron James, Dwyane Wade, Chris Paul and Carmelo Anthony Call for an End to Violence'. *ABC News*. 2016. https://abcnews.go.com/Entertainment/espys-2016-lebron-james-dwyane-wade-chris-paul/story?id=40563702

Coloured footballers have been marred by racism too. Raheem Sterling has set quite an example by his resolve and determination to prevent racial abuse from harming future generations in soccer. Sterling has been vocal about the racial abuse he has been subjected to and why he wants to bring such incidents under the spotlight so that he and his fellow professionals do not have to deal with such pain again. He advocates that spectators, players and everybody present in the stadium should be wary about the consequences of making racist comments against players or anybody else for that matter. The Manchester City forward who had been abused by Chelsea fans at Stamford Bridge in December 2018 was compelled to initiate a dialogue, wherein his plea was to set up a structure such that in the club or on the field, people think ten times before racially abusing a player. Raheem had escalated the matter to England's Football Association and had also participated in the Premier League's 'No Room for Racism' campaign. The Premier League has pursued the issue. Sterling has performed exceptionally well on the field despite going through so much pain and has proved to his racist friends that his stellar performance on the field was perhaps the best answer to their slurs.

Such display of courage and conversations are important to understand how race and racism affect us on a daily basis. Race has an effect on how certain groups develop, it impacts people living in a certain society, the kind of struggles that they have to face on a regular basis and how it affects children growing up with this reality. Their struggles in life are quite different. In fact, there needs to be more focus in social science studies on the impact such phenomena has on educational attainment, mental health and how we can reduce the effect and create a better world for everyone. We all have to work together to ensure that our children and our families do not suffer as victims of such implicit bias by understanding how such bias can affect them and is detrimental to their development. Research, conversations and open dialogues will only help us to understand the problem and, thereby, perhaps to resolve it better.

SPEAK UP!

Kumail Nanjiani[6] is known for playing the character of a programmer, Dinesh, on *Silicon Valley*. He has been a thinker and vocalist on his shows about racism. Through his stories, he has been able to stir up the voices of many. He married a white woman and has traversed a bridge across two cultures.

He tweeted in response to the racism seen in Charlottesville:

'And I know when someone is racist, the fault is theirs and not yours. But, in the moment, it makes you feel flattened, reduced & bullied.'

Nanjiani, who was born in Pakistan and moved to the US at the age of eighteen, has leveraged social media and shares his tryst with racism, having experienced it in Hollywood. Kumail is fearless, and extraordinarily ordinary like you and me. He is a global citizen who uncannily recognises these struggles and tells it like he sees it to many who listen and take the lead from him through his shows.

Zendaya[7], the twenty-year-old actress and singer is no stranger to racism or controversy. She spoke out against the violence and racism in Charlottesville, but this isn't the first time she's used social media to condemn racism. 'I feel like you're supposed to speak up on issues that you think are important,' she told *Us Magazine*. In 2015, she took to Instagram to respond to racist remarks about her hair on the show, *Fashion Police*.

Zendaya's famous supermarket incident would be something that any of us could have experienced where she raised an objection to being racially profiled. She was trying to purchase $400 worth of gift cards at the Vons supermarket. She claimed that the clerk executive was 'rude' to her at the checkout, assuming she could not afford a $400 gift card with her skin tone. Zendaya spoke up and her story went viral. The California supermarket recently issued an apology for the incident.

---

6 D Selby. 'Here Are 9 Celebrities Who Are Totally Here to Stand Up Against Racism on Twitter'. 2017. https://www.globalcitizen.org/en/content/celebrities-against-racism-twitter-zendaya-nanjian/

7 Ibid

We grow up listening to messages that tell us that there is a 'right way' to look or behave, that there is a certain way in which we should speak, that there is a gold standard for a particular kind of visual appeal. Such atypical monologues can only be broken when someone dares to discover the magic in themselves and in others. The privilege of power and its connection to certain skin colours has proven true historically and their external manifestation from time to time has given indulgence to outrage for years.

Maybe it's time we create a bit of space for those who we may not know so well, make an attempt to hear the voices that are left unheard and open as many doors as possible for every lonely soul left out there. I have opened doors for others and many others have opened it for me. I was an ordinary girl from a middle-class family who chose to dream and work hard to achieve her dreams. During my journey, I came across some who embraced me and some who shunned me. But I have not forgotten them. Some became family in an unknown territory, whilst other pushed me to prove myself harder through criticism. They have made me who I am today. There is light at the beginning, in the middle and at the end of the tunnel. We just have to find it and push ourselves out of our self-imposed darkness. Behind each person, each relationship, each association and acquaintance, there is a beautiful human bond waiting to strengthen us.

WHERE THERE IS A WILL, THERE IS A WAY!

Making life better with different shades is a lot about how people are made to feel and to react when they are with different people. The ability to enter someone's heart and the effort to understand their story will reduce the racial fissures that exist today. It can heal the pain and give us hope that the power of empathy is enough to bring people together.

As we all know, when we wish for something strongly and sincerely enough, the universe comes together to make it happen. For every racial issue, we can take solace and inspiration from how our judiciaries and governments across the world are attempting to do what is right. Legal systems across geographies are evolving, their views and thoughts are evolving too.

1. What are my rights?

The US Supreme Court dealt with an interesting case in 2017 when an Asian American band tried to trademark their name, 'The Slants', which is a derogatory term. The US Patent and Trademark Office did not accept the application because the name denigrates Asians. The band feels that being denied permission by the government to use the name is perhaps an example of violation of free speech.

The US Congress passed the Chinese Exclusion Act, which suspended the immigration of Chinese labourers for ten years in 1882. It was the first law that prevented naturalisation and immigration on the basis of race and nationality. In the United States versus Wong Kim Arkcase, Wong was denied re-entry to the US after he visited China, despite being born in San Francisco and his parents being US residents. The court ruled in Wong's favour on the grounds of his birthright citizenship.

The Uniform Rule of Naturalisation of 1790 was the first naturalisation law that was passed in the US, where one of the qualifications was that an individual had to be a free white person. The first case of Takao Ozawa versus United States challenged this law. Ozawa had lived in the US for twenty years, although he was born in Japan. In 1922, Justice George Sutherland denied Ozawa citizenship that Ozawa had filed for in 1915 under the Naturalization Act of 1906 because Sutherland believed that the word 'white' was perhaps identified or was a synonym for someone who belonged to the Caucasian race. But he changed his understanding of the word 'white' in the case of the United States versus Bhagat Singh Thind, where he said that Thind was an upper caste Hindu. But he said that to be eligible for citizenship, one had to be Caucasian and have white skin. He was denied the citizenship as well. The Immigration Act of 1952 said that immigration of a person couldn't be based on colour because it removes the restriction of 1790.

2. Being different is not wrong

Roma is a nomadic subgroup of people who prefer to remain independent of any territory identification. They do not follow historic traditions like most other races or clans who associate themselves with ancestral legacy. Nor do they claim right to a nationality or country and keep moving in groups. Freedom is core to who they are. They remain an enigma to many.

In Romania, the Roma had to face brutality for being who they were, based on unfounded views about them. They were attacked in a police raid on 15 December 2011, when the police broke into their homes pretending to be neighbours. They had guns, and beat up the men and women, torturing them in their own homes. The police claimed that these were usual raids for safety and security, but the raids were carried out on the pretext of illegally cut timber.

Some of the Roma courageously filed a complaint about police brutality, but after a year of investigations, the prosecutors decided they did not have enough evidence to open a case against the police. The case was reopened after the national courts in Romania ordered the prosecutors to investigate more thoroughly, but was eventually closed again and no further action was taken. That was when the Romani litigants turned to the European Court of Human Rights (ERRC) in June 2014.

Almost five years later, the Court delivered a judgement. According to Adam Weiss, who manages litigation at the ERRC, 'This long time frame is not unusual, but it is frustrating. The European Court assigned this case to a committee of three judges. They can do this when the case is considered so routine it does not require any special legal considerations. This is supposed to speed up the procedure. But then the case should have gone much faster than this. It makes it hard for other Roma who stand up for their rights to have confidence that their cases will be decided quickly enough to make a difference.'[8]

---

8 European Roma Rights Centre. 'Roma Win First-Ever Judgement of "Institutional Racism" in Europe'. 2019. http://www.errc.org/press-releases/roma-win-first-ever-judgement-of-institutional-racism-in-europe

Roma families waited for eight years to have the courts arrive at this judgement. This judgement is perhaps the strongest one delivered against Romania in history, which has identified the action of the police as a harsh treatment of the people. Police perception of the Roma being criminals and anti-socials has also been questioned here. The courts stated that racism was a key driver in this incident as there was a bias at play with police officers considering the free spirited Roma communities as criminals. According to the court, 'The applicants were targeted because they were Roma and because the authorities perceived the Roma community as anti-social and criminal.'[9] The court also decided that Romania violated the applicants' human rights by failing to investigate their allegations of racist police brutality.

If the judgement becomes final, the applicants will receive €11,700 in damages.

3. What matters is not what is said but what is heard

The Constitutional Court of South Africa passed a landmark judgement on racism and language by stating that the dismissal of Meyer Bester was correct by his employer, because the court observed and decided that the utterance by Meyer Bester was racially derogatory. Meyer Bester, an employee of Sibanye Rustenburg Platinum Mines (South Africa), felt that there was not enough space left to park his car in the parking bay and he raised the issue with the safety officer asking him to remove a car owned by a 'black man', thereby implying perhaps an 'inferior man' not deserving a parking space. The comment was made with an emphatic demeanour and when brought to light, his employer terminated Bester for being evidently racist. The decision by Sibanye Rustenburg Platinum Mines was sustained in May 2018 because courts opined that the use of descriptive language is not really neutral, but carries racist or oppressive implications.

Negative words or words used in a derogatory way may not adequately describe the world around us. Yet, the one who hears the words has the power to decide whether it is racist or not. The

9 European Roma Rights Centre. 'Roma Win First-Ever Judgement of "Institutional Racism" in Europe'. 2019. http://www.errc.org/press-releases/roma-win-first-ever-judgement-of-institutional-racism-in-europe

ruling further signifies the fact that the intent behind what we say does not matter, but what is of significance is how the hearer hears it. Words like the 'black' man or 'brown' woman can have a racist undertone or prejudiced implication according to the socio-cultural-historic context, especially in South Africa, which does have a history of racism. This judgement shows how sensitively the courts in South Africa now think about language, words, intentions and implications, thereby trying to constructively drive the anti-racism message across.

With these landmark judgements in some of the countries, we should indeed feel optimistic that there is hope for humanity. There are people in this world who can see the strands of racism and its impact and mitigate the same.

However, as I review some of these progressive landmark judgements, I struggle to find any in Asia or closer home in India. Is this because we have not evolved to the level of noticing or resolving such issues? Is this because we believe racism does not exist here, or is this simply apathy I see in emerging markets? Issues exist and we do acknowledge that minorities need to feel inclusive and safe. One hopes that in coming years our awareness and sensitivity levels will continue to rise.

Be it North East Indians or blacks in India, there is plenty of racial incidents reported in the media, but we still don't seem to be dealing with them at a mass level, or perhaps not as much at the forefront of social issues that need our attention. Progress in this context is to the extent where people are able to come out and report such cases and the police are registering their FIRs, hoping they will translate into judicial actions as appropriate.

With each passing incident, we are beginning to realise what we can do better to open our minds to others who look different but feel the same.

At the end of it, it is all about how we are made to feel when we are with people. The ability to enter someone's heart and the efforts to understand their story will reduce the racial fissures that exist today. It can heal the pain and give us hope—that the power of empathy is enough to bring people together. Let's shed our hesitation of the unknown and let's invest in the real person beyond colour.

Some Takeaways from My Reflections

The stories and discussions for my book helped me reflect on my journey and raised a few learnings that I hope to be able to mesh with my thoughts and actions, going forward.

1. Leave the past where it belongs

Bust the myths passed down through generations.

Racism is a choice we make. We don't challenge assumptions, if our parents told us about what different colours of the skin imply. We saw them practising it, so we assume it must be right. It is simple and convenient. Have we ever thought that we may be missing some real truths of interactions, meeting some lovely people who can make our journey even more memorable?

My grandmother would never allow a Muslim into her kitchen. It was not about their religion, but more about what she believed was a way of living, eating and dressing! She had a perception that they may not be as clean as she would like them to be to enter her kitchen. Further, cooking with hands that eat non-vegetarian meals was beyond any level of tolerance. As much as I loved her dearly, I was unsuccessful in making her believe that we as teenagers (then) were as dirty or clean as they were. It was tough for me to explain to her that her grandchildren ate meat outside the house without her knowledge, and so were equally sinful as any other Muslim she may have met.

The funny part was that she did not know too many Muslims and at some level these stories were passed down to her over generations too. She believed every bit of it and the paradigm was difficult to change, bordering on questioning not just her beliefs, but her identity.

My parents having studied in city colleges believed less in these prejudices and, in fact, loved the *biryanis* cooked in Muslim households. As for me, I have no clue what the fuss was about, given that I have some very good Muslims friends and we share so much in common. Across my global jaunts, they have been such a wonderful support for me.

When it comes to people and colour, try and see the world from the eyes of a baby who has no baggage for the first eighteen months till we teach them the connotation of colour.

Embrace what comes your way. Sometimes, start a conversation with people in gatherings without asking their name, where they live or where they are from. Just listen to what they say, how they say it, their expressions and their vibes before making an opinion.

2. Be vulnerable, be strong!

There is strength in letting yourself be seen with your vulnerabilities. It makes you more human. We need to step up and share our narrative, which helps people see us like the emotional being they are too. That creates more compassion and less exploitation. Our hopes, our fears, our joys will multiply by sharing them with others. This authenticity enlarges the circle of trust as trust begets trust.

I had a friend, Nasir, in Europe who was a great soccer player. He was a quiet sort, but very good at the game. He practised every day and aspired to get into one of the clubs. He was born and brought up in Europe and strongly identified with European ideologies. Nasir rarely got into conflicts and kept to his game and related activities. One day, the match got really fierce on the field. It seemed soccer had turned into rugby with some heated exchange of words and punches between the two teams. Things went a bit out of control and my friend, who till now was standing by, felt compelled to step in to garner peace. He held out his arms between the two captains and requested that they both have an amicable conversation. One of the captains, in his rugged accent said, 'Hey you, Paki, get out of the way, in fact get out of our country!' The other captain rolled over his eyes and said, 'That's the only thing I agree with you. This "Paki" does not get us.' Nasir was punched hard and he fell down.

More than the physical bruises it was his inner core that was hurt more. He was lost for words. This country was his home. Where did

'Paki' come from? Nasir found his voice and stated loudly to both the captains, 'That hurts bro!' One of the teammates helped him up and checked his bruises. My friend said, 'No, this is less painful than what they called me and how they called me.' He was upset, really upset, and he let them know it. He went on to demand that action be taken. The coach arrived on the scene, and his teammates were now more sympathetic with Nasir than the cause of the conflict between the teams.

A display of your happiness, sadness or disappointment makes people connect with you, as these are universal emotions. It is okay to feel vulnerable and let it energise our actions. It helps people understand what hurts you and bothers you, creating a shared understanding. I have been let down by my own and lifted up by others who I thought were not from my world. Colour can be leveraged to complete the picture of diverse friendships, complementing our weaknesses and strengths, making us stronger collectively.

3. Is blood thicker than humanity?

> *'The bond that links your true family is not one of blood, but of respect and joy in each other's life.'*
> *—Richard Bach*

Blood seems to be the reason why many prefer family over friends. Blood seems to be the reason why adopting a white baby for a black couple can be as exasperating as adopting a black baby for a white couple. Blood is the reason why we have the words 'ours' and 'theirs'. *But blood is also the reason why we all are one!*

Blood represents family, lineage and perhaps a way of being, which is why many hold it closely as an extension of themselves. It certainly has biological connectivity for genes; however, qualities that are associated with humanness may not be solely biological. The nature versus nurture debate has been there for decades so there is more to people than just where and from whom they were born. This 'nurture' shapes up who we are, our values, drivers and our behaviour. Relationships are based on these ingredients. Being born to a certain family or a race is not our decision, it is a given, but all other relationships are our gifts. We can empower ourselves if we really search our calling. It is our choice to respond to life with affection, love and empathy.

Andrea, a white Italian, worked for ChinChin, a Chinese senior manager in a Singaporean firm. Andrea found her reclusive, expressionless and difficult to understand. ChinChin spoke English, but that was when she spoke. Andrea was respectful towards ChinChin, but she kept social distance. She had a house-warming party and invited her team, but assumed ChinChin was different, not her type and not interested. She had a baby, but the celebration list did not include her, neither were the rants of her divorce discussed with her. ChinChin continued to maintain a professional relationship irrespective.

Andrea was travelling for a day. Her office phone rang incessantly. ChinChin, tired of the constant ringing on Andrea's desk, took the call. A doctor was on the phone, informing ChinChin that the nanny brought Andrea's son to the hospital. He had had a bad accident at home. He needed to undergo a surgery immediately and Andrea was not reachable as she was on a flight. ChinChin rushed to the hospital right away. She undertook the responsibility like a family member, donated blood, as she shared the same blood group with the baby, made sure good nursing care was provided till Andrea arrived forty-eight hours later. When she met ChinChin that evening, she felt she was meeting family. Her heartfelt gratitude rolled out with tears in her eyes. She had found her own in a new country. ChinChin became the godmother to Andrea's son. And from there on, their relationship became stronger than many others in the family.

We may don different colours of the skin, *but the colour of blood beneath that is always red.*

4. Respect yourself before you ask it of others

When someone behaves badly with you, you feel annoyed. When someone is rude to you, you feel bruised. When someone humiliates you, you feel shattered.

I did. It hurt. It pained and sometimes made me feel trivial and irrelevant. Till I understood the oft-heard statement that 'no one can hurt you or make you feel inferior unless you let them do that to you'. You let their words touch you. When was the last time you thought about how you made someone feel when you belittled them for no fault of theirs? Our emotional breakdowns are not visible to others, but they leave scars in our hearts. Sometimes, when faced with tough conflicts, we become submissive and we compromise. We believe that if we keep quiet, things will get better. It doesn't always work that way.

I recall when I was a new entrant in one of the offices in the western world, a white Australian woman publicly ridiculed me in front of many. She may have been furious or was having a moment, but that did not give her the right to misbehave with me. I was unsure why she thought she could do that to me. I was deeply hurt and embarrassed. My emotions and humiliation were evident on my face. Just that tears did not roll out of my eyes. Something in me rebelled, made me push back my chair and call her out firmly. I shared with her that I was truly disturbed and bruised with this behaviour. Whatever may be the issue, my self-respect and dignity had been attacked and that too publicly, and that was just not acceptable. When I got up to defend myself, a few others around the table got up too and she had to publicly apologise. Freedom of speech does not come at the expense of ridiculing others. I pushed back and all else fell into place.

We have to first respect ourselves, draw lines in terms of what behaviour can be taken for granted. We must take pride in who we are.

5. Do unto others as you would like them to do unto you
As Mahatma Gandhi said, 'Be the change that you wish to see in the world.'

What goes around comes around! Be sensitive. We need to be conscious of our behaviours, our speech and our mannerisms. Therefore, self-awareness and sensitivity to other cultures and ethnicities are important. When I meet strangers, I try and think of how I would have liked them to make me feel about myself. I then try and adapt my disposition to make them feel comfortable.

It takes more listening than talking. Drawing people out helps you understand them better. I often reminisce in such situations about when I was in an unknown environment, how intimidating and confusing it was. I craved for someone to listen to me and a few did. Sometimes we are unaware of the wonderful people around us, what they have done for us and we forget to express our gratitude.

In London, I had an Eastern European maid whose English language skills were limited to getting her around the city. She had left three young children back home to work in London and support them. As a mother, my heart went out to her. Her work was meticulous and done diligently with care. One day she came in looking depressed, informing me that she will have to leave. She needed more work and was struggling to find work in my neighbourhood, as no one wanted to employ her. She was getting work in houses further out of the city and that would make it untenable for her to reach my place. I could not really understand the struggle, given that she was a really good cleaner. After much discussion in her broken English, she explained to me that my neighbourhood was predominantly white or expats. They wanted someone local who could connect better. Even though her work was great, she was not a local. There was honesty in her eyes and a real appeal for help. I was taken aback about the 'local' and 'outsider' debate. Even I was an outsider for that matter. Connect is a matter of communication. I loaned her some money to tide over her short-term needs and took it upon myself to teach her the English language to help her connect. She was a brilliant student and in a few months improved her skills. As her connect improved, she was able to market her skills better and found a couple of other houses to clean. She continued to work with us for years and remains connected till date with my children. Her gratitude and humility have been inspiring for me. In different ways, I did what I hoped someone would do for me if I was in their circumstances.

We must experience people as people who have feelings, emotions and tears. Our lives are all intertwined today, it's a small world, and technology has made it possible for all of us to get closer to each other. Therefore, none of our relationships is finite. They do not finish with the end of our journey at the borders of a land. Once we give love, we will receive it back. It is human nature. But, if we give hate, we will receive much worse. Our behaviour, the warmth, the affection that we give to other people, will automatically prompt the other to return the same. The challenge is to remain alert and practise this all the time, in all kinds of situations.

6. Don't judge people on the spur of the moment
Have you ever been a minority anywhere? How does it feel? What do you long for when you are not among people you are familiar with? Have a think before you read on!

I have been in these situations more often than I thought I would be. They were my best self-affirmation and learning experiences. It was a mix of happy and not-so happy times. But then life is bitter-sweet too and I like it that way.

The initial days with new people in a different country made me feel a little out of place, akin to being in a new job, a new college or school. I was lost, I had to unlearn and relearn. At times I was anxious about not knowing the norms, worst still, assuming the norms. This created some awkward situations and I was misinterpreted. Being an Asian, when I started working in Europe, the relatively profuse polite email etiquettes were alien to me. In my early days, I sent off any email to a colleague without starting the email with 'Dear Neil' or 'Hi Neil', 'Hope all is well', etc. I got a rude reply to my query and a curt line at the end, saying, 'PS: I have a name and it is Neil.'

It did not feel good as my action was unintended, but a whole lot of intent was read into it. Even though this was a small incident, it came across as rude to me. The only difference was that I was new to that office, country and community, a minority, and he was not—I could have been advised of a miss or a way of working in a different way. I was ready with my email headers, grammar and appropriate signatures after that. I was determined to stay there and successfully so!

Each passing incident, each passing day made me stronger and sensitive to minorities when I was one. I then applied this sensitivity when I was in the majority group with other minorities. I could feel their pain, their isolation. Instead of judging people instantly, my experience taught me to dwell a little deeper into understanding their real intent/actions before attributing my opinion on them. It was such a beautiful unfolding to experience someone's state of being to find my own infinite limits. We have just one life, but I lived many by simply peeking into other people's journeys and their culture by reading their minds. Like colour, our reference of right or wrong is also learnt. If you can try holding your judgements for a few minutes, basis physical appearance before you are able to draw out their real self, then you will learn something new with each interaction! You will stumble on something that was not obvious.

7. Life doesn't get easier, you just become stronger

What does not kill you makes you stronger. Ups and downs are a part of life. Successes can sometimes make us complacent, so always treasure the tougher moments more. Our tough experiences with others shape up our mettle.

A friend of mine applied for her dream role in Hong Kong last year. She worked at an MNC with offices across the world. She prepared for her interview diligently, sought inputs on the role and spoke to stakeholders. And then, the final day arrived. She went into the room where all the panellists were meeting her through a video conferencing. Two hours passed by and when she came out she looked very happy. She felt she had done really well and expected a positive outcome. After a few days, she got a call from the European hiring manager who gave her some great feedback about her skills, but also communicated that there was more needed for the role. She was caught off guard. On quizzing him further, he shared that he needed a 'local' person with 'local' knowledge that she was lacking. She was devastated. In the evening, an announcement was released stating a 'local British' person has got the job, who had been in Hong Kong for the last two years. My friend's disappointment turned into anger and she was ready to escalate. As we debated the process for the selection and her ground for the escalation, we realised that all 'boxes' had been ticked and she was not able to prove her claim. She did more diligence that affirmed her apprehension that the hiring manager had hired his 'own'. He had navigated the process well to avoid issues. She raised the issue formally.

Process and policies are as good as people want them to be. We can twist them and work around them, depending on what our intent is. Work politics related isolation for a minority can be problematic, as they don't always understand the nuances. I have unfortunately been caught in that a few times. I remember thinking to myself that if I quit and go elsewhere, there is no guarantee that this will not happen there too. So I decided to persist and give it all it took before exercising the option to quit. I reached out and enhanced my network outside the team through each and every person I knew. I reached out to a senior who was credible and was known to be colour-blind and requested that he mentor me. He kindly conceded. I persisted on the project that I was tasked without letting off any adverse reactions. I was optimistically cautious and started to reach out to a couple of people in the team who I knew were easier to make connects with. This concerted effort paid up and life was infused into my continuity in the role. My learning was: *don't give up, things find a way if you persist, and with every challenge, you become stronger on the path you tread*!

8. Everyone you meet has something to teach you

People come into your life for a season and they stay for some time for a reason—to teach us something new, to be a companion through a few moments in our journey and to help us discover a side of ourselves we may not have known.

As I moved across countries through good and bad, in some ways I am grateful to all the people who treated me well as they helped me discover the compassionate side of self. They taught me what support meant when you feel lonely and hurt. I learnt from them how empathy is such a special fulfilling feeling for the giver as well as the recipient. I also want to thank people who were tough, as they taught me what tenacity and persistence meant.

Be it the US, Europe or Asia, there were good moments and tough ones. I felt underwater for being brown more often than for being a woman. Gender has not been a handicap for me as much as colour has. However, for every person who saw me as a coloured person, there was another who saw the value I could create. As I moved across geographies, I was supported and helped by another person from a different race who held my hand and helped me navigate.

I was fortunate that my path crossed with someone who saw in me the capability to work in the US when I did not. Someone who taught me to navigate the corridors of banking in Europe and someone who taught me what leadership meant in trying times when I was back in Asia. Each of them had an open mind where my race or colour was invisible to them. What really mattered to them was competence and capability. Each of these leaders was different in their own ways, yet had that basic respect for humanity. They came into my life and taught me lessons that are lifelong and agnostic of race, nationality or gender. Even today, when I am in certain situations, I literally go back to think that if they were here, how would they have managed this problem. Most times I get my answer magically.

From my experience, I would suggest that there is so much hope in the world. Pay forward. Take bets on people. Take a few risks in relationships. It is a worthwhile learning. Life is such an exciting journey of adventures. Why not challenge yourself and your ability to meet, work and connect with new people, tiding over apprehensions, which may be on both sides! We learn from each other and we grow to another level, closer to who we are meant to be.

Mistakes are the portals of discovery—don't be dismissive of people who may have unknowingly wronged you, before really knowing them. Give them a chance to help you understand life better from another perspective. Each of us deserves at least one chance, isn't it? We learn with experience and with time. Every person is unique in some ways and you can learn from their successes and failures. Our life is too short to go through these collective experiences ourselves. Ignorance ignites fear, so let's rise above that through awareness and learning.

It is about the lens we see our life through—is the glass half full or half empty? Do not colour your life's lens with black, brown or white. Shades of love have vibrant colours that we need to embrace.

We must learn to trust, we must learn to take a leap of faith with people. Remember, knowing a person is a lifelong process, but first we need to give them the opportunity to reveal their true selves. Let's be eager to overcome our fears with our strong faith in humanity and affections that nurture our race! I hope our children grow up in a world that sees 'colour' as an expression of creativity in the human race.

> *Blue skies, the yellow sun*
> *Pink morning and Orange evening on the run*
> *Purple rain and white snow on the mountains*
> *Blue oceans and gardens that are evergreen*
> *Red rose for love, glimmering silver stars in their sparkling sheen*
> *What is your colour, where do you belong*
> *For the sake of humanity, are you willing to be colour-blind lifelong?*
> *Do you see me when you see me?*
> *Let us take one step forward today, enjoy the transparent colours of joy*
> *Help each other strengthen the bonds and not destroy*

I would say that take the time to appreciate what we have and the choice we make so that no colour matters!

Here is hoping for a brighter and more 'colourful' future for all of us.

Acknowledgements

Someone once told me that one should always be thankful for what one has, and continue to strive towards what one wants.

Life has given me so much that if I were to go back in time, I would want to live my life exactly how I have lived thus far, gathering varied experiences through a quest of exploring and learning. I have moved from one milestone to another, from one country to another, from one role to another, taking life as it comes. Each of these experiences has enriched me with their diversity. I learnt, I evolved, I grew, I progressed, I failed... I started all over again, but never stopped. My journey has been enabled by various people who, along the way, created those moments that really mattered. They belonged to different ethnicities, geographies, genders but, at the core, each one of them taught me something really valuable that has made me who I am today.

Writing this book, and reflecting on experiences of many others who chose to share, has brought more life truths at the fore for me that I have humbly attempted to share with you. A lot of people contributed towards this book through their direct and indirect candour and efforts. I would like to express my heartfelt gratitude towards them.

The reflective journey whilst writing this book beckons me to thank my family, my parents (Ajit and Kiran) for letting me be who I wanted to be; and my husband, Sandeep, for supporting me every step of the way in our global sojourn and being there for me, always. My children who taught me about the new world order, given they belong to several geographies. My learning evolves with them every day.

A special thanks for all the mentors (you know who you are) for believing in me when I did not believe in myself. Thank you for supporting me, especially in places that were unfamiliar and intimidating. It made all the difference. I promise to pay forward your kindness by providing similar support to others in need.

I am grateful to friends and friends of friends from various NGOs and diversity groups who proactively reached out to me when they knew I was writing this book. They willingly shared their experiences, helped me with their inputs and connections, and, sometimes, just offered experiential banter. Like I have always said, all these invisible efforts have greatly contributed to the making of *Colour Matters?*

My intent converted to action, thanks to the encouragement and support from a few friends who felt as strongly about this topic as much as I did. Sameer Mathur, a close friend who helped me with his networking skills and connects to ensure we were set off in the right direction. Ronita Saha, a young management student, who is always brimming with innovative ideas and stories to narrate, which helped me with my thought process. Saumya Singh and George Koshy for being there to brainstorm and for helping me keep my drive and motivation going.

Finally, I am truly grateful to Bloomsbury, the publishers of this book, who were courageous and bold to work alongside me on a topic which many felt hesitant to venture into, even though it is a critical need of the hour. A special thanks to Nitin Valecha and Praveen Tiwari for their empathy, collaboration and help all along.

I owe much to you all and yet, deep within, I know, I don't— because you are family! You can count on me as much as I count on you.